Electronic Democracy

Electronic Democracy examines a range of key actors within representative democracy – political parties, pressure groups, new social movements and government bodies – and assesses how they are using new information and communication technologies (ICTs) to fulfil their traditional roles.

While political parties and local government have been the subject of increasing empirical investigation, interest groups, international organisations and new social movements have not attracted significant scholarly attention until now. The authors investigate issues such as how far the Internet will reform and revitalise political organisations and institutions, and whether or not representative democracy is under threat from the direct communication offered by these new technologies.

The book features comparative studies focusing on the United Kingdom, the United States, Sweden, Germany and Australia. It will interest both students and researchers of political communication, organisations, participation and institutions.

Rachel K. Gibson is Deputy Director of the Centre for Social Research in the Research School of Social Sciences (RSSS) at the Australian National University, Australia.

Andrea Römmele is Senior Research Fellow at the Mannheim Centre for European Social Research (MZES) at the University of Mannheim, Germany.

Stephen J. Ward is Senior Lecturer in Politics at the European Studies Research Institute, University of Salford, UK.

Routledge/ECPR Studies in European Political Science

Edited by Thomas Poguntke
Keele University, UK and

Jan W. van Deth
University of Mannheim, Germany on behalf of the European Consortium for Political Research

The Routledge/ECPR Studies in European Political Science series is published in association with the European Consortium for Political Research – the leading organisation concerned with the growth and development of political science in Europe. The series presents high-quality edited volumes on topics at the leading edge of current interest in political science and related fields, with contributions from European scholars and others who have presented work at ECPR workshops or research groups.

1 **Regionalist Parties in Western Europe**
Edited by Lieven de Winter and Huri Türsan

2 **Comparing Party System Change**
Edited by Jan-Erik Lane and Paul Pennings

3 **Political Theory and European Union**
Edited by Albert Weale and Michael Nentwich

4 **Politics of Sexuality**
Edited by Terrell Carver and Véronique Mottier

5 **Autonomous Policy Making by International Organizations**
Edited by Bob Reinalda and Bertjan Verbeek

6 **Social Capital and European Democracy**
Edited by Jan van Deth, Marco Maraffi, Ken Newton and Paul Whiteley

7 **Party Elites in Divided Societies**
Edited by Kurt Richard Luther and Kris Deschouwer

8 **Citizenship and Welfare State Reform in Europe**
Edited by Jet Bussemaker

9 **Democratic Governance and New Technology**
Technologically mediated innovations in political practice in Western Europe
Edited by Ivan Horrocks, Jens Hoff and Pieter Tops

10 **Democracy without Borders**
Transnationalisation and conditionality in new democracies
Edited by Jean Grugel

11 **Cultural Theory as Political Science**
Edited by Michael Thompson, Gunnar Grendstad and Per Selle

12 **The Transformation of Governance in the European Union**
Edited by Beate Kohler-Koch and Rainer Eising

13 **Parliamentary Party Groups in European Democracies**
Political parties behind closed doors
Edited by Knut Heidar and Ruud Koole

14 **Survival of the European Welfare State**
Edited by Stein Kuhnle

15 **Private Organisations in Global Politics**
Edited by Karsten Ronit and Volker Schneider

16 **Federalism and Political Performance**
Edited by Ute Wachendorfer-Schmidt

17 **Democratic Innovation**
Deliberation, representation and association
Edited by Michael Saward

18 **Public Opinion and the International Use of Force**
Edited by Philip Everts and Pierangelo Isernia

19 **Religion and Mass Electoral Behaviour in Europe**
Edited by David Broughton and Hans-Martien ten Napel

20 **Estimating the Policy Position of Political Actors**
Edited by Michael Laver

21 **Democracy and Political Change in the 'Third World'**
Edited by Jeff Haynes

22 **Politicians, Bureaucrats and Administrative Reform**
Edited by B. Guy Peters and Jon Pierre

23 **Social Capital and Participation in Everyday Life**
Edited by Paul Dekker and Eric M. Uslaner

24 **Development and Democracy**
What do we know and how?
Edited by Ole Elgström and Goran Hyden

25 **Do Political Campaigns Matter?**
Campaign effects in elections and referendums
Edited by David M. Farrell and Rüdiger Schmitt-Beck

26 **Political Journalism**
New challenges, new practices
Edited by Raymond Kuhn and Erik Neveu

27 **Economic Voting**
Edited by Han Dorussen and Michaell Taylor

28 **Organized Crime and the Challenge to Democracy**
Edited by Felia Allum and Renate Siebert

29 **Understanding the European Union's External Relations**
Edited by Michèle Knodt and Sebastiaan Princen

30 **Social Democratic Party Policies in Contemporary Europe**
Edited by Giuliano Bonoli and Martin Powell

31 **Decision Making Within International Organisations**
Edited by Bob Reinalda and Bertjan Verbeek

32 **Comparative Biomedical Policy**
Governing assisted reproductive technologies
Edited by Ivar Bleiklie, Malcolm L. Goggin and Christine Rothmayr

33 **Electronic Democracy**
Mobilisation, organisation and participation via new ICTs
Edited by Rachel K. Gibson, Andrea Römmele and Stephen J. Ward

34 **Liberal Democracy and Environmentalism**
The end of environmentalism?
Edited by Marcel Wissenburg and Yoram Levy

Also available from Routledge in association with the ECPR:

Sex Equality Policy in Western Europe, *Edited by Frances Gardiner*; **Democracy and Green Political Thought**, *Edited by Brian Doherty and Marius de Geus*; **The New Politics of Unemployment**, *Edited by Hugh Compston*; **Citizenship, Democracy and Justice in the New Europe**, *Edited by Percy B. Lehning and Albert Weale*; **Private Groups and Public Life**, *Edited by Jan W. van Deth*; **The Political Context of Collective Action**, *Edited by Ricca Edmondson*; **Theories of Secession**, *Edited by Percy Lehning*; **Regionalism Across the North/South Divide**, *Edited by Jean Grugel and Wil Hout*

Electronic Democracy

Mobilisation, organisation and participation via new ICTs

Edited by Rachel K. Gibson, Andrea Römmele and Stephen J. Ward

Routledge
Taylor & Francis Group
LONDON AND NEW YORK

First published 2004
by Routledge
2 Park Square, Milton Park, Abingdon, Oxfordshire OX14 4RN

Simultaneously published in the USA and Canada
by Routledge

711 Third Avenue, New York, NY 10017

First issued in paperback 2014

Routledge is an imprint of the Taylor and Francis Group, an informa business

Transferred to Digital Printing 2005

Typeset in Baskerville MT by
Newgen Imaging Systems (P) Ltd, Chennai, India

British Library Cataloguing in Publication Data
A catalogue record for this book is available from the British Library

Library of Congress Cataloging in Publication Data
Electronic democracy : mobilisation, organisation and participation via new ICTs / edited by Rachel K. Gibson, Andrea Römmele, Stephen J. Ward.
p. cm.
Includes bibliographical references and index.
1. Political participation–Computer network resources. 2. Political campaigns–Computer network resources. 3. Internet in political campaigns. 4. Internet in public administration. I. Gibson, Rachel Kay. II. Römmele, Andrea, 1967– III. Ward, Stephen, 1965– IV. Title.

JF799.E44 2004
320'.0285'4678–dc21 2003012387

ISBN 978-0-415-32482-3 (hbk)
ISBN 978-1-138-01019-2 (pbk)

Contents

Figures

Tables

Contributors

Joachim Åström, University of Örebro, Sweden

Christine Bellamy, Nottingham Trent University, UK

Rachel K. Gibson, Australian National University, Canberry, Australia

Jennifer D. Greer, University of Nevada-Reno, Nevada, USA

Stuart Hodkinson, University of Leeds, UK

Mark E. LaPointe, University of Washington, USA

Wainer Lusoli, London School of Economics, UK

Catherine Needham, Oxford University, UK

Oren Perez, London School of Economics, UK and Bar Ilan University, Israel

Jenny Pickerill, Curtin University, Perth, Australia

Charles D. Raab, University of Edinburgh, UK

Andrea Römmele, Mannheim Centre for European Social Research, University of Mannheim, Germany

Stephen J. Ward, University of Salford, UK

Thomas Zittel, Mannheim Centre for European Social Research, University of Mannheim, Germany

Series editor's preface

One doesn't have to be a Marxist to accept the notion that technology shapes our world and determines the opportunities for social change and the ways people define their positions. This platitude can be easily illustrated by pointing out to the impact of the spread of television or the usage of modern survey techniques on political campaigning. Less well known is the fact that the introduction of air-condition devices transformed political decision-making processes in Washington. In the last few years, political parties and interest groups in each and every country opened their own websites with easy accessible information. Politicians like the German chancellor Gerhard Schröder answered questions of citizens using the Internet, and all over the world members of parliaments can be contacted directly by sending an email message from the living room.

This volume does not constitute yet another fashionable account of the blessings of modern communication and information technologies. Neither does it present a simple solution for the traditional practical problems of democratic decision-making procedures by substituting the crowded marketplace of ancient Greek city-states by some multi-choice-vote-at-home referendum at the start of the New Millennium. As the editors point out in their introduction, the contributions to this volume are based on the presumption that any political use of new technologies takes place within existing institutional frameworks of parliaments, executive branches, and political parties. It is this combination of discussions about these existing institutions of representative democracies on the one hand, and the opportunities of new technologies on the other, which define the unique character of the collection of essays presented in this volume. While there is certainly no lack of research on either of these two topics, only few publications aim explicitly at the relationships between these two areas in a systematic way.

Before the opportunities for new technologies in different political contexts are examined, Rachel Gibson, Wainer Lusoli, Andrea Römmele and Stephen Ward offer an overview of the main aspects of the use of these technologies in representative democracies (Chapter 1). The following four chapters deal with the problems and prospects of information technologies in several countries. In Chapter 1, Charles Raab and Christine Bellamy discuss the changes in parliamentary decision-making processes and the use of new technologies from a theoretical perspective. The core chapters of this part consist of comparative studies of the ways technologies are used in different contexts. Catherine Needham compares the integration of new technologies in the working of central governing institutions in the United States and the United Kingdom (Chapter 3), while Thomas Zittel focuses on the parliaments in the United States, Sweden and Germany (Chapter 4). The gap between expressed intentions of politicians and the actual initiatives to use new technologies to improve democratic decision-making processes is clearly illustrated by Joachim Åström in his analysis of Swedish local governments. The second set of four contributions is addressed to the meso level. Jennifer Greer and Mark LaPointe analyse the use of web communication in US-Senate and gubernatorial elections (Chapter 6). The opportunities for involvement in international organisations are, first, shown by Oren Perez in his analyses of participation experimentation processes in organisations like WTO or ISO (Chapter 7) and, second, by Stuart Hodkinson in his study of the impact of the Internet on labour organisations (Chapter 8). From Jenny Pickerill's enquiry into the differences between Australian and British political-action groups it is clear that especially activists organised in small autonomous groups can use new technologies more effectively than established lobby groups (Chapter 9). The editors' summary and interpretations of the main findings are presented in Chapter 10 and do not have to be reproduced here.

Despite the limited number of cases investigated, the contributions to this volume show that the chances for the use of new technologies depend heavily on existing political institutions and the way they function. Several important questions arise from reading the contributions to this volume and the concluding chapter by the editors. As with every technology, the use of new technologies cannot be restricted to benevolent improvements of representative democracies or the strengthening of social and political involvement only. For instance, Dutch hooligans already discovered the opportunities of new communications techniques to arrange violent battles. Racist and extremist right-wing political propaganda is spread over websites in many countries and pornographic pictures of very young children are distributed in simple ways on electronic highways. Besides, prominent political theorists like Benjamin Barber unambiguously reject the use of 'innovative technologies' such as interactive television as a panacea for the problems of modern democracies. In his view, these technologies are detrimental to democratic decision-making, because they '...could further privatise politics and replace deliberative debate in public with the unconsidered instant expression of private prejudices'. It is this tension between the enormous opportunities of new information and communication technologies and the dangers of anti-democratic, fragmented and privatised public opinion that forces us to reconsider the ways we have been thinking about representative democracy and democratic citizenship.

Jan W. van Deth
Series Editor
Mannheim, June 2003

Preface and acknowledgements

This book has a long history with the ideas behind it emerging first at an ECPR research session in Uppsala, 1999 and being continued in a workshop on 'electronic democracy' held as part of the ECPR Joint Sessions in Grenoble, France 2001. The build-up to the workshop in Grenoble served to confirm the growing academic interest in this topic since we received a large number of proposals on a wide range of topics. While we faced a hard job in selecting the workshop papers, in turn, the number of papers we could actually include in this volume was even fewer. A number of them, not published in this volume, have since been published in a 2003 special issue of Party Politics.

Although not all workshop participants are represented in this edited volume, the book clearly represents a joint effort by all those who contributed in Grenoble, and we want to express our deep thanks to them. The paper presentations and the lively discussion were invaluable in helping stimulate and shape our thinking about the structure and content of the book. The participants included: Joachim Åström, Christine Bellamy, Kees Brants, Andrew Chadwick, Rod Hague, Stuart Hodkinson, Natalya Krasnoboka, Christopher May, Catherine Needham, Jim Newell, Pippa Norris, Oren Perez, Charles D. Raab, Holli A. Semetko, Seung-Yong Uhm, Eric Uslaner and Thomas Zittel. Jan van Deth also attended an early session to present a very thought provoking 'key note' paper on the evolution of the studies of democratic participation in the representative context.

We also want to thank the contributors for their patience in dealing with our numerous requests for revision, and the Routledge team, Heidi Bagtanzo and Grace McInnes, for their guidance, patience and support throughout. Our special thanks are directed to Series Editor, Jan van Deth, and the two referees of the proposals for their helpful comments and advice.

Proposal preparation and early stages of manuscript production were facilitated by the TMR 'Political Representation in Europe' scheme, directed by Hermann Schmitt, which brought Rachel Gibson to the Mannheim Centre for European Social Research (MZES) during 2002. The final stages of editing the chapters and writing the conclusion was also made possible due to the support of the MZES and the Volkswagenstiftung, which hosted Rachel Gibson for a visit in Spring 2003. Finally, Rachel Gibson and Stephen Ward acknowledge the support of the ESRC's Democracy and Participation programme in funding their

'Internet, Political Organisations and Participation' project (L215252036), which provided much of the theoretical background and ideas informing the book. Andrea Römmele acknowledges the support of the Volkswagenstiftung.

Rachel K. Gibson, Andrea Römmele and Stephen J. Ward

1 Introduction

Representative democracy and the Internet

Rachel K. Gibson, Wainer Lusoli, Andrea Römmele and Stephen J. Ward

Introduction

The Internet is now firmly established in the realm of mass communication for many advanced industrial societies. In the course of less than ten years its use has expanded dramatically from being a specialist tool of computer programmers and academics to an everyday means for ordinary citizens to conduct a wide range of daily activities such as sending messages to one another from home and/or work, checking news headlines or movie times and buying and selling products. Paralleling the rapidly increasing diffusion of the technology at the mass level has been the use made by political actors at the organisational and institutional levels. From the more embedded legislative and executive structures of representative democracy to the more fluid forms of political parties, pressure groups and more recently single-issue campaign networks, there has been an increasing enthusiasm for using Internet technology to communicate and coordinate activities. Despite these developments, micro- or individual-level analysis has tended to predominate over studies of innovation at the macro and particularly, meso levels. Such an oversight is due to a number of factors not least of which is the difficulty in collecting data, relying as one does on the openness of the organisations and institutions to divulging details of the changes and innovation they are undergoing. The neglect has a more substantive basis, however, in that the first wave of theorising about the role of the Internet in democracy focused very much on its capacity to promote direct democracy. In such models political mediation was largely dispensed with as the new technology allowed for more frequent in-depth communication between individuals. The Internet forms a global network, free from centralised control with intrinsically empowering characteristics – costless, space-less, timeless. As the barriers to mass communication were eroded citizens could participate more fully in decision-making. Indeed, many observers applauded such moves, seeing them as removing the need for the creaking and increasingly underperforming units of representation such as parliaments, parties and other political organisations.

These early theories, it would seem, have failed to predict the direction and momentum of change. The first wave of Internet adaptation has taken place and the machinery of representative democracy is still standing, indeed on a surface level, very little seems to have really changed. Parties still campaign, politicians are elected and governments are formed, although their governing credentials are coming under increasingly critical scrutiny. This book seeks to shift the lens back towards these intermediaries of government and provide an understanding of how they are functioning using the new information and communication technologies (ICTs) in a variety of democratic contexts. Rather than continuing with radical hypothesising on the disappearance of the state and its ancillary organisations, therefore, we argue a shift in focus is needed to a more explicitly empirical and institutionally determined understanding of the nature of change induced by new ICTs. One that consciously contains the debate to questions about adaptation rather than wholesale reform and that begins with an awareness of the limitations faced by established political actors in opening up via new ICTs, rather than an extolling of the range of technological possibilities.

To that end we have assembled a range of perspectives on the use of new ICTs by the key bodies of representative government, each of which brings to bear knowledge of their pre-existing practices or current *modus operandi*. Some are explicitly comparative, such as Chapters 3 and 4 by Needham and Zittel, others cover a particular level of government or type of political actor in a specific national context. Overall, we seek to build a picture of adaptation across democratic systems and also an understanding of the pace of change across representative structures. How much change is it realistic to expect within such entities? Are the more formalised units of government, such as bureaucracies and parliaments, slower and more inflexible in their approach to using the new media than pressure groups or individual parliamentarians? Given the range of national experiences presented, what can we deduce about the importance of contextual factors at the systemic level as levers of reform? The answers to these questions do of course lend themselves to more normative speculation about the process of adaptation and whether the new ICTs could lead to the improved performance of our representative system. However, the focus of this volume is on description and explanation rather than prescription. This introduction begins that process of analysis by identifying the main actors within the representative system within two broad categories: (1) micro-level individual online engagement and (2) meso/macro-level online mobilising by different institutions/organisations, and then assessing the research to date on their adaptation to new ICTs.

The micro level: individual engagement and the Internet

The idea of the media acting as a mobilising force, as opposed to being seen as a malign or enervating influence on public interest in politics has long since proved to be intriguing. Television in particular has been seen to simplify and personalise politics to voters, focusing on the horserace aspect of who was winning and the moral failings of the candidates while contributing little to individuals' knowledge base (Crotty and Jacobson 1980; Graber 1988; Putnam 2000; Eveland and Scheufele 2000). In addition, the rise of more depersonalised strategies of direct communication by parties such as telephone banks and mass mailing in place of grass roots campaigning have been seen as heightening this disconnection between voters and the political system (Bimber 2001; Römmele 2002). Even social movements – the eleventh-hour saviours of late-twentieth-century democracy – stood accused of not just failing to challenge public apathy but actively fuelling it by leaving little room for members' participation beyond dues paying. As Jordan and Maloney described it, the environmental movement has become little more than a 'protest business' (1997) for the vast bulk of members, meeting citizen/consumer needs for a quick 'feel good' return on a limited financial investment. The Internet, however, with its interactivity, opportunities for user control and independent publishing was regarded as a new and radical force that could help to counter and possibly reverse these negative trends.

Some of the earliest evidence on individual users was compiled by the Pew Research Center for People and the Press in 1996. Their study of the US population revealed that there was indeed a social and economic divide between those who did and did not have access to the Internet. The former were far more likely to be male, highly educated, wealthy and white than their non-wired counterparts. Not surprisingly, given this demographic split, the so-called 'digital divide' meant that those who were online were more active and interested in politics than the average voter. Crucially, however, further studies found that after controlling for the higher socio-economic status of users, Internet use was not associated with any marked improvement in political activity (Bimber 1998).

This story was confirmed by updates from Bimber using data from 1996 to 1999, collected in random digit dial (RDD) telephone surveys that found no significant increases in a range of behaviours such as donating money and attempting to influence others vote decision among those accessing the Internet (Bimber 2001). This was seen as particularly disappointing by advocates of what was now termed 'e-democracy' since the demographics of Internet users had begun to broaden quite markedly, particularly in terms of gender and income. Schuefele and Nisbet (2002) offered similarly uninspiring conclusions from their telephone survey of New York residents, which examined the effects of different types of Internet use on a range of political behaviours and levels of factual knowledge. None of the modes of Internet use, including political information-seeking was found to have any significant effect on individuals' proclivity to engage in politics, either in a conventional sense (i.e. voting, contacting) or in more participatory forums.

Positive effects were not entirely dismissed, however. Norris (2001), following her analysis of survey data from the United States and Europe up until 2000 argued that Internet use was linked to higher levels of mobilisation but that this was largely confined to those who were already active, pulling them further into an upward spiral or 'virtuous' circle of participation. She concluded:

> the rise of the virtual political system seems most likely to facilitate further knowledge, interest, and activism of those who are already most predisposed toward civic engagement, reinforcing patterns of political participation.
>
> (p. 228)

Although, politically the story of the net seemed to be lacking much of a punchline, more pessimistic pronouncements emerged regarding its social effects. A number of studies began to emerge highlighting the damaging effects of the online life for social relationships and the underlying fabric of civil society. Studies of Internet effects on various measures of social capital revealed a reinforcement of existing trends towards disengagement among voters, producing isolation and alienation. Nie and Ebring (2000) reported negative effects of Internet use on individuals, levels of sociability and increasing feelings of alienation and connection to society. Kraut *et al.* (2000) echoed these findings, with the latter characterising the heavier users of the Internet as a 'newer lonelier crowd' in cyberspace. Other studies, however, such as those by Putnam (2000) and Uslaner (2001) reported a more negligible picture. Putnam, reporting on data from the DDB Needham Lifestyle survey, said that after demographic controls were applied Internet users and non-users did not differ significantly in their levels of civic engagement. Uslaner (2001) in his analysis of data from 1998 and 2000 Pew Center survey and the 1996 American NES has argued for a largely 'nil' effect of Internet use on social capital. 'The Internet…is not a reservoir of social capital' nor does it deplete the amount already in existence (p. 22). While there appear to be some positive associations in that the heaviest users of the Internet have wider social circles, those engaging in online chat appear to be more distrustful of others. Overall, he argues, 'there is little evidence that the Internet will create new communities to make up for the decline in civic engagement that has occurred over the past four decades in the United States…' (p. 22). Using data from the 1998 National Geographic Web Survey, Wellman and his colleagues arrive at similar conclusions (Wellman *et al.* 2001). Notably, a positive association is found to exist between online and offline participatory behaviour with higher rates of participation in voluntary organisations and politics being associated with heavier use of the Internet. However, they also found that people's interaction online supplements their face-to-face and telephone communication, without increasing or decreasing it.

Overall, therefore, the verdict that emerged from the initial analyses of the Internet and individual engagement in public life was at best, ambiguous. Basically, it was not possible to specify any one universal type of Internet effect on participation. One thing was clear, however, Internet use by itself was clearly not transforming inactive people into participators with regard to 'real world politics'.

More recently, attention has shifted towards investigating specifically online forms of participation, both in terms of those engaging in it and attitudes towards it among non-users. Significantly, here there has been a more uniformly positive story uncovered. A 2001 Hansard Society/MORI survey shows that almost four in five UK non-Internet users would engage in online interaction with their MP and online surgery to raise problems with MPs via the Internet as well as via an email address, so that constituents can contact him/her through a consultation forum where he/she can read constituents' views. Equally promising, the study found that younger respondents were more enthusiastic for these features to be introduced (Coleman 2001). Data from the Pew Internet Survey of online communities (2001) shows equally interesting results as regards youth, traditionally a non-political group. Youngsters are indeed slightly more likely to be in contact with political groups or organisations online than other age groups, which assumes more relevance given that only one in three respondents reported being in contact with the group before contacting them online, vis-à-vis two in three for the oldest reference group.[1] Such findings have also been confirmed from national opinion data gathered in the United Kingdom during 2002, which revealed that young people were significantly more likely to engaged in online participation than offline forms, including voting and more active types of participation (Gibson *et al.* 2002). A more recent Hansard survey confirms this point, finding that younger voters (18–24-year-olds) were significantly more likely to have visited the Westminster website (34 percent) and were much more likely to do this than writing to their MP (Coleman 2001). Broader reports on youth participation following the 2001 UK election from the Electoral Commission (2002), Demos (2002) and the Government's Children and Young Peoples Unit (2002) have also indicated the usefulness of technology in engaging younger voters. Of course, these positive findings do raise the prospect of the disadvantages faced by older voters if participation moves more into the online environment. In addition, one needs to be careful not to ascribe too much power to the technology itself as the solution to what are underlying problems of motivation. Finally, while young people may be more susceptible to Internet-based invitations to participate they are also likely to be quite scathing of technological gimmicks. Thus, parties and political organisations need to be careful that they don't actually lose supporters in their efforts to promote themselves in cyberspace. However, one can also argue for the greater validity of these findings than those from the offline environment. The Internet presents a wholly new environment for participation with its emphasis on user control and immediacy. These studies capture these context-based effects more fully by examining political activities that are embedded in it.

Thus, the micro-level data on the Internet's impact on participation while it is abundant and growing, is at present, somewhat inconclusive. This is no doubt due partly to the fact that it is still too early to assess the long-term effects of the new technology. At the individual level, ICTs should be viewed as a tool for political socialisation, particularly of younger citizens. As the Internet becomes part of life for increasing numbers of people, it enters various domains of the domestic, the personal, the social and the political. As a result, ICTs shape, and are shaped by, the forces of societal modernisation that underpin the latest evolution of participation patterns, at least in advanced democracies (Norris 2002). Certainly, we should not rule out the Internet as a means of politicisation for individuals. Given its strong appeal among the younger age group it clearly has mileage as a useful means to target apathy and cynicism among our newer citizens. However, in the short term, before accepting the null hypothesis of nil effects, more direct study would seem to be required of online political activities. As Wellman and his colleagues have noted, 'it is time for more differentiated analyses of the Internet, and analyses, which embeds it in everyday life, offline as well as online' (2001: 22). Certainly if current practice is any guide then as participation moves more into cyberspace then it would appear that there may be a more positive story yet to emerge. One obvious development in individual-level uses of the new technology that could have widespread effects on participation patterns and theory is the introduction of Internet voting. With task forces established in the United States and the United Kingdom to assess the possibilities for online general elections and a number of pilot schemes at the local and state levels taking place across Europe, North America and Australia (Solop 2000; Gibson 2002a,b) there is clearly mounting interest in the prospects for Internet voting. However, with the security concerns and problems of lower turnout among minorities and older citizens (Alvarez and Nagler 2000) the idea of Internet voting from home look to be some way off. Beyond voting, however, it is clear that patterns of participation are undergoing change worldwide.

The meso and macro levels: new ICTs and representative structures

Much of the work that has been done on the adaptation of institutions and organisations to the new technology has been generated from the political communication perspective rather than from institutional specialists. Thus, there has been a tendency for focusing on websites and email communication, and on discussions of the varying styles of communication taking place, such as interactivity versus information dissemination. As we have indicated elsewhere (Gibson *et al.* 2003) this literature has spawned varying claims about the potential use and value of new ICTs to political institutions and we group these into four basic scenarios: full-scale erosion; limited erosion; modernisation and reform; and radical regeneration.

- Erosion. Much of the early literature on e-democracy or cyberdemocracy has focused on the possibilities for direct democracy and closer connection of individuals to government and policy-making. Work by Rheingold (1993) and Grossman (1995), for example, extolled the possibilities of the Internet for forging new and stronger forms of political engagement by citizens. One consequence of this focus on the nexus between citizen and government was to question the continuing relevance of representative institutions and organisations. Among the more radical commentators of the time there was a tendency to regard them as antiquated structures and regarded the interactive capabilities of the new ICTs as paving the way to more direct forms of mass rule (Becker 1981; Grossman 1995; Negroponte 1995; Rheingold 1993; Morris 2000). Self-governing would supersede state machinery as Internet based systems of voting, referenda and discussion were set up. Details of how such systems were to work remained sketchy, however, and as the empirical evidence of a lack of interest in politics online accumulated (Norris 2001; Bimber 1998), the dreams of a return to the Athenian agora appeared to have faded.
- Limited erosion. In place of full-scale erosion, a more limited usurping of government institutions was envisaged. Electronic communication channels would provide for more direct communication between executives and

citizens. Online consultation and polls by government would streamline the political process, reducing the reliance on unwieldy intermediary bodies such as legislatures and parties (Bellamy and Raab 1999). Single-issue groups and direct-action politics would increasingly dominate society as the role of aggregative structures declined (Bimber 1998).

- Modernisation. Taking a rather more positive view of the impact of the new technologies on our representative structures, some accounts saw them as offering the possibility for reform and modernisation (Gibson and Ward 2000). New ICTs could improve the image of representative institutions particularly with younger people who are the least likely to vote or to see the relevance of the representative system. The website could act as a modern marketing tool for all parts of our representative system. Furthermore, efficiency gains should also be possible with websites serving as rapid, 24-hour, 7 days a week, service delivery points and information archives for the public replacing some of the need for expensive and slower personal, telephone or postal transactions.
- Reinvigoration. Finally, some commentators have adopted a more radical view of the restructuring possibilities surrounding the introduction of new ICTs. If properly developed, the communication technologies could sit at the core of a reinvigorated representative institution that could truly listen and thus re-engage the public (Coleman 1999a,b). Rather than just modernising internal practices, this would provide more opportunities for the public to participate in the political system and would reconnect representative organisations with the public. ICTs provide institutions and organisations opportunities for engagement through their own websites and email, such as live question and answer sessions, and discussion fora and could seek feedback on particular issues via email or electronic polls. Legislatures, parties, trade unions and the like, could all employ e-consultation and discussion allowing citizens to feed in more formally their experiences and knowledge to policy debates. All of this could potentially open up representative organisations to new audiences, since it has been argued that use of ICTs could lower the costs of participating and act as more attractive channels of communication for some groups in society such as the housebound or those with childcare responsibilities.

The systematic empirical testing of these various development paths has thus far been rather limited. Very few comprehensive and/or comparative studies of various government/political structures in terms of their presence and styles of communication on the Internet have been undertaken.[2] In the following we consider some of the main trends from the empirical evidence collated so far in relation to the different parts of the representative political system from the formal governmental through to informal parts of civil society.

Executive branch: e-government

The idea of e-government has spread rapidly across the globe, even countries that lack basic infrastructure often profess an attachment to goals of e-government

(Norris 2001). In the main, governments, e-government strategies have tended to concentrate on e-commerce, Internet regulation and in particular, making government services available online. Underlying the provision of e-services is the notion of modernisation (see earlier) creating a leaner more efficient state (see the modernisation scenario) where services actually meet citizen demand and citizens can actively shape those services through online feedback mechanisms. Such a viewpoint is summarised by one advocate who claims:

> Public organizations are rapidly becoming networked, and they are using these networks to produce and deliver services. This will ultimately lead to efficiency improvements much as happened in the private sector. Government bureaucracies will gradually become flatter, faster, and more customer friendly. Services will become better integrated and customized, with rich self service options.
>
> (Mechling 2002: 155)

Whether e-government or e-service provision has much to do with participation or democracy is, however, questionable. Advocates argue that through e-government citizens will gain additional rights and additional chances to input into the policy process (akin to the idea of consumer democracy; see Chapter 2 by Bellamy and Raab), which should eventually increase their trust in the political system. However, critics suggest that e-government represents little more than modernisation without any necessary democratic improvements (Bellamy and Taylor 1998).

Certainly, so far, we can see rapid progress in meeting headline targets of placing services online. A recent report issued by the office of the e-envoy in the United Kingdom on the readiness of governments around the world to develop the e-economy provides extensive information on a range of related topics including regulatory frameworks and roll-out of broadband.[3] Overall, the study concludes that United States, Sweden and Canada lead the world in the extent to which they have moved services online and further, established mechanisms for gauging the effects of such policies. Yet, as a number of recent studies indicate, deep-rooted problems remain in some government structures, which limit any democratic potential (Margetts and Dunleavy 2002). The inflexible, hierarchical and closed nature of large government bureaucracies mean they are often ill-suited to a more open networked style of government. Similarly, government concerns about security of public records has slowed the pace of experimentation with electronic provision.

Legislatures and legislators

The spread of legislative websites whilst less universal than government sites has nevertheless also been rapid. Norris (2001) found that over half the countries in her global survey had some form of legislative website. Whilst in the United States, congressional sites for legislators have become virtually universal (see Chapter 4 by Zittel) by contrast, in the United Kingdom, less than a third of MPs have their own personal websites (Jackson 2002). Again the political context, broad systemic rules and institutional history and resources have all been cited as important factors in the uptake and use of the technology by the legislative branch of government. It has been commonly argued, for example, that new purpose built parliaments have an advantage over those with longer historic traditions and buildings, since they can more easily incorporate ICTs into their agendas and infrastructure. For example, the newly established Scottish Parliament (Smith and Gray 1999) sought to define itself as a new and more participatory parliament appropriate to the New Millennium and (at least rhetorically) made Internet technology a key feature of its communications strategy, allowing for submission of online petitions and running e-consultation. Overall, in terms of participatory usage, the series of case studies presented in a special issue of *Parliamentary Affairs* (Coleman *et al.* 1999) revealed that whilst legislative experimentation is taking place with regard to new ICTs, participatory uses are still quite rare. Where e-consultation has taken place it has met with mixed results. The Westminster Parliament has undertaken ten e-consultations between 1998 and 2002. The Hansard Society has thus far released in-depth analysis of two of these experiments. On the whole the findings are generally positive – new voices were heard in parliamentary process, the quality of evidence and debate was relatively high and MPs found the process valuable. However, on the down side participants were disappointed with the lack of response from MPs and perhaps crucially it did not appear to improve participants, opinion of the parliamentary system (Coleman *et al.* 2002).

Whilst there has been a number of studies of parliamentary activity and also public response to it there has been limited study of the views of representatives. Peter Chen presents the most comprehensive survey when he examines the opinions of Australian elected officials at four levels of government – members of parliament of the Commonwealth, States, Territories and local government councillors and aldermen (2002). Compared to the average Australian citizen, representatives are 'high users of new media technologies, and have very positive outlooks as to the future importance of this media form' (p. 61). There are three more specific findings, as to the impact of new media on the democratic process. First, representatives do not consider new media as important as traditional media for their information distribution and electioneering activities. Second, new media has replaced traditional media for a number of functions related to the representative office, only for the more ICT skilled, urban representatives. Furthermore, three in four members of this category do not rule out the idea of e-voting, and around 65 percent consider new media important or very important for consulting with citizens. Finally, there are still a number of barriers to the use of ICTs, 'especially for rural representatives, ATSIC and local government councillors, and councillors with relatively low skill levels' (p. 61).

Disparities in the perception and adoption of ICTs between different branches of the legislative and executive are also reported in the United States (Ault and Gleason 2003). Results from interviews and focus groups show that Members of the House and their support staff are not very concerned about ICTs and their implications.[4] On the other hand, senators, their office staff and staff of Senate committees 'seem to be more aware of both the potential and the hazards of information technologies' (p. 72). Finally, government administrators have already been through an ICT 'reality check'. They routinely use information technologies within their agencies, ICTs being included in plans for future development. These different adoption dynamics, it is argued, respond directly to organisational logics related to the aims, routines and function of specific legislative and executive bodies.

Political parties

Parties have increasingly merited a degree of attention. Early work on the US and UK parties (Margolis *et al.* 1997; Gibson and Ward 1998) has been followed by studies in other countries such as the Netherlands (Voerman 1999), Italy (Newell 2001), Russia and Ukraine (Semetko and Krasnoboka 2003) and Japan (Tkach 2003). From such studies a general consensus has emerged regardless of country. First, that parties like other formal institutions have moved online in large numbers between 1994 and 1998. Second, that parties' public websites tend not to exploit the participatory elements of new ICTs. Much of the information provided is one-way, top-down, party to voter rather than two-way interactive communication. Third, that the sites are often aimed at either an elite audience of opinion-formers (journalists/researchers) and/or at the converted party members. Consequently, the value of party sites as a mobilising force for the non-partisan voter has been questioned (Norris 2003). Fourth, that although parties are beginning to use technology for internal party debate (via closed intranets, bulletin boards, email lists) these rarely widen participation extensively (Gibson and Ward 1999; Voerman and Ward 2000; Löfgren 2001; Pederson 2001), nor do these electronic channels necessarily empower ordinary members since such channels rarely play a formal role in decision-making and for a large part are controlled by central party HQ. Nevertheless, recently conducted research suggests that parties may gain at least two benefits from using ICTs: technology can help parties reach a younger audience than otherwise would be the case through traditional media (Gibson *et al.* 2002, 2003) and also ICTs can be useful in deepening the participatory activities of activists, that is, allowing them to conduct additional party activities more often (Gibson *et al.* 2003). Both these factors could be crucial in maintaining parties as participatory vehicles over the coming decade.

New social movements and protest networks

Less formalised political organisations such as protest networks or flash campaigns whilst attracting considerable media coverage have gained less coverage from academic surveys. In part, this reflects a methodological problem of how to study rather amorphous, often anonymous and rapidly changing protest campaigns. Nevertheless, a number of studies have indicated that the most likely beneficiaries of the new media are loosely organised ad hoc protest campaigns

(Bonchek 1995; Bimber 1998; Hill and Hughes 1998). In part, this is because of the relative low cost of the net and the lack of editorial control, which means that fringe campaigns have greater opportunities to voice their concerns and get their message across than they do via the traditional media. Moreover, email and hypertext links make it easier than before to mobilise protest quickly and link together previously unconnected individuals even breaking down traditional barriers of time and space. The potency of email and the net as a mobilising tool has been seen in a number of recent mass demonstrations and rallies, not least the anti-globalisation protests in Seattle in 1999 and the Stop the War rallies in 2003 (Cisler 1999; Doherty 2002).[5] Arguably, it is these decentralised formalised types of networks that offer greater flexibility to experiment with the technology and exploit its interactive potential, since they are not held back by formal organisational rules or hierarchical chains of command. Thus some of the more novel uses of the technology such as political hacking, virtual sit-ins and blockades have come from informal protest networks, particularly in environmental and human rights and social justice fields (Wray 1998; Pickerill 2000).

Whilst it is relatively easy to provide examples of novel practice amongst protest campaigners, it is more difficult to generalise or assess the wider impact. Critics have argued that far from levelling the playing field for such organisations, a process of normalisation is at work in cyberspace where creeping corporate ownership of the Net and surveillance of online users' habits have become important (Guidi 1998). The entry points to the Internet offered by big media corporations such as AOL, Time Warner and Microsoft in terms of portals can be seen as 'walled gardens' – controlled environments where subscribers' choices as to what they see and do online are predetermined and also tracked (Wilhelm 2000). Such developments mean that it becomes increasingly difficult for alternative and independent organisations and sources of news to gain a mainstream audience. The idea that the WWW is actually simply replicating the offline dominance of the major political and economic organisations has gained considerable support from some studies (Margolis and Resnick 2000).

Overview of the chapters

The aim of the book, therefore, is to examine a range of key actors within representative democracy – political parties, pressure groups and new social movements, plus executive and legislative government bodies at the national and local levels – within different national contexts and assess how they are using the technology to fulfil their traditional roles. By doing so, we aim at connecting to the debate on new institutionalism, which appears with growing frequency in political science. We argue that the use of new ICTs, experimentation and innovation will take place within the existing institutional frameworks and any study of parliaments, executive agencies or political parties will need to take that into account. Put simply, context matters. Of course, such institutionalism does not preclude these bodies from making bold advances in using the new tools available to them and exploiting the possibilities offered by the new media (March and Olson 1989;

Hall and Taylor 1996). While some of these structures have been the subject of increasing empirical investigation such as political parties and local government, others such as interest groups, international organisations and new social movements have not attracted significant scholarly attention. Second, they assess the extent to which they are seeking to expand on that role in any way, that is in a more participatory direction due to the new interactive communication possibilities offered by the net.

Chapter 1 by Charles Raab and Christine Bellamy opens up the volume by discussing the problems as well as opportunities that new ICTs present for today's centralised but increasingly strained 'post-parliamentary' governments. Raab and Bellamy theoretically lay out the possible consequences new ICTs can have on political institutions, on intermediary organisations, on policy networks and finally, on the state in general by focusing on the use of new ICTs by individual citizens. Chapter 2 by Catherine Needham presents an empirical content analysis of government websites and web-based consultation in the context of government policy commitments in the United States and Britain. Through surveying the contents of government websites, evaluating previous web-based consultations and analysing government policy commitments on their own Internet presence, an assessment can be made of the government's commitment to net-based consultation. These findings are then compared with an evaluation of the extent to which these governments are using the Internet to facilitate state–citizen interaction through other channels – such as online service provision and information dissemination. In Chapter 4, 'Electronic Democracy and Electronic Parliaments', Thomas Zittel considers the importance of technological developments versus the institutional setting by looking at the US House, the Swedish Riksdag and the German Bundestag. Zittel defines the term electronic democracy as an (ideal) three-layered concept that encompasses three different levels of political analysis: a general conception of democracy, an institutional/structural dimension (democratic design) and a behavioural dimension (participatory behaviour). This concept enables thorough empirical analysis by drawing from a quantitative content analysis of all websites in the three parliaments and from numerous background interviews with members, parliamentary staffers and outside experts.

This first section concludes with Chapter 5 by Joachim Åström, examining the relationship between ideas, intentions and initiatives in the process of wiring Swedish local governments. Do local politicians in Sweden believe in the use of the Internet in the political process? How far do local government websites provide comprehensive information and opportunities for interactive communication? Åström analyses the ideas and experiments of Swedish local government through an attitudinal survey of local politicians towards ICTs and then compares the responses with the actual content of municipal websites.

The second part of the volume examines the use of new ICTs at the meso level, focusing on the adaptations taking place among more formal political organisations such as parties and trade unions to the more fluid and loosely organised pressure groups. Chapter 7 by Oren Perez examines the globalisation process and emergence of largely autonomous, global institutions (WTO, International

Organisations for Standardisation and ICANN). It puts forward the argument that there is a need for innovative institutional structures that would enable the public to scrutinise such global organisations and their organisational norms. It has been suggested that the Internet offers one such potential vehicle for transnational public debate. The author reveals how the Internet while not eliminating the traditional problem of collective public action can contribute to the creation of transnational communities. Greer and LaPointe (Chapter 6) bring the focus down to the national level and examine the changing use made by candidates of the web during the 2000 and 2002 US senate and gubernatorial elections. Candidates as current and future leaders provide a particularly relevant insight into how well the representative system is adapting to the challenges and opportunities presented by the new ICTs. While the questions posed focus on the influence of party on the uses made of the web, attention is directed towards the impact of broader external factors such as the closeness of the election race, as well as individual factors such as candidates' gender and age or status as an incumbent. Chapter 8 by Stuart Hodkinson focuses on non-governmental actors and discusses the role of new ICTs in reviving trade unionism. The essay profiles the decline of unionism in the face of globalisation and the potential benefits of the Internet to bring about a new internationalism among organised labour. Finally, Jenny Pickerill, in Chapter 9, compares the response of two different forms of environmental organisation: the well-established pressure group Friends of the Earth UK and the protest network Woomera2002 in Australia. The chapter assesses the differences that organisational structure, participatory culture and political context make in terms of the deployment of ICTs. In short, Pickerill analyses whether loose, non-hierarchical networks are better able to exploit the technology for mobilisation purposes than more established formalised pressure groups.

In combining macro- and meso-level data from different contexts we aim to provide a snapshot, albeit a non-systematic one, of how well the organs of representative democracy are utilising the new communication tools, as well as raising the question of how far context matters. Specifically, the chapters investigate how far these intermediaries are encouraging participation with the new ICTs, versus opting for the more static information provision model. While it is hoped that signs of proactive participatory uses for the technology emerge, the amount of interactive communication taking place is not presented as a yardstick for giving the thumbs up or down to certain bodies. The point that is returned to in each of the chapters is that context matters. Depending on their size, age and function there will be differing systemic and technological opportunity structures within which democratic organisations and institutions operate. We need to adjust our expectations for innovation and change accordingly. A long-established legislative chamber would inevitably be slower to incorporate the Internet into its operations compared with a newly started environmental movement filled with young computer-literate individuals. Now that representative democracy has withstood the predicted erosion, it is the existing organisational and institutional capacity and incentives we argue that provide the best guide to predicting the implications of the new ICTs for democracy.

Notes

1 The figures presented here were elaborated from the 2001 Pew Internet and Community Survey. The questionnaire, data set and basic cross-tabs are publicly available for academic research at <http://www.pewinternet.org> from 8 February 2002.
2 One exception is Pippa Norris's global survey *Digital Divide* (2001), which explores some of these issues in terms of both individual-level participation and institutional and organisational mobilisation.
3 'International E-economy Benchmarking: The Worlds Most Effective Policies for the e-Economy,' Booz Allen Hamilton, November 2002. Available at <http://www.e-envoy.gov.uk/oee/oee.nsf/sections/esummit-benchmarking/$file/whole_report.pdf>, accessed on 26 November 2002.
4 The results are based on a restricted *n*, and should be taken as exploratory only.
5 For a good account of Stop the War campaign's use of the technology see Alistair Alexander 'A Revolution for Revolt,' *The Guardian*, 20 February 2003.

References

Alvarez, R. M. and Nagler, J. (2000) 'The Likely Consequences of Internet Voting for Political Representation', paper prepared for presentation at the Internet Voting and Democracy Symposium, Loyola Law School, Los Angeles, CA.

Ault, J. T. and Gleason, J. M. (2003) 'U.S. Government Decision Makers' Expectations and Patterns of Use of Emerging and Existing Information Technologies', *Government Information Quarterly*, 20 (1), 63–76.

Becker, T. (1981) 'Teledemocracy. Bringing Power Back to the People', *The Futurist*, December, 6–9.

Bellamy, C. and Taylor, J. (1998) *Governing in the Information Age*, Buckingham: Open University Press.

Bennett, W. L. (1998) 'The Uncivic Culture', *PS*, December, 741–61.

Bimber, B. (1998) 'The Internet and Political Transformation', *Polity*, 31 (1), 133–60.

Bimber, B. (2001) 'Information and Political Engagement in America', *Political Research Quarterly*, 54 (1), 53–68.

Bonchek, M. (1995) 'Grassroots in Cyberspace', paper presented at 53rd Annual Meeting of the Midwest Political Science Association, 6 April, Chicago.

Chen, P. (2002) *Australian Elected Representatives' Use of New Media Technologies*, Centre for Public Policy, University of Melbourne.

Cisler, S. (1999) 'Showdown in Seattle', *First Monday*, 4 (2), <www.firstmonday.dk/issues/issue4 12/cisler/index.html>, first accessed 4 January 2002.

Coleman, S. (2001) *Democracy Online*, London: Hansard Society.

Coleman, S., Taylor, J. and van de Donk, W. (eds) (1999) *Parliament in the Age of the Internet*, Oxford: Oxford University Press.

Coleman, S., Hall, N. and Howell, M. (2002) *Hearing Voices*, London: Hansard Society.

Crotty, W. J. and Jacobson, G. C. (1980) *American Parties in Decline*, Boston: Little, Brown and Co.

Doherty, B. (2002) *Ideas and Actions in the Green Movement*, London: Routledge.

Eveland, W. P. and Scheufele, D. A. (2000) 'Connecting News Media Use with Gaps in Knowledge and Participation', *Political Communication*, 17 (3), 215–37.

Gibson, R. K. (2002a) 'Elections Online: Assessing', *Political Studies Quarterly*, Winter 2001–2002, 116 (4), 561–83.

Gibson, R. K. (2002b) 'Internet-Voting and the European Parliamentary Elections of 2004', E-voting and the European Parliamentary Elections Conference, The Robert Schuman Centre for Advanced Studies, Florence, Italy.

Gibson, R. K. and Ward, S. J. (1998) 'UK Political Parties and the Internet', *Harvard International Journal of Press Politics*, 3, 14–38.

Gibson, R. K. and Ward, S. J. (1999) 'Party Democracy Online', *Information Communication and Society*, 2 (3), 340–67.

Gibson, R. K. and Ward, S. J. (2000) 'Conclusions: Modernising without Democratising?', in Gibson, R. K. and Ward, S. J. (eds), *Reinvigorating Democracy? British Politics and the Internet*, Aldershot: Ashgate, 205–12.

Gibson, R.K., Lusoli, W. and Ward, S. J. (2002) 'Online Campaigning in the UK', American Political Science Association Annual Meetings, Boston, Mass, September 2002.

Gibson, R. K., Nixon, P. G. and Ward, S. J. (eds) (2003a) *Political Parties and the Internet*, London: Routledge.

Gibson, R. K., Lusoli, W. and Ward, S. J. (2003b) 'Virtually Participating: A Survey of Party Members Online', *Information Polity*, 7 (4), 199–215.

Graber, D. (1988) *Processing the News*, New York: Longman.

Grossman, L. K. (1995) *The Electronic Republic*, New York, NY: Viking.

Guidi, L. (1998) *Bologna 'Civic Network'*. Web Document, G8 Government Online <http://www.statskontoret.se/gol-democracy/italy.htm>, first accessed 9 February 2000.

Hall, Peter A. and Taylor, R. C. R. (1996) *Political Science and the Three New Institutionalisms*, MPIFG Discussion Paper 6.

Hill, J. and Hughes, K.(1998) *Cyberpolitics*, Lanham: Rowman & Littlefield.

Jackson, N. (2002) 'MPs and Web Technologies – An Untapped Opportunity?', paper presented to the UK Political Studies Association Conference, University of Aberdeen.

Jordan, G. and Maloney, W. (1997) *The Protest Business*, Manchester: Manchester University Press.

Kraut, R. *et al.* (2000) 'Information and Communication', *Information Systems Research*, 10, 287–303.

Löfgren, K. (2000) 'Danish Political Parties and New Technology', in Hoff, J, Horrocks, I. and Tops, P. (eds), *Democratic Governance and New Technology*, London: Routledge, 57–70.

March, J. and Olson, J. (1989) *Rediscovering Institutions*, London/New York: Simon & Schuster.

Margetts, H. and Dunleavy, P. (2002) *Better Public Services Through E-Government*, London: National Audit Office.

Margolis, M., Resnick, D. and Tu, C. C. (1997) 'Campaigning on the Internet: Parties and Candidates on the World Wide Web in the 1996 Primary Season', *Harvard International Journal of Press Politics*, 2 (1), 59–78.

Marlin, A. S. (1999) 'Politics on the Web, Why and Where?', *Campaigns and Elections*, 20 (3), 11–12.

Mechling, J. (2002) 'Information Age Government: Just the Start of Something Big?' in Kamarck, E. and Nye, J. S. (eds), *Governance.Com*, Washington, DC: Brookings Institution Press, 141–60.

Morris, D. (2000) *Vote.Com*, Los Angeles: Renaissance Books.

Negroponte, N. (1995) *Being Digital*, London: Coronet.

Newell, J. L. (2001) 'Italian Political Parties on the Web', *Harvard International Journal of Press Politics*, 6 (4), 60–87.

Nie, N. H. and Ebring, L. (2000) 'Internet and Society: A Preliminary Report', Stanford Institute for the Study of Quantative Society <www.stanford.edu/group/siqss>

Norris, P. (2001) *Digital Divide*, Cambridge: Cambridge University Press.

Norris, P. (2002) *Democratic Phoenix*, Cambridge: Cambridge University Press.

Norris, P. (2003) 'Preaching to the Converted', *Party Politics*, 9 (1), 21–46.

Pedersen, K. (2001) 'Ballots and Technology in the Danish Parties', paper presented to the ECPR Joint Session Workshops, 6–11 April, University of Grenoble.

Pickerill, J. (2000) 'Environmentalists and the Net,' in Gibson, R. K. and Ward, S. J. (eds), *Reinvigorating Democracy?* Aldershot: Ashgate, 129–50.

Putnam, R. (2000) *Bowling Alone*, Simon Schuster: New York.

Rheingold, H. (1993) *The Virtual Community*, New York, NY: HarperPerennial.

Römmele, A. (2002) *Direkte Kommunikation zwischen Parteien und Wählern*, Opladen: Westdeutscher Verlag.

Schuefele, D. and Nisbet, M. (2002) 'Being a Citizen Online', *Harvard Journal of Press/Politics*, 7 (3), 55–75.

SDA (2001) *World Internet Project Italy*, Milan: SDA Bocconi <http://www.economiaemanagement.it/Universita/Allegati/wip8english.pdf>

Semetko, H. and Krasnoboka, N. (2003) 'The Political Role of the Internet in Societies in Transition: Russia and Ukraine Compared', *Party Politics*, 9 (1), 77–104.

Smith, C. F. and Gray, P. (1999), 'The Scottish Parliament in the Information Age' in Coleman, S., Taylor, J. and van de Donk, W. (eds), *Parliament in the Age of the Internet*, Oxford: Oxford University Press, 67–79.

Solop, F. I. (2000) 'Internet Voting and the 2000 Election, A Case Study of the Arizona Democratic Party Primary Election', Paper presented at the 55th annual conference of American Association for Public Opinion Research, Portland, Oregon, USA, 18–21 May.

Tkach, L (2003) 'Politics @ Japan: Party Competition on the Internet in Japan', *Party Politics*, 9 (1), 105–23.

Uslaner, E. (2001) 'Trust Civic Engagement and the Internet', paper presented to the ECPR Joint Session Workshops, 6–11 April, University of Grenoble.

Verba, S., and Nie, N. H. (1972) *Participation in America*, Chicago: The University of Chicago Press.

Voerman, G. (1999) 'Distributing Electronic Folders: The Digital Electoral Campaign of 1998 in the Netherlands', Documentatie-centrum Nederlandse Politieke Partijen, University of Groningen.

Voerman, G. and Ward, S. J. (2000) 'New Media and New Politics', in Voerman, G. and Lucardie, P. (eds), *Jaerboek Documentatiecentrum Nederlandse Politieke Partijen 1999*, Groningen: University of Groningen, 192–215.

Wellman, B., Quan Haase, A., Witte, J. and Hampton, K. (2001) 'Does the Internet Increase, Decrease, or Supplement Social capital?', *American Behavioral Scientist*, 45 (3), 49–64.

Wilhelm, A. G. (2000) *Democracy in the Digital Age*, New York and London: Routledge.

Wray, S. (1998) 'Electronic Civil Disobedience and the World Wide Web of Hactivism', <http://www.nyu.edu/projects/wray/wwwhack.html>, New York University.

2 Electronic democracy and the 'mixed polity'

Symbiosis or conflict?

Charles D. Raab and Christine Bellamy

I have a fantasy in which a modern Constitutional Convention assembles a group of fifty-five men or thereabouts whose commitment to democracy and whose wisdom are not in doubt. Their task is to design democratic institutions suitable for this small planet in the year 2000. And so they come to the problem of the unit (Dahl 1967: 957–8).

Introduction: the problem of democracy in the 'mixed polity'

Dahl's wise men disagreed about which unit was the most suitable for democracy, on a scale ranging from the very local to the global. Yet, because politics occurs at all these different territorial levels, Dahl argued that we ought to consider different democratic models for units of different size and kind. The arguments for democracy at the local end of his scale turned, as they have always done, on the prospect for direct citizen participation in collective decision-making, while the necessity for representative institutions was plain at any level beyond the very small.

Here we are, past the year 2000. The implications of ICTs did not enter into Dahl's thinking, nor did – or could – the prospect of a postmodern, post-parliamentary politics. Nevertheless, the central thesis of this chapter is that 'the problem of the unit' remains with us still. Indeed, it has been made much more complex by enhanced possibilities for direct participation through ICTs, and by the postmodern vista that brings into view a wider variety of collectivities. In post-modern thinking about the networked society, moreover, these collectivities are increasingly defined not simply in terms of territory, but in terms of interests, affinities or identities of all sorts. Some collectivities are 'real', while others are 'virtual', existing only in cyberspace, and some might be very short-lived. Some aspire to some degree of autonomy, to the right to decide matters for themselves. Certain of these matters are internal, relating to deliberation and implementation of rules, policies and issues relating only to the collectivity in question, while others are concerned with their relations to other polities, including states. For some groups, it is difficult or impossible to estimate the size of membership, or to establish clear criteria for joining or exclusion. For some, too, it is impossible to identify a leader or leadership group, because such roles are eschewed, rather like student movements in the late 1960s.

In this kind of thinking, cyberspace subverts spatial boundaries, including those of territorial political communities at all levels. It empowers affinity groups that cut across jurisdictions, and vastly increases the possibilities of forming temporary or longer-lasting collectivities. This notion of a partly connected, partly disconnected, interweaving and shifting constellation of political forums and arenas makes Dahl's problem look simple, grappling as he did with a set of less inclusive, more stable, more territorially defined political arrangements than would be possible in the postmodern scenarios. It also makes the design and reform of democratic processes – especially considering how they might be experienced by persons who are involved in more than one of these collectivities – far more interesting, but much less tractable.

Our purpose here is to cast light on the issues that are involved, by exploring the relationship between the 'modern' politics that Dahl took for granted – especially its characteristic orientation to representative democracy – and an ICT-powered, postmodern politics characterised by more diffuse structures and less commensurable political norms. In order to explore this relationship, we conceive of politics as increasingly taking place in a 'mixed polity'; that is, a polity composed of a mixture of different, and not obviously compatible, political forms, some that bear obvious affinities with postmodern politics and others that continue to be shaped by the legacies of the modern period. In the history of Western constitutional ideas, 'mixed government' was usually conceived as a mixture of (pre-modern) monarchical and aristocratic elements with (modern) democratic elements, but we borrow the term to denote a polity composed at once of modern *and* postmodern elements. *If* postmodern practices are emerging – and we think that this is probably the case – then they must be taking root amidst an institutional framework that has been shaped in modern times. Their juxtaposition thus creates a mixed polity of considerable complexity.

We conceive of the mixed polity, then, as a welter of jurisdictions, networks and domains, some defined in terms of recognised territories, some defined in formal institutional terms, some based on interests and affinities, some constituted online, but many defined in hybrid terms. We argue, too, that the study of the mixed polity cannot for long evade or ignore classical questions to do with membership, accountability, representation and the legitimacy of decisions. In political structures of traditional, territorial units that have persisted from the modern into the postmodern era, there is a continuing pressure to maintain processes that make possible some kind of aggregative and integrative functions in and among the different networks and sectors in which politics takes place. We assume, however, that these processes are not likely to enjoy the kind of centrality and primacy that classical constitutional theory, at least, accords institutions in the 'electoral chain of command' that connects citizens to central institutions of decision-making.[1] Instead, democratic processes focused on electoral politics, representative government and parliamentary debates will have to fight for a place amidst a growing array of competing, cross-cutting forums and countervailing ideas. How, and indeed whether they can be expected to do so successfully, is a question we begin to address here.

Various scenarios are taking shape in contemporary thinking about the fluid politics of the mixed polity. They involve ICTs to different degrees. Some democratic forums – such as established policy communities – are strongly institutionalised and provide the means of participation for insider groups in policy-making within conventionally defined, territorially referenced units, albeit often in ways that are both closed and opaque. Other groups operate in the well-established structures of civil society, at different levels, including the grass roots. Their political influence upon the wider polity is probably best described as limited and sporadic: it is certainly far from non-existent but tends to be issue-specific and contingent, although it is also oriented towards formal political processes. Beyond these well-recognised scenarios is a postmodern one in which still other groups function at the margins of civil society, with almost no connection to conventional public decision-making arenas and almost no awareness of, or contact with, the machinery of parties or parliaments. Some of these may constitute themselves solely as virtual, cyberspace 'communities' detached from place and from the political issues and processes of territorially based politics.

The (as yet empirically unproven) premise behind much postmodern writing (e.g. Holmes 1997) is that, in principle at least, it will be easier for groups – however transient and ephemeral – to flourish in the 'virtual society' formed in cyberspace. By this reading, the virtual society can support a much more inclusive politics, one that is capable of sustaining large numbers of such groups and involving individuals in multiple memberships, defined by their particular mix of special interests. At the very least, 'real-world society' in general may become more aware of their existence and demands, so that they are enabled more easily and confidently to assert and negotiate their claims. For this postmodern scenario to come to pass, however, it is necessary to assume some kind of connectivity between the politics that takes place in these different groups – virtual, territorial, affinity-based or whatever. Will this really be the case, or will postmodern politics simply grow in the interstices of the modern constitutional state, with no more heed to its health or demands than that paid by postmodern critics who have simply written it off? If territorial boundaries give way in cyberspace, does it follow that what must give way as well is the idea that politics has essentially to do with decision-making within, and on behalf of, a discrete and bounded collectivity? If it does so follow, does it mean, first, that postmodern politics undermines the possibility of holding any institutions or persons to account for the consequences of decisions, or for the probity and technical quality of governmental processes. Second, does it mean, too, that, if decision-making is a matter only for each of these polities in and for itself, then the need for debate, discussion, argument – in short, the aggregation or reconciliation of the views or interests of any wider collectivity – is obviated?

ICTs: reinvigorating or marginalising formal political institutions?

These questions arise from the disjuncture between the significance ascribed to formal political institutions in modern and postmodern writings, a disjuncture that lies in their intrinsically opposed views about the significance and desirability of social complexity and political order, and in the implications of these views for the ways in which they relate to evolving concepts of representation, aggregation and accountability. At some danger of oversimplification, it may be said that, as it developed in western Europe in the late eighteenth and nineteenth centuries, representative and responsible government promoted a concept of order that placed a premium on hierarchical, top-down control of the demands made by civil society on the political world. The practice of representation (better understood perhaps as 're-presentation') emerged as a device for simplifying the way the political elite conceived of society as well as for classifying the sets of views that came to be expressed. In other words, constitutional models such as mixed government and then representative democracy held an emergent pluralisation at bay by structuring and legitimating the kinds of interests that were given a voice and the channels through which they were able legitimately to express their demands. They served, therefore, to reduce the volume and scope of issues that the political system was obliged to process and resolve, as well to restrict the range of acceptable solutions. It can therefore be argued that representative democracy emerged as a particularly orderly and mostly successful device for reducing political complexity in an era when the growth of the electorate, the growth of the mass media, and the growth in the range and scope of the administrative state could be expected to increase massively the range of demands on the political system. To a significant but – as we argue later – decreasingly successful extent, representative democracy has served to channel, and therefore to restrict, these demands while providing a legitimate democratic front. Above all, representative democracy has secured for governments a degree of freedom and space to deal with social problems by negotiating in sometimes relatively closed networks with powerful interests on which, however, they have therefore become increasingly dependent. In other words, representative democracy buttresses the primacy of central political institutions and protects them by providing legitimate mechanisms for managing complexity (Easton 1965).

This is a solution to the problem of order that has also carried a high political price, not least in increasing exclusion, public disillusionment and apathy. It is also one that has become increasingly less convincing as representative bodies and elected governments have become less able to monopolise and control processes of public decision-making. In previous writing (Bellamy and Raab 1999a,b; Bellamy 2000), we analysed the problems faced by representative democracy at the end of the twentieth century and examined how far ICTs offer scope for its reform and renewal, with particular reference to its British parliamentary form. In particular, we were concerned to probe the significance of ICTs for the management of complexity. Two key questions arose. First, will ICTs serve, for example, to encourage the emergence of a wider range of more open, less easily manipulated interactions between parliamentary elites and members of the public, thus reinvigorating representative democracy? Second, will they provide governments with the means of re-centring public decision-making on the 'electoral chain of command' or will they simply reinforce existing problems and trends?

To examine the first of these questions, we surveyed the possible uses of such devices as telephony, digital TV, personal computers and networked terminals in public or commercial spaces, and analysed the democratic significance of ICTs, using a four-rung 'ladder of informatisation' of a politics based on parliamentary institutions (Bellamy and Raab 1999a,b). This 'ladder' is reproduced in the Appendix. We concluded that the application of ICTs *could* well improve parliamentary procedures and bring representative institutions closer to the public. But we also found that there are few signs that representative institutions are, as yet, much interested in innovations on the higher rungs. This is not surprising, for a number of reasons. Not least of these is the severe challenge that the development of new information and communication flows pose to what are often deeply entrenched infrastructures and processes for handling information and communications, and for controlling the uses to which they are put. The 'reinforcement' thesis (Danziger *et al.* 1982) holds that existing institutions tend to tame new technologies and shape them to their own purposes: technology thus becomes a tool for the reinforcement of existing power structures. Democratic institutions find it easier and less threatening to innovate – and particularly to embed innovation into their day-to-day routines – in ways that are commensurate with existing communication paradigms, established structures of political control and well-established organisational roles.

It follows that we should expect parliaments, too, to focus more effort on 'informatising' their own internal business arrangements and on the delivery of information to the public, with much less interest being shown in stimulating and incorporating more open democratic interaction. We therefore believe that, especially in the longer term, the significance of ICTs is more likely to lie in the service of direct, non-representative forms in which citizens interact with each other in ways that do not presuppose the existence, or even the primacy of, central political institutions. In such a context, attempts to 'wire up' parliaments might be better seen as futile, rearguard actions by deeply conservative institutions jealous of their prerogatives and legitimacy. For these reasons, our overall thesis was that informatisation can go only so far in adapting conventional political institutions to the politics of a diffused, pluralist, postmodern society.

This conclusion is reinforced by a broad-brush assessment of the implications of ICTs in relation to five trends that are commonly perceived to be undermining the primacy and legitimacy of the 'electoral chain of command' in Western representative democracies. These trends are:

- the overtaking of conventional politics by electronic media;
- the power of party discipline over representative institutions;
- the control of representative institutions by political executives;

- the displacement of decision-making into policy networks;
- the 'hollowing-out' of the state.

We next examine each in turn.

The overtaking of conventional politics by electronic media

The Internet is often regarded as a *pluralising* medium, facilitating the creation of more diverse sources of information as well as new, independent channels of political communication and debate. Far from reinforcing trends to more highly managed forms of democracy, cybersociety, it is widely believed, could subvert or supplant the power of politicians, bureaucrats and media tycoons. There has been considerable excitement, therefore, about the burgeoning of community networks, electronic public squares and online bulletin boards (Tsagarousianou *et al.* 1998). Petitions are organised electronically; electoral campaigns are revitalised by online access to candidates' information and electronic hustings; and electronic channels are used to disseminate dissident information and views from within repressive, closed regimes.

The potential significance of such opportunities for democratic participation may be inestimable, for many of them bear directly upon the core processes of accountability and representation. However, practice is lagging, especially insofar as it bears on the quality of interaction among citizens, elected representatives and governments. For many years to come, most people will continue to receive a significant proportion of their political communication from old-style broadcast media. Moreover, the increasing convergence of communications and entertainment media, together with the growing competition between their service providers, could seriously challenge traditional public service broadcasting. Unless they can convey the view that politics matters and is interesting to citizens, ICTs will have failed to overcome the apathy that corrodes the current system of representative democracy. But, beyond this consciousness-raising effect, the new technologies must provide the means for greater participation, on the one hand, and accountability on the other. Supporting these functions might well be within the scope of ICTs, depending upon how they permeate society and are designed with political accessibility in mind, not just as 'consumer' tools for fun, shopping, receipt of state benefits and the like, and certainly not as instruments for top-down surveillance and control.

The power of party discipline over representative institutions

In principle, ICTs could easily support a variety of new channels of communication *within* political organisations, through which the patterns of information flows might be changed and powerful resources made available to ordinary members to help them challenge party machines. On the other hand, party elites might be equipped with a more extensive and effective armoury of electronic tools that might reinforce their communicative supremacy; history attests to the difficulty of reforming party organisations. There is evidence that party bureaucracies are alert to the possibilities of ICTs for strengthening central control, improving the efficiency of electoral campaigning and reaching supporters and voters. Whether they are using ICTs for creating party structures that are more open to influence from below is less certain (Ward and Gibson 1998). Moreover, as we will discuss in the following, in the information age traditional parties are as likely to be side-stepped by new political processes, or 'hollowed out', as they are to reinvent themselves with new ICTs.

The control of parliaments by political executives

The executive's control of parliament is built into the bones of Cabinet systems such as that of the United Kingdom, where it is a consequence of the development of party-political discipline over a century or more. This control is not likely to be easily loosened simply by the informatisation of representative institutions, especially if this means little more than enhancing government's ability to give information to parliament, MPs' ability to communicate with individual citizens or parliament's ability to broadcast to the public. Recent and cautious reforms of parliamentary procedures within the United Kingdom, although not without important effects on the scrutiny of the executive and on the ability of some citizens to affect decision agendas more effectively, have so far failed to bring about fundamental change in the relationship between parliament and government. To the extent that ICTs have been involved in these changes – for example, the televising of proceedings (utilising the technologies of the 'first media age'), the greater availability of documents and reports on the Internet (utilising the technologies of the 'second media age') and procedures for petitioning legislatures – they offer only modest comfort to the 'optimistic' school. Reports from other countries – for example, the United States, Denmark, Slovenia and others (Coleman *et al.* 1999; Margolis and Resnick 2000) – point to a similar conclusion. Improving the ability of representative institutions to hold executives to account depends more on structural and procedural changes, perhaps assisted by ICTs, than on ICTs themselves.

The displacement of decision-making into policy networks

The fragmentation of the governmental system into specialist policy communities or 'subgovernments' embracing both public and private interests has long been recognised, for example, in the seminal work of Richardson and Jordan (1979) who coined the term 'post-parliamentary politics' to underline its significance for the 'electoral chain of command'. There has been rather less comment on the de-centring of democracy that may result from this trend, as opposed to tacit acceptance of it as an inevitable way of managing complexity and interdependence in the modern world (but see Kooiman 1993; Kickert *et al.* 1997). The question arises, then, as to how ICTs could help to reverse, or at least help to manage, the trend towards decision-making in what are often closed, non-transparent networks outside the main arenas of parliamentary democracy. This question directs us to consider the extent to which the policy elites that have become integrated into these networks are themselves subject to democratic control and renewal.

This issue resonates, therefore, with the growing preoccupation in recent democratic theory with strategies for democratising the multiple centres of power and decision-making in the complex, interdependent structures of modern governance (Etzioni-Halévy 1993). Insofar as new kinds of electronically supported information flows and resources, including those generated by new kinds of civic networks and bulletin boards, could help to support such strategies, then informatisation could mitigate counter-democratic tendencies associated with policy networks.

There are, however, two important qualifications to be made about such optimistic scenarios. The first is that by enabling speedier communication and sharing of information in and around networks, ICTs may themselves be implicated in the proliferation of networking as a form of governance, masking complexity and fragmentation by reducing the costs and inconvenience in managing relationships across boundaries. In facilitating the trend towards networks, ICTs also conspire in producing its political consequences. It is likely that some players will develop better ICT infrastructures than others and – other things being equal – that they will be able to win more often in the political games played in networks. The growing dependence on ICTs means that these tools will play an important part in modifying power balances amongst participants: ICTs, like money or votes before them, are becoming a powerful resource for political competition. There are likely to be new sets of 'haves' and new sets of 'have-nots' in the networked polity. What Schattschneider (1960) called the 'mobilisation of bias' – in which some issues, and the interests associated with them, are organised into politics whilst others are organised out – might well persist in the networked polity, even taking new forms, as ICTs rewrite the rules of the game. That would hardly be a democratic outcome.

Second, even if networked technologies could increase the inclusiveness of at least some kinds of decision-making processes, we need to consider what kind of democratic politics would ensue. Democratising the internal processes of political parties, strengthening and democratising civil institutions (some perhaps in a virtual sense) and enhancing the accountability and circulation of elites within networks all speak to the *aggregative* as well as the *expressive* functions of representation and accountability. But they would do so mainly in relation to each of the many dispersed centres of power in a complex world. What is largely unanswered is whether and how such scenarios could map onto, or help to reinvent, the processes of electoral politics and political debate in traditional political units, especially the core processes of representation and accountability.

The 'hollowing-out' of the state

The preceding discussion provides specific illustrations of a more general point, that governing may be too complex and societies too diffuse to be steered effectively, at least through the traditional structures of the Weberian state. One version of this argument is that the state is being 'hollowed out' both from without and within (Rhodes 1996). In this view, power shifts away from centralised state institutions in downward, outward and upward directions, although there are serious doubts that central governments are quite so rapidly and extensively losing their grip over policies and their implementation in many fields (Pierre and Peters 2000). What is the case, however, is that the constraints on states' autonomous power over strategic and economic decision-making have become more apparent as governments become increasingly entwined in the management of international interdependencies. Internally, too, governments are confronted by policy networks, as discussed earlier, in which the role they play ranges from uncertain leadership to deep dependence (Weller *et al.* 1997).

In addition to these problems, governments operate within multi-centric societies, with shifting modes of influence and multiple sources of power. Moreover, diversity and complexity go beyond the structural to the cultural: society is not only multi-centric but multicultural and varied in its values. The processes of representative democracy cannot be unaffected by such changes, and attention must therefore be directed to the cultural provenance of the accounts and stories that are brokered in representative institutions. How are they negotiated, and by whom? Whose narratives do they represent? Even to pose these questions is to doubt whether all voices can be equally represented, heard and reconciled through the restricted and highly managed channels of representative democracy. They might be more faithfully articulated through new, more direct, more pluralised modes of democratic politics.

The argument here is that democratic practices must change to accommodate a socially diverse society, just as they must also respond to the emergence of more diffuse and complex governing arrangements. Flexible ICT networks appear to offer the technical means for acknowledging and coping with such complexity. But for this very reason, they raise important normative issues. Without new forms of coordination and aggregation, there is a real danger that ICTs will simply amplify the fragmentation of public space, balkanising politics into multifarious and shifting constituencies that cannot be aggregated by any obvious means into collective decision and action. Moreover, cybersociety transcends national boundaries as the parameters of political activity, reinforcing trends towards the globalisation of politics. It is far from clear that the representative institutions of individual states can find an adequate response. Representatives may, for example, wish to consider the extent to which, and the means through which, they should take notice of the outcomes of political debates conducted in the public squares and bulletin boards of cyberspace. However, such efforts at incorporation may – rightly perhaps – be seen as forlorn attempts to tame new technologies and resist the possibility of legitimising new democratic forms.

The conclusion to be drawn from this brief survey of the declining health of representative democracy is that there are few reasons to suppose that informatisation will either greatly disturb or accommodate the main lines indicated by these five trends. If anything, it is people operating outside the context of representative institutions who are the most enthusiastic about ICTs, and they appear to see more exciting possibilities for a politics without representative democracy (e.g. Holmes 1997; Poster 1993, 1997). They are therefore bent either on replacing it or paralleling it with what they deem to be more authentic, or direct, democratic forms that are better suited to a post-parliamentary politics.

But what kind of 'politics' can that be? Politics as a process concerned with the making and implementation of decisions by governmental institutions figures only vaguely in images of postmodern politics, in which the emphasis is far more on discourse and communication than on deliberation, decision and execution. Where parliamentary decision-making aggregates and condenses, political discourse about a postmodern world disaggregates and expands, celebrating variety and the rich pluralism of opinion. That discourse, in itself, aims at no terminal point of aggregative decision. It therefore aims at no action for which anybody can be held accountable under any code of accountability. It is also, therefore, of course, a politics in which 'representation' seems to have little real meaning or resonance as part of a legitimising theory of democracy, and in which 'accountability' is hard to locate, either conceptually or empirically. This implies serious consequences for the aggregative and accountability functions that lie at the heart of representative democracy in large-scale societies – at least, as that form of democracy has been traditionally understood.

Does this matter and, if so, why? Answering these questions needs to start with confronting a set of underlying issues to do with the nature and locus of power and decision-making in the virtual polity, the continuing role and nature of the modern 'state' and how we should think about the relationship of one to the other. To go back to Dahl (1967): what are the political units in which the practice of participation and accountability in the mixed polity could and should be articulated? Before we open up these issues, let us revisit the discussion of a prior question: what are representative political institutions *for*?

Integration, plurality and collectivity

The traditional answer to this question is that democracy is not simply about providing opportunities for individual citizens to express their personal opinions, to promote their private interests or to seek redress for individual grievances – or indeed to join together with other citizens to mobilise the power to do these things – though it must certainly embrace all these possibilities. Individuals also hold interests in common as a *collectivity*, a 'public', that shares goods and values in common, makes rules for collective life, and establishes widely accepted principles for promoting mutual well-being. This recognition of the importance of the 'public domain' has certain crucial implications for assessing the claim that a political system is 'democratic'.

First, a democracy must establish open, inclusive processes by which public issues can be not only *aired* but also *resolved*, and through which the value system underpinning them can be constantly tested and renewed. Second, the decisions that are made, and the actions that are undertaken, on behalf of the public must be open to public display, scrutiny, challenge and revision. Third, the damage that those decisions and actions might do to individuals and groups must be preventable or at least remediable. Thus, representative democracy involves an inclusive process, in which participants display certain moral qualities, especially tolerance of each other's perspectives and interests and a willingness to mediate them with reasoned argument. The ideal that is often put forward is a form of *deliberative democracy*, involving a search for the best outcome for the collectivity as a whole, one that is acceptable to, or at least not harmful for, all participants (Fishkin 1991). 'Deliberative democracy', of course, can mean different things, as recent discussions show (Elster 1998), but most theorists adhere to a core definition, which:

> includes collective decision-making with the participation of all who will be affected by the decision or their representatives: this is the democratic part. Also...it includes decision-making by means of arguments offered *by* and *to* participants who are committed to the values of rationality and impartiality: this is the deliberative part.
>
> (Elster 1998: 8; emphasis in original)

Our understanding of aggregation *includes* deliberation (or discussion, or debate) as the means for arriving at a (perhaps voted) conclusion of decision- and policy-making. In using this term, we wish to avoid the connotation of 'mere' aggregation through voting, though we part company with any notion of deliberative democracy that suggests that all can be resolved simply by maximising opportunities for rational discussion.

All this means that there is a necessary duality – and therefore an important and inescapable tension – at the very heart of the notion of the 'public'. Ranson and Stewart (1994: 60) observe that '[p]ublic means not only "the public as a collectivity" (the whole) but also "the public as plurality" (the many)'. Thus a 'citizen' is, at once, both a member of a society with collective interests and an individual within an aggregation of individuals all of whom have private and partial interests. The exercise of citizenship therefore implies not only the power to influence decision-making and to hold decision-makers to account, but to engage in both of these processes in ways that acknowledge and accommodate the interrelationships between public purposes and private concerns. Viewed from the 'top', private interests are not only those held by individuals, but also include sectoral interests formed by, and defining, groups below the level of the collectivity as a whole, as in most accounts of 'pluralist' politics. Viewed from below, however, the issue is not so simple. Faced with a multitude of arenas, interests and roles, how can individuals handle their relationships with the diverse and diffuse communities and networks to which they potentially belong?

As we have seen, Dahl (1967) discussed the problem of recognising and accommodating a range of territorially defined collectivities within a single state. Most 'modern' democratic theory assumes that the collectivities in question are coterminous with fixed, constitutionally recognised, political units, such as those bounded by a nation, a province or a local authority area. Such theory is usually couched, therefore, in terms of a simple, one-dimensional relationship between individual citizens and the unit(s) in question, a relationship that is mediated primarily if not exclusively through processes of representation and accountability, channelled through representative bodies. Thus, as we have seen, the political significance of the representative democracy project lies in the way it reinforced the ideal of a highly integrated, geographically defined polity, even as the world became a more complex place. Representative democracy assumes both the possibility and desirability of a single political sovereign ('parliamentary sovereignty') conceived usually in centralised and hierarchical terms. It therefore assumes a unified and unitary structure of command, such as the 'electoral chain of command'. Above all, it assumes a single and inclusive forum of the political nation, reflected, for example, in the primacy of the House of Commons in the UK political system. This arrangement is constitutionally compatible with the existence of lesser territorial political entities, which nest within the overall national polity, although in practice there may be unresolved tensions among levels. In the UK, once again, where local governments are creatures of Acts of Parliament rather than having entrenched constitutional status, relationships have been highly conflictual over long stretches of time, and many issues concerning the relationship between Westminster and the devolved systems of Scotland, Wales and Northern Ireland remain unresolved.

Assumptions about the primacy of the overarching polity have been institutionalised through long-standing practices. They emphasize the role of elected representatives as gatekeepers as well as conduits of democratic opinion, filtering both the number and range of opinions and issues that come into political account. They also assert the desirability of simplifying and aggregating opinions and issues to the point where they are capable of being re-presented and resolved in a single forum, and they establish administrative arrangements capable of guaranteeing the primacy, inclusiveness and effectiveness of feedback. These institutional assumptions are also reflected in how we think about the polities nesting within the state. In these ways, the rhetoric and practices associated with representative democracy may be seen as important techniques for *controlling* and making more manageable the political effects of social complexity and diversity at each level of a territorially defined state.

In contrast, however, political theorists have recently become much more conscious of the growing mismatch between the confinement of democratic politics within the restricted channels of representative politics, and the multiple nodes of power to be found in complex systems of governance. These nodes include many that transcend the increasingly blurred and shifting boundaries between state and society, and between one state and another. At the same time, what has become more apparent is the plurality of connections experienced by individuals to the multifaceted social and governmental worlds they inhabit. The 'collectivities' through which individuals seek to pursue their interests are plural, contingent, overlapping and often transient: they are neither simply defined nor fixed, and they are not circumscribed by geography alone. They are constituted by a variety of criteria, of which the territorial is only one. They are also far from being uniformly dominated by formal state institutions or by conventional political channels.

Parliaments and postmodernisation

Most accounts of postmodern society and politics dwell upon the transformation of the state, and upon the shift of public decision-making away from the primacy of central institutions in a more fragmented, diffuse polity. Here there are plural nodes of decision-making, as networks and markets supplant or coexist with bureaucracies and hierarchies (Maidment and Thompson 1993). In some versions, there are no normatively privileged ruling institutions and no central core of agreed public purposes or moral values. For some writers, this shift is inevitable and is viewed dispassionately: because collective goals cannot be pursued in the postmodern polity, it is meaningless, and *merely* nostalgic, to give them much further thought. It is futile, moreover, to fret about the design of institutional forms that might give them effect (see, e.g. Frissen 1999: chapter 5, commenting on recent Dutch parliamentary reform commissions). Indeed, for theorists such as Poster (1997), it is useless to try to imagine a postmodern 'democracy': even to employ this term is to imprison the future in the worn out categories of modernism. For writers such as these, the stance has to be one of *letting go*. For others, however, these trends are to be regretted not least because they empty politics of collective content, meaning and morality. The danger is not so much that politics will transmute into a war of all against all, but that:

> it will not be about anything in particular. There is no inquiry, no debate, no agreed-upon grounds for asserting truth-claims, no propositions to be tested, no persuasion, no refutation, and no requirement that words connote the same phenomena for everyone.
>
> (Fox and Miller 1995: 69)

The postmodernisation of politics would cut society adrift from the prospect of improvement guided by generally agreed aims, including the pursuit of egalitarian ends (van Stokkom 1992, cited in Frissen 1999: 107). Furthermore, postmodernists view ICTs as the handmaiden of these accelerating trends. 'Cyberspace' is virtual, and cannot be tied to or mapped onto the formal institutions of the Weberian state. 'Cyberdemocracy' can be developed in all kinds of ways that owe nothing to the territorial collectivities that their members may inhabit. The very concepts of 'membership' or 'citizenship' are unclear and elusive; so too, in consequence, are 'decision' and 'policy'. The very notions of 'representation' and 'accountability' appear, then, to be irrelevant, embarrassingly outmoded and of little value in these postmodernising political scenarios.

If this scenario does accurately describe an emergent future, then, as we have speculated before, the application of ICTs to reinvigorating representative democracy amounts to 'wiring-up the deck-chairs' on a ship of state that is doomed to sink below the waves (Bellamy and Raab 1999a). But what, then, are we to make of democratic innovations such as the historic re-creation of a devolved Scottish government – one, moreover, that is replete with plans for the extensive use of ICTs in its parliamentary and governmental organisations, as well as facilitating communication between these organisations, citizens and social groups? Is this simply to provide the deckchairs with tartan cushions? The very centrepiece of the new devolved arrangements is the establishment of a representative body – a parliament – one that is related to an accountable executive, and one of a type that, we are increasingly told by postmodernists, is fast being consigned to redundancy or oblivion.

This question brings us back to the issues at the heart of this chapter. What role can there be for central political institutions in the mixed polity, and how (and how effectively) could the performance of this role be subjected to democratic involvement and accountability? A scan of contemporary political theory suggests that it is possible, in principle, to adopt one of four broad responses to these questions in the literatures on postmodernism and pluralisation. The *first* – associated with certain post-Marxist literature (see variously, Miller 1989; Mouffe 1992; Hirst 1994) – finds it impossible, in the end, to let go of the concept of the Weberian state, however hollowed out it becomes. This writing continues to see the state as a special kind of association that can and should control the terms on which all other associations exist and act. The talk in this literature is of a continuing process of pluralisation, in which the state itself fosters a more diverse, participative, inclusive society as a continuous act of political will. It devolves more of its own functions, for example, to voluntary associations in civil society, and takes positive steps to nurture a wider range of communities. It may thereby come to recognise a much wider range of identities and demands, including those from hitherto excluded groups. However, the overriding claims of social justice mean that it must ultimately retain both the right and capacity for regulating civil society and mediating among the different constituencies that compose the polity. In other words, there is a powerful if residual notion that the state, and therefore democratic institutions within the state, should continue to provide a forum for deciding what is good and just for the collectivity as a whole. The assumption is that democratic debate can continue to take place on the basis of common values, bringing, for example, equality and justice to the fore. It follows that parliaments, however limited their powers, should and could still aspire to serve as symbols of political integration and as important sources of coherent policy.

The *second* response is more commonly associated with post-communitarian and liberal theorists further to the Right (e.g. MacInytre 1988; Rawls 1972). It acknowledges – not always with complacency – the multiplicity and diversity of identities and values in contemporary society and, in consequence, denies that there is a common platform of values capable of supporting a widely accepted notion of what is socially just. Indeed, the assertion of such a notion is bound to be oppressive to those who do not share in the dominant value system. However, they believe that it might, nevertheless, be possible to agree on a set of procedures that could permit different groups to compete in the political arena on terms that could be generally acknowledged as 'fair'. In this formulation, central institutions take overarching responsibility for mediating and supervising relations of competition and exchange that exist among groups and networks. Aggregation is important, but it amounts to no more than an agreement about procedure. Voting, for example, is good enough.

The *third* response – which, as we have seen earlier, is mainly associated with postmodernism as a theoretical perspective (Connolly 1991; Poster 1993; Fox and Miller 1995; Frissen 1999) – is the belief that aggregation in either of these senses is neither a feasible ambition nor normatively desirable. Formal governing institutions may survive, but have no generally accepted prior claim to regulate or mediate among other associations, groups or networks. Postmodern society is seen, rather, as a web of affinities and affiliations, often shifting and never permanently fixed. Social bonds are formed from webs of meaning that are constantly renegotiated and always contingent. From this perspective, any attempt to re-centre politics on the state, to impose an overarching set of values or procedures, is therefore bound to be partial and oppressive: aggregation is an inherently dangerous aspiration. What, however, is there to prevent this ambition being realized? What, too, is there to ensure that webs are open, or to prevent the emergence of new forms of exclusion? At this point, postmodern theory tends to fall back on the assertion that postmodern politics are likely to be associated with new dispositions and attitudes, ones that are capable of fostering new connectivities and more open, more welcoming political discourses and communicative orientations. It therefore fosters a hope that postmodern society can engender greater mutual respect. Whether this hope is based on anything more solid than unfounded optimism is as yet far from clear.

The *fourth* response – one to which our own analysis tends – acknowledges postmodern tendencies to fragmentation and balkanisation, and agrees that they cast important doubts on the practical competence of the modern state. But, at the same time, it is much more sceptical about the possibility of an unproblematic, universal shift to a new postmodern political style. It seems more likely that the emerging polity will be a hybrid or mixed social form, in which the contradictions between modernity and postmodernity set up tensions that will prove to be impossible to resolve. On the one hand, the mediative, aggregative, aspirations of the state and its central machinery will never finally wither (though the capacity to fulfil them may well become severely attenuated), and the traditional functions of representative bodies – aggregation, representation and ensuring accountability – will never become entirely redundant. On the other hand, the pluralisation of society, the growing complexity of decision-making, the diffusion of governance and the growing popularity of anti-foundationalist discourses will make it increasingly difficult to sustain the legitimacy and the effectiveness of the 'electoral chain of command'.

The end of parliamentary institutions?

It might seem, on the one hand, that the effort and money spent on reinventing representative institutions amounts to little more than a sentimental clinging to an outdated tradition, to a much-loved political teddy bear. Who *really* believes in them any more? No need to pension them off, however: time will take its toll, despite all the effort devoted to modernising and informatising these bodies. Political and governmental institutions correspond to the societies they inhabit and lead. When – even in Scotland or other places seized with a new-found sense of political identity – we can no longer be certain what constitutes the 'collectivity'; when its manifestation is no longer uniquely tied to an identifiable territory coterminous with a contemporary 'state'; when interests can be aggregated at global and sub-state levels; when deliberation and decision-making can take place in multiple arenas at many levels or at no 'level' at all; then the claims of the parliamentary-democracy project look increasingly threadbare.

On the other hand, it is possible to assert that, though in practice representative bodies may be of small relevance to the making of decisions and to the exercise of power, they nevertheless play an essential part in bestowing meaning and legitimacy on governance, however dispersed and diffused. Indeed, it may be argued that this role will become more, not less, important in conditions of political change, fragmentation and unpredictability. In the proper sense of Bagehot's (1867/1963) famous term, parliaments, and the party politicians who strut across their floors, have become 'dignified' parts of the political system, exercising few direct powers but playing an equally important role in focusing interest and fixing popular attention. Their most significant function is to act as the front offices of politics, displaying the issues of the day, and influencing and reflecting the changing political climate which is, at bottom, the only effective restriction on the powers of back-office networks. For example, it is not necessary to believe that the Scottish people fell victim to a delusion that a self-governing nation collectively required an 'efficient' deliberative body in order to argue the case for the establishment of the Scottish Parliament. Rather, by this view, the Scottish Parliament is a symbolically necessary institution, acting both as a powerful source of legitimation of, and a lodestone for, Scottish aspirations both inside and outside the Scottish political world. It is also, obviously, a working legislature, but it would be to underestimate its full significance to see this as its sole function.

This argument assumes, then, that representative institutions are still perceived as a special source of democratic legitimacy, capable of establishing the democratic credentials of a regime in a way that no other institutions can. It assumes, too, that postmodern politics has not yet established its own claims to legitimacy or transcended what is still, largely, a modern or even pre-modern political culture. Elements of postmodern politics must coexist with the modern consciousness of a past in which the achievement of the representative franchise was the distinctive mark of political belonging, and in which the attrition or abolition of parliamentary institutions signalled important dangers. It is true, of course, that, in the recent past, these dangers were more often associated with the assertion of centralised, authoritarian regimes rather than the splintering of power in an array of disparate networks and groups. But can we face a postmodern future without the blessing of representative institutions? On what objects should political legitimacy now come to rest? A diffuse agglomeration of self-governing, sometimes transitory, fragments?

Parliaments in the mixed polity: still an efficient part of the political system?

This discussion gives force to our view that the most salient feature of contemporary government is that *we are situated between parliamentary and post-parliamentary forms of governance in a mixed polity that uncomfortably embraces elements of both.* The future, indeed, is just as likely to consist of diverse combinations of these forms, as it is to witness either the replacement of modern politics by postmodern politics or the successful resistance of the postmodern by the modern. Elements of modernity will persist into a postmodernising world, which will exhibit varying kinds and degrees of accommodation and tension. In this mixed polity, networks may proliferate but will not have entirely supplanted older, bureaucratic structures of policy-making and implementation. Central administrative machines may continue – altering in shape and scope, reinventing their modes of steering or rowing, hiving off some functions, decentralising others and devolving still more – but they will neither wither away nor become irreversibly hollowed out. In practice, networks tend to adjust to and incorporate these machines, rather than entirely displace them. Markets may be playing a more prominent role in the allocation of values, but they do not normally stand alone and are entwined with other arrangements (Thompson *et al.* 1991). Indeed, one interesting manifestation of the mixed polity is that 'co-production' between the state and society is coming to be seen as a favoured way of making and implementing policy (Kooiman 1993; Kickert *et al.* 1997) even though, from a democratic point of view, many commentators are concerned with their democratic legitimacy (e.g. Rhodes 1997). The main point we make here is that governments are far from irrelevant or invisible in both the literature on and the practice of governance, although their role, influence and accountability are often unclear.[2]

The scenario of postmodern governance is of a *kaleidoscope* of many forms, including those that reflect older concepts of policy-making, representation and deliberation. Its elements are sometimes conflicting, often tailored to the influences of different domains and often inappropriately applied. But it is always variegated rather than uniform, and *that is what is 'postmodern' about it.* Above all, the postmodern polity *celebrates* complexity. As we saw earlier, the modern polity recoils from it, denying it or trying to reduce it, and representative democracy has offered important techniques for bringing this about. The mixed polity, on the other hand, must search for ways of accommodating complexity while also coming to terms with the far from unspent legacies of representative democracy.

It may be, too, that parliaments will still have, and *should* have, a substantive, as well as a legitimating, role to play, in helping to provide for representational, aggregative and accountability functions in the mixed polity. Or perhaps a better way of expressing this is that the performance of a 'dignified' role (in Bagehot's terms) necessarily involves the possibility that representative institutions will continue to have a powerful, if not always easily and directly measurable, influence on public policy and governmental decision-making. As Judge

(1999: 140; emphasis in original) writes, citing a host of supportive literature:

> To conclude that parliament's substantive contribution to law-making is limited, even peripheral in the case of detailed formulation and implementation, does not mean that parliament is peripheral to the process of policy making itself. Often the contribution of parliaments are [*sic*] indirect..., or perform a 'climate setting' role, or, through oversight of policy implementation, contribute to the 'next round' of policy development... But, even if it is conceded that, despite all of this, parliament's practical contribution to policy making is relatively restricted, the crucial point remains that parliamentary representation is still of *paramount importance* in the legitimation of public policy outputs.

The functions of representation and accountability

This argument points to the conclusion that representative bodies will continue to remain (however peripherally) part of the 'efficient' element of the polity, relevant to the direct exercise of whatever effective power still accrues to the Weberian state. We assess this assertion, by exploring what the concepts of representation and accountability might mean, why they might still be important and how they might be operationalised, in the mixed polity. Perhaps unsurprisingly, our tentative conclusion will be that the tensions and contradictions in such a polity make it much more problematic to see how representative institutions can help to make them work but – more contentiously perhaps – we nevertheless assert the continuing importance of these concepts to the democratic health of the contemporary polity. This then, is a conceptual and practical problem that needs to be more thoroughly addressed in relation to the postmodernisation and virtualisation of democracy.

As we have seen already, representation can be seen as a way of coping with overload by simplifying and aggregating demands made upon decision-making bodies, as systems models such as Easton's (1965) show. Structures outside or at the boundary of the 'black box' do not transmit raw pressures or messages; instead, they filter, combine, restate and select them in ways that can then be processed by the government machine. Although systems approaches oversimplify and thereby distort the nature of politics and policy-making, they nevertheless serve a useful purpose by pointing up the role of gatekeeping institutions in the political system. In particular, they set out the rationale for aggregative functions that help to keep the system's fuse from blowing. Representative institutions play a significant gatekeeping role, but elected representatives transform what they 'represent'. The degree to which they distort (misrepresent) the views, interests and demands that they 'stand for', and the reasons why they take-up some while rejecting others, is an important evaluative question, one that exposes the extent to which the frustration of unalloyed popular demands is legitimate in a democratic polity. Representative government is government in which no one person or section can get all they want. Compromise is not only functionally crucial but is thereby cloaked in legitimacy to the point where it is seen as a positive virtue.

In such a system, no one wins outright but some potential issues lose outright by not even getting past the gatekeepers. Depending on the electoral importance of different mixes of interests, the skill of the gatekeeper lies in convincing losers that they have at least had their interests taken into account – a problem that is best pointed up in the Burkean notion of virtual representation. As has been well understood for many years, the success of gatekeeping skills depends upon there being a substantial degree of popular deference to, or trust in, the system – in its processes and incumbents – in order to reconcile as many groups as possible to a process in which they can never entirely win and may sometimes badly lose.

More recently, the crucial, complexity-reducing function of trust has been examined by Luhmann (1979), and its importance is now being rediscovered in the proliferating literatures on co-production, power-dependency, and networks. In the networks of the mixed polity, the mutual negotiation of roles and the critical role played by the exchange of resources, involves trust in the willingness and ability of partners to work to mutual advantage (Raab 1992). In its further development of these relationships into 'contingent interdependency' (Frissen 1999: 227), postmodern governance does not obviate, but may even extend, the need for trust. Frissen writes:

> Administration . . . should primarily rest on a trust in autonomy. Not because autonomy self-evidently produces what is good but because confidence in autonomy is both intelligent and pleasant. It is intelligent because the administration links up with processes of social fragmentation in a flexible fashion . . . It is pleasant because it avoids the administrative perversions . . . of totalising intervention and the destruction of variety. It thereby eliminates the need for fraud, deceit and calculation on the part of autonomous actors and domains towards the central planners . . . But this is not a trust in some ideal of basic democracy or in some naive anarchism. It is a trust based on a respect for contingency, an appreciation of fragmentation and the hope for connections.
>
> (Frissen 1999: 226)

What has changed in the concept of 'trust' is that its use and meaning has shifted over time. No longer are we so concerned as were Burke, Bagehot or Almond and Verba, for example, with the trust of the people in the 'system' as a whole – vertical, bottom-up, generalized trust, if you like. Instead, we have become much more interested in how trust is created in the context of specific relationships for particular purposes. Some examples are the establishment of popular trust relations within a pervasive but specific functional regime (e.g. governments' current concern with establishing popular trust in e-commerce (Raab 1998); the establishment of trust between partners in a public/private partnership; and, as in the quotation above, the establishment of trust between tiers within devolved political or managerial arrangements. What all these examples illustrate well is that this growing interest in trust reflects the more diffused, flexible and contingent nature of contemporary governance, and this must include the exquisite difficulties of establishing trust relationships in the virtual world of cyberspace.

At first sight, at least, it seems obvious that while postmodern life may create an increasing need for trust, it may, at the same time, place decreasing emphasis on the effectiveness of – or indeed, the need for – gatekeeping. In contrast to hierarchical conceptions of order that were embedded in the model of representative democracy, complexity is not a problem for postmodern politics; indeed it may even be positively welcomed as reflecting more accurately the complexity of postmodern societies. The problem that has preoccupied theorists as diverse as Hobbes, Burke, Crick and Easton – that of reconciling diversity and order – seems to disappear. The idea that politics has to do with the difficult task of making authoritative decisions within, on behalf of and with the acceptance of the members of a collectivity fades away. Whereas gatekeeping inevitably frustrates desires, the plural segments and arenas of the postmodern polity hold out the prospect of gratifying and indulging them. There is no gatekeeping because there is no certain place to erect the gates; by the same token, there can also be no 'black box'. But this means, too, that postmodern politics undermines the possibility of, and indeed ceases to nurture the ambition for, holding anyone to account for the probity, quality or consequences of public acts. If no one is in charge, the concept of 'stewardship', a concept that is inherent in the liberal emphasis on accountability (Gray and Jenkins 1985), is also extinguished.

None of this can be shrugged off as of little or no consequence for the quality of governance and the health of democracy. For all its faults, the system of representative democracy classically recognises the need to provide political authority for making and implementing binding decisions at the 'macro' level, whatever or wherever that level may be for the decision in question. It provides, for example, a well-recognised means for establishing and renewing an overarching legal framework, for the democratic control or regulation of public goods. Above all, perhaps, it supplies a legitimate technique for extracting and allocating money and other resources for purposes that exceed the scope and capacities of smaller or less inclusive domains. It also provides authoritative constitutional and political arrangements for mediating relations between these collectivities.

But if social action or public decision-making is simply a matter for each one of a plethora of social fragments, the possibility of collective deliberation or even transparency about transcendent issues is thrown into doubt. If the public sphere is splintered into a pluralistic array of transient groups, the wider repercussions of actions in one domain on other domains will be difficult to recognise and control. Perhaps this could be done simply by *ad hoc* connection and local negotiation and exchange. If so, it is not clear how these processes could be made to involve the most appropriate stakeholders, or how outcomes could be implemented and enforced, whatever the material, organisational and political resources available to the unit in question. It may be that central institutions carry residual responsibilities for seeing that questions such as these are addressed, and that the implementation of outcomes is adequately supported and resourced. But what would give them the legitimacy and – just as important – the political capability to do so, is problematic.

Conclusion

Such issues serve to point up the true importance of ICTs for the emerging mixed polity, and for our understanding of post-parliamentary democracy. The significance of electronic means for political participation is often seen to lie in the circumvention of the need for representation or mediation. But such a shift towards direct democracy does not *by itself* necessarily pose a threat to the public realm or its central institutions. Participatory democracy (Pateman 1970; Budge 1996) still involves decision-making by and for the collectivity as a whole, and therefore still involves the ideals of representation and accountability. It is rather the *de-centring* of those institutions in postmodernity that challenges the centrality of these concepts, whether democratic processes are supported by ICTs or not.

If a representative institution is a *centripetal* force, the *centrifugal* force of cyberspace is its antagonist. In the mixed polity, we can expect that the processes of mutual adjustment between sectors, groups or interests will increasingly take place outside the central arenas of representative democracy. This shift inevitably obscures both the locus and processes of decision-making, making it impossible for members outside these forums to fix responsibility or influence outcomes, though in practice much might depend on what constitutes domains or fragments within the mixed polity and the extent to which their memberships overlap. Thus it might depend on which categories or groups are involved; whether they are mutually exclusive or cross-cutting; whether the sectors are horizontally or hierarchically aligned or nested; what the criteria are for membership and who, in the end, determines and enforces them; and what kinds of internal processes and leadership are extant in various domains. But these contingent approaches to participation and representation are silent on a central question: whether the interest of the wider polity in the affairs of each domain can and should be recognised. Is anyone responsible, for example, for ensuring that the interaction of the parts adds up to something approaching fairness, equity and coherent policy?

As we have seen, our working assumption is that we will be faced with a mixed polity in which postmodern novelty will coexist with the political legacies of modernity. In particular, the political machinery associated with the modern state will continue to exist, even if many of its functions are devolved or dispersed. Governments will continue to raise taxes and allocate expenditures, representative bodies will continue to legislate, nation states will continue to conduct diplomacy, maintain armies and go occasionally to war, and territorially defined collectivities will still function and assert their authority. However attenuated, it is the machinery of government – as that term has been customarily understood – that will probably bear the brunt of mediating, cohering and regulating the diffuse, overlapping networks of governance. The paradox is that, far from withering away, central institutions, including parliaments and the like, may be faced with *intensified* problems of managing political complexity. These problems are born of the assumption – which we share – that there may be circumstances in which it is desirable to hold some rings, at least, between disparate elements, and that it will be important to do so in ways that are recognised to be democratic and legitimate. Whether in the end, politics in the mixed polity *can* be centred in these ways, remains, of course, to be seen.

Appendix: applying a 'ladder of informatisation' to parliamentary democracy

Online participation in proceedings of parliamentary committees
Online participation in citizen juries and deliberative panels
Online participation in focus groups
Participation in political forums in civil society, such as electronic public squares and village halls
Mobilisation of opinion through online petitions and political campaigns
Online participation in election hustings

Online advice bureaux held by MPs
E-mail correspondence between MPs, citizens and the Executive

Publication of MPs' voting records and position papers
Information about the availability of MPs
Parties' election manifestos and candidates' position papers
Broadcasting of parliamentary proceedings
Publication of records of parliamentary proceedings and votes
Publication of official and parliamentary reports, policy documents and draft bills

Expert-systems support for legislation
Electronic voting for MPs in parliamentary votes
Online access for MPs to draft bills, minutes of debates, committee agendas, etc.
Online access for MPs to library and information services
Electronic voting in parliamentary elections

Source: Bellamy and Raab, 1999b.

This ladder is designed to illustrate the broad distinction between the use of ICTs to strengthen the efficiency and effectiveness of the state in controlling and serving citizens, and the use of ICTs as 'citizen technologies'. On the lowest rung are proposals for strengthening parliamentary democracy by enhancing the efficiency and effectiveness of elected representatives, thus enhancing the influence and prestige of parliaments. Such innovations respond to the claim that a major source of parliaments' failure to deliberate wisely and to scrutinise government effectively lies in the low quality and independence of information possessed by elected representatives. ICTs could redress such problems by, for example, providing online access to significantly enhanced library and research services. However, whilst these measures may be valuable improvements in the way in which representatives work, they do not necessarily widen citizen participation or significantly improve the processes of parliamentary democracy.

On the second rung, better provision of information to the public is available through networked technologies, such as the Internet or digital TV, which offer fast, cheap and effective ways of disseminating a wide variety of information. This might include records of parliamentary debates; draft legislation and committee papers; information about MPs, including their availability to constituents, voting records or position statements; information from Ministers, such as answers to parliamentary questions; and information about elections, including party manifestos and campaign materials. Potentially, at least, the wider and greater availability of such material could enable citizens to undertake their roles as electors and constituents more competently and intelligently, but it also increases their reliance on point-to-mass, 'broadcast' channels of information dissemination and thus on those who control those modes.

These two rungs, and the categories of technology-mediated innovation associated with them, involve the use of technologies as accessible sources of richer, more comprehensive, more flexibly organised information resources. However, they take relatively little advantage of the interactive capabilities of ICTs for supporting qualitatively different kinds of interaction and participation in the democratic process. Our third level therefore denotes a range of proposals for exploiting, for example, the interactive possibilities of telephone helplines or email in creating new bonds between representatives and the public. The third rung, however, remains more or less within the realm of communications involving citizens as individuals who largely interact with representatives over their private concerns.

The fourth and top rung, on the other hand, involves proposals for using ICTs to offer members of the public opportunities to participate more directly and, at least as important, more collectively, in the policy 'input' processes of parliamentary democracy. These opportunities may also enable more direct and collective approaches to holding representatives and governments to account, as we will explore here. The early history of electronic democracy is littered with experiments, often termed 'electronic town meetings' or 'city forums', to use cable TV to involve voters actively in election hustings, in discussions with elected representatives or in confrontations with officials (Abramson *et al.* 1988). The Internet provides even richer, more widely available, opportunities for democratic interaction on the issues of the day, particularly in the formative stages of making policies or laws. It is not difficult, for example, to conceive of arrangements that could permit members of the public or spokespersons of pressure groups to present online evidence to parliamentary committees.

These 'higher rung' applications of ICTs appear to present unambiguously positive opportunities for strengthening the involvement, competence and power of citizens in the processes of parliamentary democracy. We enter, however, a couple of important caveats. The first is that it is by no means obvious that dissemination will necessarily be either universally rapid or egalitarian. The foregoing analysis indicates that those facilities capable of supporting the richest information services and the most convenient interactive communications media will be disseminated most quickly and intensively amongst young, educated people in the higher social classes, especially those who currently enjoy continuous, personal access to PCs and who will continue to form a significant *tranche* of the market for cellular phones. For this reason, indeed, many governments and commercial companies assume that, for several years to come, call centres – accessed, in the main, by customers using touch-pad phones connected to land-lines – will continue to provide important channels for high-volume, low-value transactions, such as claiming welfare benefits. In other words, although facilities for e-commerce and e-government will almost certainly spread rapidly in the next few years, it does not automatically follow that all sections of the public will thereby enjoy equal access to those technologies and services that are best suited to supporting more sophisticated democratising inputs.

The second caveat is that it is by no means self-evident that investment in ICTs will necessarily favour the rapid emergence of higher-level applications, so far as electronic democracy is concerned.

Notes

1 We use the term 'electoral chain of command' to capture the relationship between electorate, parliament and government in European constitutional democracies in conformity with the model offered, e.g. in Hoff *et al.* (2000: 4).

2 The following extract is taken from a recent Dutch policy document (Dutch Parliament, 2000: para. 2.1) and captures well the tensions apparent in a system caught uneasily between Weberian, social democratic and postmodernist assumptions:

> Government and citizens are increasingly operating in a network society in which they are becoming more and more equal and in which the strength of government is determined by the delivery of quality and by the joint creation and sharing of policy information. Indeed, policy can in some cases even be said to be a co-production. Yet at the same time justice must also be done to the more traditional function of government, for example maintaining law and order and exercising the monopoly on protecting safety and security, although government is also having to take on new roles such as interactive and communicative leadership. Government has, however, traditionally been a referee too, and has as such been responsible for the public interest, taking account of minority interests. A new balance must be struck in the network society between government, the market sector and civil society. With the advent of the network society, government must invest in newly shaped information relationships.

References

Abramson, J., Arterton, F. and Orren, G. (1988) *The Electronic Commonwealth*, New York: Basic Books.

Bagehot, W. (1867, reprinted 1963 with introduction by Crossman, R.) *The English Constitution*, London: Fontana.

Bellamy, C. (2000) 'Modelling Electronic Democracy', in Hoff, J., Horrocks, I. and Tops, P. (eds), *Democratic Governance and New Technology*, London: Routledge.

Bellamy, C. and Raab, C. (1999a) 'Wiring-Up the Deck-Chairs?', *Parliamentary Affairs*, 52 (3), 518–34.

Bellamy, C. and Raab, C. (1999b) 'Parliamentary Democracy and New Technology', paper prepared for the Colloque Internationale, *Les Parlements dans la Société de l'Information*, organised by the Sénat and CEVIPOF, Paris, 18–19 November 1999.

Budge, I. (1996) *The New Challenge of Direct Democracy*, Cambridge: Polity Press.

Coleman, S., Taylor, J. and van de Donk, W. (eds) (1999) *Parliament in the Age of the Internet*, Oxford: Oxford University Press.

Connolly, W. (1991) *Identity and Difference*, Ithaca, NY: Cornell University Press.

Dahl, R. (1967) 'The City in the Future of Democracies', *American Political Science Review*, 61 (4), 953–70.

Danziger, J., Dutton, W., Kling, R. and Kraemer, K. (1982) *Computers and Politics*, New York: Columbia University Press.

Dutch Parliament (2000) *Contract with the Future*, Memorandum Lower Chamber, session year 1999–2000, 26387, nr. 8, 19 May.

Easton, D. (1965) *A Systems Analysis of Political Life*, New York: John Wiley & Sons.

Elster, J. (ed.) (1998) *Deliberative Democracy*, Cambridge: Cambridge University Press.

Etzioni-Halévy, E. (1993) *The Elite Connection*, Cambridge: Polity Press.

Fishkin, J. (1991) *Democracy and Deliberation*, New Haven: Yale University Press.

Fox, C. and Miller, H. (1995) *Postmodern Public Administration*, Thousand Oaks, Calif.: Sage.

Frissen, P. (1999) *Politics, Governance and Technology*, Cheltenham: Edward Elgar.

Gray, A. and Jenkins, W. (1985) *Administrative Politics in British Government*, Brighton: Wheatsheaf Books.

Hirst, P. (1994) *Associative Democracy*, Amherst: University of Massachusetts Press.

Hoff, J., Horrocks, I. and Tops, P. (eds) (2000) *Democratic Governance and New Technology*, London: Routledge.

Holmes, D. (ed.) (1997) *Virtual Politics*, London: Sage.

Judge, D. (1999) *Representation*, London: Routledge.

Kickert, W., Klijn, E-H. and Koppenjan, J. (eds) (1997) *Managing Complex Networks*, London: Sage.

Kooiman, J. (ed.) (1993) *Modern Governance*, London: Sage.

Luhmann, N. (1979) *Trust and Power*, London: John Wiley & Sons.

MacIntyre, A. (1988) *Whose Justice? Which Rationality*? London: Duckworth.

Maidment, R. and Thompson, G. (eds) (1993) *Managing the United Kingdom*, London: Sage.

Margolis, M. and Resnick, D. (2000) *Politics as Usual*, Thousand Oaks, Calif.: Sage.

Miller, D. (1989) *Market, State and Community*, Oxford: Oxford University Press.

Mouffe, C. (ed.) (1992) *Dimensions of Radical Democracy*, London: Verso.

Pateman, C. (1970) *Participation and Democratic Theory*, Cambridge: Cambridge University Press.

Pierre, J. and Peters, B. (2000) *Governance, Politics and the State*. Basingstoke: Macmillan.

Poster, M. (1993) *The Second Media Age*, Cambridge: Polity Press.

Poster, M. (1997) 'Cyberdemocracy: The Internet and the Public Sphere', in Holmes, D. (ed.), *Virtual Politics*, London: Sage.

Raab, C. (1992) 'Taking Networks Seriously', *European Journal of Political Research*, 21 (1–2), 69–90.

Raab, C. (1998) 'Electronic Confidence', in Snellen, I. and van de Donk, W. (eds), *Public Administration in an Information Age*, Amsterdam: IOS Press, 113–33.

Ranson, S. and Stewart, J. (1994) *Management for the Public Domain*, Basingstoke: Macmillan.

Rawls, J. (1972) *A Theory of Justice*, Oxford: Clarendon Press.

Rhodes, R. (1996) *Understanding Governance*, Milton Keynes: Open University Press.

Rhodes, R. (1997) 'Foreword', in Kickert, W., Klijn, E-H. and Koppenjan, J. (eds), *Managing Complex Networks*, London: Sage.

Richardson, J. and Jordan, A. (1979) *Governing Under Pressure*, Oxford: Martin Robertson.

Schattschneider, E. (1960) *The Semisovereign People*, New York: Holt, Rinehart and Winston.

van Stokkom, B. (1992) *De Republiek der Weerbaren*, Houten: Bohn Stafleu Van Loghem.

Thompson, G., Frances, J., Levacic, R. and Mitchell, J. (eds) (1991) *Markets, Hierarchies and Networks*, London: Sage.

Tsagarousianou, R., Tambini, D. and Bryan, C. (eds) (1998) *Cyberdemocracy*, London: Routledge.

Ward, S. and Gibson, R. (1998) 'UK Political Parties on the Net', *Harvard International Journal of Press/Politics*, 3 (1), 14–38.

Weller, P., Bakvis, H. and Rhodes, R. (1997) *The Hollow Crowns*, Basingstoke: Macmillan.

3 The citizen as consumer

E-government in the United Kingdom and the United States

Catherine Needham

Introduction

New information and communication technologies (ICTs) have the potential to radically reconfigure the state–citizen relationship. The Internet, in particular, has the scope to have an enormous impact on state–citizen dialogue, given its capacity to surmount geographical barriers and allow interactive and simultaneous mass transmission. Forms of state–citizen interaction that have been dominant for over a century, such as constituent surgeries, public meetings and face-to-face consultative hearings can be replaced by email and online discussion forums. Such developments have led Grossman to argue, 'Interactive telecommunications technology makes it possible to revive, in a sophisticated modern form, some of the essential characteristics of the ancient world's first democratic polities' (Grossman 1995: 48).

The extent to which this transformative potential is being realised depends to a large extent on how established institutions are responding to the opportunities being provided by the new ICTs. As the introductory chapter to this volume has highlighted, context matters, and the adaptability of conventional actors in the political system is expected to be shaped in large part by their existing internal norms and patterns of behaviour. This chapter addresses this issue through an evaluation of the 'electronic government' programmes of the United Kingdom and United States. The term electronic government here refers to all forms of government–citizen interaction online but excludes participation on election or party websites, or citizen-to-citizen interaction.[1] The goal is to assess how extensively central governing institutions have integrated new technologies into their patterns of working. In order to do this the online activity of the executive and legislative branches of government are analysed to identify the priorities that the two governments have set in establishing their online presence, and then assessed against the empirical evidence. The first section of the chapter discusses the theoretical debates surrounding electronic government, outlining the implications of different forms of online operability for democracy and citizenship. The model of the active citizen, providing input into policy-making via online feedback channels, is contrasted with the citizen-consumer, a passive recipient of electronically delivered outputs from the state.

The chapter then goes on to examine the design and implementation of e-government strategies in the United Kingdom and the United States, to see how far individuals are encouraged to be citizens or citizen-consumers in their electronic interactions with government. Policy documents on electronic government are analysed alongside a review of current online provision to measure the extent to which priority is given to service and information provision, or to consultation and feedback. On the basis of this, the two governments' online presence is evaluated against both their own stated policy objectives and against normative standards regarding democratic engagement with citizens. Finally, conclusions are drawn about the extent to which the moves towards e-government in these two countries conform to the models of adaptation outlined in the introductory chapter. How far does the evidence support the idea of a decline and erosion of the familiar aggregative structures of executives and legislatures in society, as opposed to the prospect of renewed relevance and revitalisation?

New ICTs, democracy and the citizen

Predictions about the impact of new ICTs on democracy range from the sceptical to the optimistic. Some, such as Barber (1999) and Hague and Loader (1999) have highlighted the scope for ICTs to be used to nurture 'strong democracy', enabling citizens to become active participants in the political community. Others, such as Elshtain (1982), reject the democratising potential of such technologies, arguing, 'interactive systems encourage social atomisation and…foster the impression that an electronic transaction is an authentic democratic choice' (Elshtain 1982: 109). Some, including Margolis and Resnick (2000) and Davis (1999) highlight the potential for the new technologies to be co-opted by governments and used to consolidate existing political power structures. Across these different perspectives there is agreement that technology is not deterministic in its effects; the impact of technological change is mediated by the political and cultural context. As Noveck puts it:

> It is not technology per se which either fosters or denigrates the connection between communications media and participatory democratic culture. Technology exists within a framework of values and ideals both inherent to it and imposed by the external legal and institutional structures.
>
> (Noveck 2000: 20)

The impact of new ICTs on democracy and citizenship depends to a large extent on how governmental institutions choose to develop their online presence and set their priorities for web-based interaction. Whilst citizenship can flourish outside the institutional context, it is through institutions that government–citizen interactions are controlled and mediated by government. Governmental actors both initiate interactions and configure the channels through which citizens can contact government. As governments develop publicly available websites they must make a choice about which aspects of these interactions to move online, and decide how far the opportunities presented by technology should reshape the *content* of these interactions as well as their form. The extent to which technology will be democratising in its potential will depend in large part on the willingness of governments to act as leader and facilitator of expanded democratic participation.

In developing an online presence, governments choose whether to move their offline functions online, or to transform those functions to take full advantage of the opportunities presented by new technologies. Such a choice must take into account the three primary mechanisms through which governments interact with citizens: the provision of public services, the provision of information and consultation on policy. Government must decide how to move these three processes online and which of them to prioritise in developing online operability. This choice has implications for citizenship and democracy because these processes impact differently on the experience of citizenship. Service provision involves a bilateral transaction between government and user, often with little user-control over the process. The citizen as service recipient acts as a citizen-consumer, and the role is passive in the sense that service users have little scope to influence the set of choices on offer. As Gyford puts it, 'consumption is an act of receipt rather than creation' (Gyford 1991: 169). Through posting information online a government tells citizens about what it is doing, allowing users to make more informed choices about the services they use and expanding accountability. Again, however, there may be little scope for citizens to control the content and comprehensiveness of this information. Consultation is a more expansive role, in which the citizen becomes an active participant in government rather than a passive consumer. If consultation is used extensively it can mark a shift towards more participatory forms of democracy.

The range of options facing governments is shown in Table 3.1. At its least expansive, the Internet can be used as a tool to deliver government services and to process transactions, without offering any scope for enhanced participation. At this extreme lies pure representative democracy, a Schumpeterian model in which citizens are asked only to vote in periodic relations and are expected to be passive recipients of government services (Schumpeter 1965). At the other end of the scale, governments can use the interactive potential of the Internet to bring in innovative forms of deliberative democracy, allowing the citizen to participate fully in policy-making processes. This could involve a shift towards direct democracy, with representative institutions supplemented or replaced by mechanisms that allow ongoing consultation of the citizenry. In between these extremes of transactional efficiency and radical institutional transformation, lie opportunities to deepen citizen participation within the boundaries of representative democracy, through the expansion of consultation opportunities.

The sections that follow investigate where executive and legislative institutions at central level in the United States and the United Kingdom lie on this continuum and whether their position is static or moving. The chapter surveys policy statements on e-government and the content of central government websites. It discusses the extent to which governments have developed online sites with

Table 3.1 Impact of electronic government on institutions and democracy

Form of electronic government	*Institutional impact*	*Model of democracy*
		Representative
Service delivery	Executive branch coordinates online service delivery	Citizen acts as citizen-consumer; no active role between elections
Information provision	Executive and legislative branches post information online	Citizen can become more informed about government and its functions
Offline consultation moved online	Executive and legislature use Internet to facilitate and open up existing consultation mechanisms	Citizens have new channels to communicate with government, which shadow offline equivalents
Advisory online forums of citizens and policy-makers	New consultative institutions set up to advise on policy	Citizens can participate in new institutions; government controls range and impact of consultation
Decisions taken by online forums	Deliberative institutions established to supplement or replace representative institutions	Direct citizen control replaces representative democracy on some or all policy questions
		Direct

a consolidating rather than transformative effect, using technology to move their offline functions online rather than embracing a more deliberative model of democracy. It also looks at how far such outcomes conform to or conflict with governments' own policy statements on e-government.

Policy objectives

It was in the mid-1990s that central governments in the United States and the United Kingdom began to issue strategy documents as a basis for developing their online presence. Prior to this, government policies in the area of new telecommunications had focused on establishing a regulatory framework and widening access to the Internet, rather than on how the new technologies might impact upon the role of government itself. As these governments began to develop their online strategies, three trends were discernible in both countries:

- Electronic government was detached from wider telecommunications strategies and sited in an executive agency or department with a managerial rather than a business focus.
- The domain of electronic government was conceived of in functional or service delivery terms rather than in the participatory terms.
- Users of electronic government services were designated as consumers or customers, terms that were used interchangeably with that of citizen.

The movement of electronic government from the broader telecommunications arena to a managerially focused executive agency or department has been prominent in both countries. In the United Kingdom, responsibility shifted from the Department of Trade and Industry to the Cabinet Office. The first major policy statement on electronic government in the United Kingdom, the 1996 green paper *Government Direct: The Electronic Delivery of Government Services*, was issued through the Office of Public Service in the Cabinet Office. In 1998, the government established an e-Envoy's office, also within the Cabinet Office, with the remit of 'leading the drive to get the UK online'. The office now employs approximately 200 people, working on different aspects of e-government under the 'UK Online' initiative. In the United States, electronic government was positioned within the Reinventing Government agenda established by the incoming Clinton administration in 1993, and overseen by the vice president's office. Since the 2000 election, the coordination of electronic government has shifted to the Office of Management and Budget, which appointed an interagency task force in August 2001, led by an associate director for Information Technology and e-Government.

The second prominent feature to emerge regarding electronic government was an emphasis on service delivery or information provision rather than consultation or interaction. In the United Kingdom, the 1996 green paper *Government Direct: The Electronic Delivery of Government Services*, made its orientation towards service delivery evident in the title. Opportunities for citizens to use the new technologies to offer feedback to government receive scant attention. In the foreword to the document, Roger Freeman, the minister for Public Services in the Cabinet Office wrote, 'I believe that it will help to bring government closer to the individual and give citizens . . . more control over their dealings with government' (Cabinet Office 1996). Yet, as Chadwick and May point out:

> Only one sentence in the whole document (which runs to some thirty-eight pages in the downloadable version) makes direct mention of how ICTs might provide for greater citizen influence on policy-making: 'E-mail will also make it easier for people to contribute views to the policy-making process.'
>
> (Chadwick and May 2001a: 20)

In the *Modernising Government* white paper, published in March 1999, the Labour administration, newly elected in 1997, outlined its broad e-government strategy. It called for an improvement in government service delivery, and highlighted online provision as the best way to achieve this. The document emphasised the potential for information technology to 'enable government to offer services and information through new media like the Internet or interactive TV' (Cabinet Office 1999). The deadline of 2002 was set for a list of transactions that would be available online, including booking driving tests, submitting self-assessment tax returns and getting information and advice about benefits. Full electronic service provision was promised by 2008, a deadline that was later reduced to 2005. Opportunities to use the interactive potential of the new technologies to bring citizens more directly into policy-making were not covered by the document. Citizen input was limited to 'market research and user feedback', in order to 'improve the design and organisation of services and other processes, and focus them more firmly on citizens and businesses' (Cabinet Office 1999).

A more detailed strategy for 'Information Age Government' in the United Kingdom was published in spring 2000, entitled *E-Government: A Strategic Framework for Public Services in the Information Age*. It emphasised the potential of new technologies to bring about a 'transformation of the way government and citizens interact' (Cabinet Office 2000a). Again, as the title implies, the focus was on service delivery. In the foreword to the report, Cabinet Office Minister Ian McCartney said, 'We are at the start of an information revolution which is changing the way companies do business and the way citizens get many of the services and goods they need' (Cabinet Office 2000a). References to expanding consultation of citizens within the document are limited to loosely framed calls for 'greater democratic participation and openness' and a 'better informed and more participatory democracy through electronic consultation and better responses to feedback' (Cabinet Office 2000a). Strategies for achieving these goals are not discussed.

The e-Envoy's office published the UK Online's first annual report in the autumn of 2000. The document listed twenty-five aims of the UK Online strategy. Of these, fifteen related to e-commerce, aimed at facilitating business transactions online; five related to service delivery (such as moving services and procurement online); four were oriented towards improving access and skills training for net users. Only one could be categorised as relating to greater citizen involvement. This called for the government to: 'Drive forward citizen participation in democracy as part of the UK Online citizen portal' (Office of the e-Envoy 2000). Again, no details were given about how this forward momentum would be achieved.

In the United States, the service orientation has also been explicit as the government has developed its online strategy. The administration committed itself to establishing a strong online presence for government as part of the National Performance Review (NPR), set up by the new Clinton administration in March 1993. Vice President Al Gore pledged that knowledge received from the information superhighway would 'spread participatory democracy' (Davis 1999: 21). As the opportunities to harness the Internet to deliver services became apparent in the mid-1990s, online delivery became a goal of the NPR and the subsequent Reinventing Government initiative. The *Access America* report published in 1997 spoke of creating a government, 'where all Americans have the opportunity to get services electronically and where, aided by technology, the productivity of government operations will be soaring' (National Partnership for Reinventing Government 1997). Sally Katzen, the deputy director at the Office for Management and Budget – with oversight of the electronic government agenda – gave a speech in October 2000, in which she defined e-government as involving 'access to government information and services 24 hours a day, 7 days a week' (Katzen 2000).

The service orientation has continued under the Bush administration. Bush's budget proposals for 2001–2002, published in February 2001 in a document entitled, 'A Blueprint for New Beginnings', include a section on Government Reform, which outlines the next phase of e-government. The document states, 'The

President believes that providing access to information and services is only the first step in e-Government'. It goes on to discuss the need to establish 'citizen-centered' government, but the primary route through which this is to be achieved is via better user control of online services. According to the document, 'By enabling individuals to penetrate the Federal bureaucracy to access information and transact business, the Internet promises to shift power from a handful of leaders in Washington to individual citizens' (Bush 2001: section ix). The document does stress the importance of allowing citizens 'to go online and interact with their Government' (Bush 2001: section ix). However, there is no indication given of what form this interaction will take and how it will be achieved. When Bush's budget proposals were being discussed in front of the Senate Committee on Governmental Affairs, Sean O'Keefe, deputy director of the Office of Management and Budget gave the Committee more detail about the impact of e-government proposals on individual citizens, saying, 'We are focused on building easy to find one-stop-shops for citizens – creating single points of easy entry to access high quality government services' (O'Keefe 2001). The US government like its UK counterpart, envisages interaction in terms of better access to services rather than enhanced opportunities to participate in decision-making.

The third common feature of the development of government websites in the United States and the United Kingdom has been the increasing identification of users of the sites as consumers and customers, alongside, or even instead of, 'citizen'. The 1996 UK *Government Direct* green paper, states that the aim of the government's electronic strategy should be 'to make electronic direct delivery of services the preferred option for the majority of government's customers (both citizens and businesses)' (Cabinet Office 1996). In the 1999 *Modernising Government* white paper, the minister for the Cabinet Office, Jack Cunningham, calls for government to recognise that people are 'consumers as well as citizens' (Cabinet Office 1999). In the foreword to the *Information Age* strategy paper, Cabinet Office Minister Ian McCartney states, 'Information Technology is a powerful enabler but the starting point should always be to identify what the customer wants and then to look at how we use IT to identify this' (Cabinet Office 2000a).

Policy statements in the United States have also favoured consumerist language. One of the goals of the National Performance Review was to make the federal government 'customer driven', according to an executive order issued by Clinton in September 1993. The order stated, 'The standard of quality for services provided to the public shall be: "Customer service equal to the best in business"'. In the Introduction to the *Access America* report, Al Gore argued, 'Information technology (IT) was and is the great enabler for reinvention. It allows us to rethink, in fundamental ways, how people work and how we serve customers' (National Partnership for Reinventing Government 1997).

On the basis of the policy documents, it appears that governments have sought to harness the consolidating opportunities of the Internet rather than its transformative potential. Government websites are primarily expected to be mechanisms through which governments can perform their existing service-based functions rather than as an alternative channel through which government and citizen can communicate. Although consultation and participation are mentioned in several reports they receive scant attention, with little detail provided about how the Internet can be used as a medium to expand citizen consultation. In both countries there appears to be some rhetorical support for expanding consultation online, but no clear strategy or timetable outlining how this is to be achieved. There is a tension between the consumerist language of the policy documents and the accompanying claims that the Internet can be a tool for the expansion of citizenship.

Overall, therefore, these patterns of development suggest a commitment to the overall project of e-democracy on the part of the US and UK governments that is functional, at best. The orientation of the policy-makers and bureaucrats has been largely utilitarian, driven by an understanding of the technology as offering a means to do more of the same, in a quicker fashion, rather than on unleashing its inherently interactive and democratic potential.

Delivering e-government

Service delivery

Governments have invested substantial resources and political capital in expanding online service delivery. In the United Kingdom, in March 2001, the government announced that, with the aid of Microsoft, it had set up a new server designed to ensure that the 2005 target of full online service delivery would be met (Martinson 2001). Douglas Alexander, the e-commerce minister, announced in June 2001:

> The most recent survey of departments shows that for the whole of central government there are 521 services provided to the citizen or to business. Of those 218 services are enabled [online] now, 384 services will be enabled by 2002, and 517 services will be enabled by 2005.
>
> (Alexander 2001a)

The UK Online portal was launched in February 2001, allowing citizens to conduct a range of transactions online. It is now possible for citizens to apply for a passport, notify government of a change of address, fill in self-assessment tax forms, buy a TV licence and even report certain crimes to the police (Office of the e-Envoy 2001a).

In the United States, an early priority of the Clinton administration was online delivery of benefits (via the Electronic Benefits Transfer System), including social security, Medicare and Medicaid. In 1996, Clinton and Gore launched a 'Commonly Requested Services' feature on the White House home page, allowing users to access an electronic form and transmit it directly to the Social Security Administration (National Partnership for Reinventing Government 1997). In a 1999 memorandum, Clinton required that 'the heads of executive departments and agencies shall, to the maximum extent possible, make available online, by December 2000, the forms needed for the top 500 Government service used by the public' (Clinton 1999). This medium-term guarantee reinforces the commitment to full online service delivery by 2003. In January 2001, the *Access America's* e-Gov site published a statement on Electronic Government, asserting, 'Today e-gov is putting people "online, not in line"'. It claimed, 'By the end of 2000, nearly forty million Americans were doing business with government electronically. On a regular basis, people are accessing information to solve problems themselves through the Internet, via telephones, and through neighbourhood kiosks' (National Partnership for Reinventing Government 2001). A survey for Brown University published in September 2001 found that 34 per cent of federal sites offered some form of online service transaction. The most heavily used services were online tax filing and vehicle registration (West 2001). In August 2001, President Bush signalled his support for the expansion of e-government with the creation of the e-Government Task Force within the Office of Management and Budget (OMB). The associate director is charged with distributing the president's proposed $100 million e-government fund for interagency initiatives over the next three years (Office of Management and Budget 2001).

In developing their online service capabilities, central governments in the United Kingdom and the United States have sought to organise services around user need, rather than mirroring the organisational structures of government. UK Online, for example, aims to 'pull together packages of information and services focused around those experiences from the citizen's point of view'. For people moving house, for example, 'there's a life event that leads to sites with information about house prices, to local schools and transport and the government's pilot change of address service which streamlines the process of telling key departments when you've moved' (Cabinet Office 2000b). According to Cabinet Office Minister Ian McCartney, 'In time the portal will help revolutionise the relationship between government and citizens by turning public services inside out. Instead of being organised around government bureaucracy, they'll be organised for the citizen's convenience' (Cabinet Office 2000b). In the United States, the *Access America* report called for the integration of services across different federal agencies so citizens can 'custom-tailor' government to their specific need, developing websites such as 'Access America for Students' and 'Access America for Seniors' (National Partnership for Reinventing Government 2001).

In the area of service delivery, both governments have made substantial progress in moving their capabilities online. Future plans include greater customisation of sites and the extension of online transactions. The drive to customise services is attributed, in both countries, to a claim that users will expect government sites to match the scope for customisation and responsiveness that is delivered by non-governmental sites. In launching the Electronic Government Act 2001, for example, US Senator Joe Lieberman stated, 'The people are demanding the same 24-7 access to government information and services now available to them from the private sector online' (Lieberman 2001). Jack Cunningham, minister for the Cabinet Office in the United Kingdom, in the introduction to the *Modernising Government* white paper, argued, 'We need to make sure that government services are brought forward using the best and most modern techniques, to match the best of the private sector . . . especially electronic information-age services' (Cabinet Office 1999: 5). People's experiences as consumers are assumed to shape their expectations as citizens.

Information provision

Service delivery is the responsibility of the executive branch of government, and hence its online expansion has been spearheaded by the executive, whereas the provision of information online has been shared between executive and legislative branches.

Executive branch

It is now possible to find an extremely wide range of information on departmental and agency sites – ranging from the full text of government bills to local road traffic information. In the United Kingdom in 1994, as government departments began to establish their own websites, the 'open.gov' portal was established, which aimed to create a single point of entry for people who wanted access to government information. By December 1994 open.gov was receiving 35,000 hits a week; by August 1999 this had increased to over 14 million per week. The site has been criticised for its non-intuitive name, and an unwieldy search engine, but it does provide an organisational index of all public bodies on the Internet, a topic index, a list of what's new on government sites and links to other government portals. In summer 2001 open.gov was consolidated with the UK Online site to create one central portal.

The National Audit Office's *Government on the Web* report, published in December 1999, surveyed the information facilities provided by UK government websites. It found that almost 90 per cent included a statement of current activities; 67 per cent included a 'what's new' section; 60 per cent contained a mission statement; and 56 per cent included a list of basic responsibilities (National Audit Office 1999). Three-fifths of sites included a designated contact route, but often this was by fax or telephone rather than email. Over a fifth of sites included details of how citizens could complain or appeal against decisions. The report found, however, that 'Features that allow more extended interactive communication of information with citizens are still weakly developed in public agency sites. Only one in six sites allowed any forms to be downloaded by users, and only one in eight allowed users to submit forms to the agency online. Chat rooms or forums for outsiders to discuss issues were provided by less than a tenth of sites' (National Audit Office 1999).

Beyond the provision of departmental information, the UK Online site operates a daily news service. The *Sunday Times* likened this news component to the government printing its own newspaper – something last done during the general strike of 1926 – and alleged that civil servants have dubbed UK Online 'Pravda.com' (Carr-Brown 2001). Applicants for editorial positions on the site were told that they will 'work with No 10 on developing the presentation strategy of cross-government news' (Carr-Brown 2001). The news service presents information in a format very similar to that used on the BBC website, creating an impression of impartiality, although the site does little more than reproduce departmental press releases.

Like its UK equivalent, the US government's portal provides access to a high volume of information. Via the 'Firstgov.gov' portal it becomes possible to navigate through the fragmented federal bureaucracy, with organisational charts providing an indication of the structure of the government, including the proliferation of agencies attached to it (Firstgov 2001). The site links to 30 million pages of information, services and online transactions. Most divisions within agencies and departments maintain their own website; the Department of Defence alone has 3,000 websites with about 1.5 million pages (National Audit Office 1999). There are links to Congress, the judiciary and state and local governments. A link entitled 'Doing Business with Government' takes the browser to a list of the online transactions for citizens, including filing a tax return and reserving campsites at a national park. The Brown University study found that 80 per cent of federal sites incorporated a search engine and 41 per cent allowed interested browsers to register for email updates about changes to the site (West 2001).

Agency sites in the United States provide a range of information, which Davis categorises under four headings: mission description (i.e. general statement of what the agency does); mission activity (ongoing updated information about activities of the agency); consumer information (details of specific services agency provides); and interactivity (links allowing citizens to interact with agency staff). Davis points out that it is the last element – the interactivity – that is usually missing:

> Nearly every site volunteers agency e-mail addresses or, in many cases, even displays forms that users can complete to transmit e-mail messages... Citizens are given the impression that they are important to the agency's mission. But that interactivity has not been used to affect the agency's decision-making process.
>
> (Davis 1999: 138)

These findings closely match those of the National Audit Office's content analysis of UK websites, discussed earlier. Davis is highly critical of the quality and content of information carried online in the United States. He argues,

> Each level or branch of government, or individual agency or member office, is using the Internet to fulfil the same functions carried on offline – primarily touting the accomplishments of the office or individual, and/or soliciting public support for policies. All of these activities are carried out at the taxpayer's expense. The Internet thus is a public relations rather than a public participation tool.
>
> (Davis 1999: 146–7)

Legislative branch

Government information in the United States and the United Kingdom is also provided on sites managed by the legislative branch of government. The parliamentary website in the United Kingdom includes the full text of parliamentary proceedings, with an online version of Hansard. The site also publishes parliamentary bills and votes, details of issues under investigation by select committees and their reports and library research papers. The search engine is cumbersome, however, and the site is difficult to navigate for those who are not familiar with parliamentary structures and procedures. These shortcomings have been recognised by site designers and a redesign to make it more user-friendly began in summer 2002.

Congressional sites offer much the same information, but it is presented in a more user-friendly format. As in the United Kingdom, full transcripts of floor proceedings are available, along with roll call votes and the text of committee hearings. Via the 'Thomas' search facility, operated by the Library of Congress, browsers are able to view online versions of the *Congressional Record*, read historical documents such as *The Federalist Papers* and get a tutorial on how Congress works. The extensive search facilities ensure, as Owen *et al.* point out, that, 'Today, any user can check the status of any bill or amendment – a capability formerly held only by lobbying firms and interest groups' (Owen *et al.* 1999: 13).

Consultation

Executive branch

In both the United States and the United Kingdom, consultation on policy questions is routinely practiced by executive agencies and departments, allowing experts and interested parties to give detailed feedback on proposals between elections. Governments are usually keen to involve those groups whose compliance is required for policy enforcement, and to take the temperature of public responses to proposed legislation. In moving their consultation functions online, governments have been faced with a choice between maintaining offline consultation, moving existing forms of consultation online or developing new forms of consultation.

In the United Kindom, the first e-envoy Alex Allan, appeared to show a keen awareness of the consultative potential of the Internet, arguing:

> It is in the promotion of online consultations and forums that the Internet offers truly novel means of communication. A means of communication where messages and themes can emerge in ways that may not be expected, as the participants bounce ideas off each other.
>
> (Allan 2000)

In developing web-based consultation processes, the executive branch of government in the United Kingdom has, however, tended to move existing procedures online, rather than to use the interactive potential of the Internet to design innovative consultation. In 1996 government departments began to post consultative information on the web, supplementing offline information provision. Early in 1996, a joint Department of Health/Welsh Office consultation on the Mental Health Act 1983 Revised Code of Practice was uploaded onto the web in a zipped file. The site was not highly publicised, however, and the information was accessible only to those who were capable of unzipping a file. Submissions to the consulting department could only be done by conventional mail (Finney 1999: 363).

More interactive forms of consultation began to be introduced towards the end of 1996. In November of that year the government's Advisory Committee on Genetic Testing (ACGT) posted its draft code of practice on over-the-counter devices for genetic testing (such as commercially available tests for cystic fibrosis) on the web along with a discussion forum. Interested parties could participate either by joining the discussion forum or by making a written submission. Participation rates were low, which probably reflects the narrow and specialised subject matter and the limited publicity given to the consultation. Only twenty responses were posted on the discussion forum (Finney 1999). The interactive features of the Internet were utilised more fully in December 1997, when the Home Office in association with the independent, non-partisan public online forum UK Citizens Online Democracy, consulted over the government's *Right to Know* (Freedom of Information) white paper. The online consultation was well publicised in offline media and ran in parallel with a traditional printed consultation. Background resources were provided on the site, and respondents were given a range of ways to submit their views. One hundred and sixty nine submissions were made online (Finney 1999: 371).

In both consultations, the sponsoring agency or department had agreed to include submissions made via the electronic discussion forum in its analysis of the consultation results. Yet, in the case of the ACGT, when the Committee Secretariat published its summary of consultation responses in January 1997, submissions made within the discussion forum were not included. Finney concludes: 'there was no indication that submissions made solely on the website . . . were ever formally considered in the final code of practice' (Finney 1999: 370). The outcome of the Freedom of Information consultation was also disappointing. Stephen Coleman, director of the e-democracy programme at the Hansard Society, describes his frustration with the outcomes of what he describes as a 'model consultation':

> This was exactly how a consultation should work. Lots of people came on . . . something like 80 per cent of people who came on to the site had never submitted anything previously to government before. What happened at the end of the consultation? The white paper was withdrawn, the legislation didn't go through. And when the freedom of information bill came back it was in a spirit completely opposed to anything the consultation had suggested.
>
> (Coleman 2000)

In both these cases there was no discernible impact on the outcome of the consultation. It is unclear, however, whether this arose from a lack of commitment to the online consultation exercise within the sponsoring department/committee, or whether it reflected hostility to the findings of the consultation.

The next stage in the development of online consultation came in 1998, when departments began to make consultation materials available on their websites and to provide email addresses to enable respondents to give electronic feedback. This process became standardised when the UK Online site went live in December 2000. The site includes a 'Citizen Space' portal, which offers users the opportunity to participate in online policy discussion forums and to view ongoing departmental consultations. The discussion forums are well used, containing over 30,000 postings on issues from sport to food safety. A commitment is given by administrators of the forum that a summary of the discussions will be sent to the prime minister, although one interviewee described this – off the record – as 'nonsense'.[2]

In addition to the more generalised discussion forum, visitors to the Citizen's Space portal are provided with a register of all ongoing departmental consultations, with hyperlinks to relevant consultation documents and an email feedback procedure. The register shows whether the consultation is currently open, pending or closed, whether consultation results are posted and whether a discussion forum is linked to the consultation.[3] Of the consultations, less than 1 per cent provided a discussion forum, where citizens could browse the submissions made by other visitors to the site, and contribute to the discussion. In all other cases the only opportunity to participate was through sending an email to the consulting department. Of the closed consultations, approximately one-quarter provided results, but in most cases these results only summarised the submissions to the consultation process rather than explaining how submissions fitted into the decision-making process. This is despite a promise made on the site that, 'you will be able to read a summary of the views expressed and the reasons for the decisions taken' (UK Online 2001).

The UK Online register offers an efficient gateway into e-consultation through the provision of a central portal. By limiting responses to email submissions, however, it fails to develop the full interactive potential of the net. There is little scope for respondents to exchange views between themselves or with public officials. The absence of feedback about the impact of email submissions on departmental decision-making makes it difficult to estimate the effect on legislative outcomes. These findings run counter to the pledges given in the government's new code of practice for written consultation in November 2000 (including Internet-based consultations), which emphasised the need for accessibility, adequately lengthy consultation processes and feedback on consultation responses (Cabinet Office 2000c). All departments were expected to work to these standards from January 2001. An insight into the government's view of online consultation was given during the pilot stage of UK Online where it was stated, 'The responses are weighted according to who has sent them in. This means that the views of the organisations and experts, who have been invited to respond, count for more than the view of other organisations and people'.[4] This revealing paragraph appears not to share the faith in public participation expressed by the 6th Report of the Neill Committee on Standards in Public Life, which emphasised that 'Without the consultation of a wide cross-section of the public the openness and accountability of Government can be impaired' (Neill Committee on Standards in Public Life 2000). The paragraph was removed from the UK Online site when it was officially launched two months later in mid-February.

There are some suggestions that the UK Online site will be developed to allow greater interactivity in the future. Early in 2001, a Policy and Best Practice team was established within the office of the e-Envoy, which refers to itself as the 'e-Democracy team' although not formally designated as such. Ways to expand and redevelop the Citizen Space element of UK Online are being explored within that brief. The e-Commerce minister, Douglas Alexander, gave a speech in October 2001 in which he called for the Internet to be used to broaden and deepen democratic participation, and stressed the potential for new technology to establish a new relationship between government and citizens. He said:

> We must open up new democratic channels, through which government and representatives can relate to citizens. We must make citizens feel democratically empowered beyond their few seconds in the polling booth. I believe that it is now time to set all this activity into a clear policy framework and put e-democracy on the information age agenda. Government should set out what it means by e-democracy and how it intends to use the power of technology to strengthen democracy.
>
> (Alexander 2001b)

The speech coincided with a new campaign to publicise the UK Online initiative. Yet, the campaign itself offers no new ways to interact with government, and indeed is designed to offer 'an integrated consumer focused publicity campaign' (Department for Trade and Industry 2001). Alexander's speech was, however, heralded by Steven Clift as 'a completely new phase in the evolution of thought about government's democratic role in the information age' (Clift 2001a).[5] It was supplemented by the appointment of a ministerial committee, chaired by the leader of the House of Commons, Robin Cook, which has been asked to 'consider ways of strengthening the democratic process by engaging the public and their elected representatives through the use of the internet and other electronic means'. Alongside a study of the viability of e-voting, the committee will look at 'the use of new technologies to give citizens enhanced opportunities to participate in the democratic process between elections' (Leslie 2001). This is the first time that a national government has established a Cabinet-level committee on e-democracy. Until ministers earmark funds and set a timetable for developing the consultative aspects of the Internet, however, their level of commitment will remain unclear.

The US central government currently lags behind the United Kingdom in its use of net-based consultations, perhaps surprisingly given the advanced broadband technology and the high penetration rates of the Internet in the United States. As yet, however, there has been little evidence of a centrally coordinated strategy to mobilise citizens through online consultation. The Brown University survey found that 86 per cent of federal sites offered email links, and 19 per cent allowed browsers to post comments on message boards or discussion forums. However, actual interactivity was limited (West 2001). The Firstgov portal does not offer the register of consultations that is provided by UK Online. Feedback is limited to comments on service provision; links to consultations are absent. A survey of the 131 feedback links offered by agencies listed on the Firstgov site on 7 December 2001 found that 82 per cent of the links offered only contact information, allowing users to communicate with the relevant agency by email, telephone or post. The remaining 18 per cent invited feedback on specific issues (such as the experience of visiting a national park), provided a complaint form, invited the reporting of problems or crimes or asked for responses to an online survey (Firstgov 2001). None of the links connected the user to legislative consultation. According to Steven Clift of the Minnesota-based Democracies Online website, 'When you compare the availability of online interactivity from the US government with the UK, the lack of US government interest stands out. There is no real chance to be an e-citizen on the government's online turf here, for now we can only participate in commercial and non-profit online spaces' (Clift 2001c).

In part the absence of interactivity may reflect the structure of US government. Government departments do not have the jurisdictions of their UK counterparts, and most legislative initiatives are drafted at state level or in Congress. Agencies or departments are more likely to consult on a new regulation than a major piece of legislation. Despite these limitations, Americans utilise national government websites more heavily than state or local websites, signalling that such sites represent an important point of contact. A survey for the Council for Excellence in Government found that 54 per cent of Internet users had visited federal government websites, whereas 45 per cent and 36 per cent had visited state and local government websites respectively (Council for Excellence in Government 2001: 9).[6] If people are going to be brought into consultation exercises, particularly where the issues are of national significance, federal government sites can reach a wide sample of the American population.

An indication of the potential public interest in online consultation can be seen in the first such exercise undertaken by a federal agency, which attracted widespread public participation. In 1997, the US Department of Agriculture (USDA) initiated an electronic consultation process following the publication of a proposed standard on the marketing of organic agricultural products. The government's online journal *Govexec.com* described it as, 'the first fully electronic rule-making for a major regulation in federal history' (Shulman 2000). It attracted considerable media attention. According to Shulman, 'Following publication of the proposed rule over the Internet, the USDA received over 275,000 public comments by e-mail, www, fax and postal mail'. Indications are that it did lead to a change of policy on the part of the Department of Agriculture. At the end of the initial consultation process in May 1998, Agriculture Secretary Dan Glickman announced that 'fundamental' changes would be made in the proposed rule, promising, 'If organic farmers and consumers reject our national standards we have failed' (Shulman 2000: 4). The revised code of practice that emerged in March 2000 was very different in tone from the original draft consultation, which had been heavily weighted towards the interests of food producers rather than consumers. Dr Margaret Mellon of the Union of Concerned Scientists, a persistent critic of the USDA's original proposal, expressed her support for the new rule, arguing that it 'could turn out to be the most important rule the USDA has issued in 20 years' (Shulman 2000: 4).

Following the USDA experiment in electronic consultation in December 1999, the Clinton administration issued a memorandum that underscored the importance of upgrading 'the capacity of regulatory agencies for using the Internet to become more open, efficient and responsive' (Clinton 1999). Each agency head was required to 'permit greater access to its officials by creating a public electronic mail address through which citizens can contact the agency with questions, comments or concerns' (Clinton 1999). However, there was no requirement that agencies use the Internet to extend their formal offline consultation procedures.

Since that date a number of agencies have held online discussions. The Environmental Protection Agency (EPA), for example, held a consultation on how to improve public involvement in EPA decision-making. This process involved over 500 individuals, including citizens, representatives of industry, environmental groups, small business, states, local governments, tribes and other groups. Participants could discuss the draft Public Involvement Policy and offer suggestions on how EPA should implement it (Environmental Protection Agency 2001). The Welfare to Work agency within the Department of Labour published a new regulation in March 2001, and allowed browsers to submit comments online using a standard form. However, neither of these consultations is clearly linked from the Firstgov portal; neither are they signposted on the home page of their respective departments. This suggests that people have to know what they are looking for and be familiar with the site design if they are able to participate in online consultation, making it hard to engage the wider, non-expert community in the process. The lack of a central register of consultation on the US federal government site means that consultation exercises must get media attention if they are to ensure high levels of participation. The USDA participation on organic food was successful in securing this level of publicity, probably due to the wider media debate on organic and genetically modified food. Less media-friendly subjects are not likely to be adequately publicised without strong government backing.

As in the UK, there have been recent moves in the US to emphasise the democratising potential of new technologies. Mark Forman, the associate director of the Office of Management and Budget for information technology and e-government, speaking at the Council for Excellence in Government's Imagine E-Government Awards ceremony in July 2001 said:

> The next step in electronic government will be to transform it into an 'e-democracy,' in which the public uses the Web to get direct access to the government... The Internet allows communication between communities and

> the government on a larger scale than has ever been possible. Communication is really the heart of e-government – communication between citizens and the government.
>
> (Vasishtha 2001)

As in the United Kingdom, however, tangible policy commitments on defining and expanding 'e-democracy' have not thus far been forthcoming.

Legislative branch

Legislatures in both the United States and the United Kingdom act as arenas for public consultation over legislation, supplementing the consultation undertaken by the executive branch. In both countries, web-based interaction between citizens and their representatives is possible both through members' own Internet sites and through initiatives undertaken by legislative committees. In the United Kingdom, around one-fifth of MPs have their own websites, although a survey rated those that did exist very poorly – branding them 'inept', 'flaccid' and 'bland' (Steinberg 2000). All MPs now have publicly available email addresses, but the fear of overload has made most MPs very circumspect in their usage, and until constituency screening processes are in place they will probably continue to be so (Coleman 2001: 8).

The expansion of consultation at parliamentary level has been spearheaded by parliamentary select committees, a number of which have piloted e-consultation projects in collaboration with the Hansard Society on issues ranging from domestic violence to data protection.[7] Unlike executive-based consultations, which are formally open to all, the Society-run consultations have followed the 'expert witness' tradition of select committee hearings. A data protection consultation, for example, was held in 1998 in collaboration with the Parliamentary Office of Science and Technology (POST), and was limited to invited participants from the data protection field, including lawyers, IT specialists and people involved in privacy legislation in other countries. Similarly, in October 1999, the Hansard Society again worked with POST to coordinate a consultation with scientists and engineers as part of the House of Lords Science and Technology Committee Inquiry into Women in Science. According to Coleman:

> When we started talking to parliamentary committees about running consultation over the internet, the assumption that we had was that if the consultations are going to result in real evidence for committees the only way we can produce that evidence is by thinking very carefully about how we get people to deliberate and who we invite to do that. So the first thing we did was rule out opening a website and say to everyone and anyone come on and speak, because you can extend democracy without opening things up to everyone. And if you can extend democracy in this way the question is who needs to be involved, who currently is not being heard, how do you help them have their say in a useful way.
>
> (Coleman 2000)

Sometimes the closed aspect of the online consultation proved a necessity given the sensitive nature of the material discussed. The initiative on domestic violence in spring 2000 run by the Hansard Society on behalf of the All Party Parliamentary Group on Domestic Violence was limited to female victims of domestic violence. Participants were identified via the Women's Aid organisation, and then provided with a special password and PC access. Security and anonymity were essential given that most participants were living in refuges and needed to protect their identity and location. MPs from the Domestic Violence Group logged onto the website periodically to follow the online debate, a factor Coleman believes encouraged participation: 'We asked people why they participated and whether they felt more motivated to participate in the domestic violence consultation because they were speaking to parliamentarians. And they said yes, no doubt whatsoever' (Coleman 2000). The Hansard Society has also run a consultation in conjunction with the Social Security Select Committee on tax credits, and assisted the House of Lords Select Committee on Stem Cell Research with an online consultation forum. Stephen Coleman, project director, predicts that such consultations will in the near future become a standard part of committee hearings (Coleman 2000).

The extent to which these legislative consultations have an impact on outcomes is difficult to assess given that select committees and parliamentary groups are charged with making recommendations and scrutinising departmental actions, rather than making policy. Coleman acknowledges that the findings of the Women in Science consultation did not match the needs of the sponsoring committee, and so was not effective. The data protection consultation took place at a late stage in the policy process, with respondents being asked to comment on an existing code of practice rather than being brought in at the design stage, which led to criticisms from some participants about the consultation's effectiveness (Parliamentary Office of Science and Technology 1998). Following the domestic violence consultation, Margaret Moran (chair of the All-Party Group) requested government action to improve the protection of children in situations of domestic violence in a Commons statement in June 2000 (Moran 2000). The Children Act sub-committee of the Lord Chancellor's advisory board on family law agreed to take into account the findings of the consultation when looking at proposed change to the act (Kennedy 2000). The findings of the tax credits and stem cell consultations were formally presented to the select committees involved, but appeared designed to enhance the committee members' understanding of the issues rather than to feed directly into legal changes.

In the United States, in contrast to the UK experience, all members of Congress have their own professionally designed site, with biographical details and links to committee and floor activity. From each member's website, a centrally administered link generates a form through which browsers can send an email to a chosen Senator or Congressman. Both Congress and Parliament face the common problem of how to process the number of emails received by members. In the United States, this was estimated by the Congress Online Project to be 48 million in 2000, and growing by an average of 1 million messages per month (Congress Online Project 2001).

As in the United Kingdom, it is at the level of committee hearings that online consultation has been introduced into the legislative process in the United States. Given the size and dispersion of the US population and the traditionally open nature of the committee system to outside interests, one might expect the idea of Internet-based submissions and discussion to be well advanced. However, as is the case with the executive branch of government, the US legislature has not shown the willingness of its British counterpart to experiment with online consultation procedures. The first Congressional online consultation was launched in May 2001 by Senators Fred Thompson and Joseph Lieberman, respectively the chairman and ranking member of the Senate Governmental Affairs Committee, which aimed to 'improve the access of the American people to their government'. The website invites comment on 'ways to advance the cause of digital government, to promote innovative uses of information technology and to expand citizen participation in government' (Lieberman 2000). Browsers can view fifty-nine proposals for the expansion of e-government, and offer comments on linked discussion forums. In a survey of the site on 7 December 2001, it was found that 445 comments had been posted. The most popular topic, accounting for almost a quarter (23 per cent) of total responses, was that of 'citizen's access', in which respondents were asked whether there should be more citizen access to government officials and activities. The vast majority – perhaps unsurprisingly – called for greater citizen involvement in decision-making.

All proposals on the site are exploratory rather than tied into specific legislation so it is not possible to review the impact of the site on legislative reform at this stage. At the same time as the site was launched, an Electronic Government bill was introduced into the Senate. Its expressed aims are 'To establish measures that require using Internet-based information technology to enhance citizen access to Government information and services, improve Government efficiency and reduce Government operating costs, and increase opportunities for citizen participation in Government' (Electronic Government Act 2001). The participative element of the bill refers to expanded access to information, which is a narrow interpretation of participation. The launch of the website on Electronic Government *after* the bill had been drafted is, perhaps, an indication of the extent to which consultation is as yet peripheral to the policy-making process.

Conclusion

The experience of electronic government in the United Kingdom and the United States is one of limited ambition and mixed achievement. The policy documents issued by both governments display a pronounced lack of radicalism. In both countries, electronic government has primarily been conceived as a way to expand the provision of services and information. Consultation and participation are discussed as general goals but little detail is provided about how the Internet can be used as a medium to expand citizen consultation. Where greater interactivity is proposed it often refers to better access to services rather than enhanced opportunities to participate in decision-making. Policy-framers reserve their detailed commitments for service delivery, whilst the expansion of citizen involvement remains a vague aspiration. Policy documents juxtapose the language of the service consumer with that of the participatory citizen, but indicate that it is the consumer's demand for online services that will be satisfied before any participatory yearnings of the citizen.

The practice of e-government largely reflects these policy objectives. In developing their websites, governments have shown a focused approach to online service provision and a more tentative attitude to online consultation. In the area of service delivery, both US and UK governments have made substantial progress in moving their capabilities online and have established deadlines for full online service provision – although it may be that as the deadlines approach the definition of 'full' starts to be refined.

The provision of online information is also an area where governments have made substantial progress. It is possible for citizens to become much better informed about government, its organisation and outputs, than was the case before the development of the Internet. Documents that previously were available only in public libraries, if at all, can now be downloaded directly to the user's PC. The provision of information is a key tool in ensuring government transparency and equipping interested citizens to challenge decision-makers, and its expansion constitutes an important step towards improving government accountability.

Progress in the development of online consultation has been tangible, if slow. In both the United States and the United Kingdom, offline consultation exercises now have an online component, with interested parties able to read and respond to policy documents online. Legislators in both countries have established mechanisms to allow online submissions to committee hearings. The appointment of a ministerial committee on electronic democracy in the United Kingdom, and signals from the US Office of Management and Budget that 'e-democracy' represents the next step in electronic government, may signal a new interest in using the Internet as a tool for consultation and interaction.

If the records of these governments are judged on their own terms they can be declared a cautious success. There are some areas in which the government has failed to match its own commitments, however. The information provided has tended to be promotional rather than discursive, and has been oriented towards enhancing service usage rather than consultation. For online information to be useful to the citizens it has to be logically organised and available via an effective search engine, and this is not yet the case across government. Many sites expect browsers to have extensive knowledge of internal government organisation to access relevant data.

The expansion of online consultation has been limited by inadequate feedback mechanisms. Interactive sites where users can discuss documents with other browsers or government officials are less common than those that simply post information in a downloadable format. Often the only response a citizen can give is via an email link, which disappears into the ether leaving the citizen unclear about how far their views will be taken into account by policy-makers. The UK Online site has expressed a commitment to improving feedback mechanisms but more efforts need to be made to uphold and widen this commitment.

There are clear similarities but also important differences between the countries in their implementation of e-government. The US government, especially at congressional level, offers a wider range of information online with more user-friendly portals and search engines than its UK counterpart. The more extensive Freedom of Information laws in the United States create a legal presumption in favour of disclosure, which may support a different attitude towards information provision than in the United Kingdom. The incoming Freedom of Information law in the United Kingdom may create pressures to expand the information provided online, although the law equips ministers with a range of tools to block exposure. Online consultation is better developed in the United Kingdom than in the United States, with the UK Online's consultation register providing an entry point into consultative processes, which is missing in the United States.

From the normative perspective, neither the policy nor the practice of e-government has matched the radical transformative effects envisaged by the technological utopians. In both countries, central governments have failed to develop any really extensive and influential mechanism of citizen input via the Internet. Online interactivity is not yet a standard element of consultation exercises at executive or legislative level. The provision of email addresses has made one-way communication easier, but has served as a complement to traditional written submissions rather than signifying a shift to a quicker and more interactive style of operation. Very few consultation exercises offer interactivity between citizen and state, in which MPs, bureaucrats or government ministers provide feedback to consultation respondents. Neither has there been any evident terminal erosion of governmental bodies as a result of harnessing the new technology. From the perspective of the models of adaptation outlined in the introduction to this volume, therefore, it would not seem that any one has been followed religiously. The basic fabric of the state is very much intact and it does not appear that the arrival of new ICTs has raised any serious questions about its continuing relevance. Neither has there been a vigorous embracing of the possibilities presented for deepening and widening citizen participation, in any practical sense. At best one can say that a strategy of limited utilitarian reforms has been engaged in, with parliament and the executive branch focusing on accessibility to information and service provision.

The lack of radical transformation should not come as too much of a surprise, however. As the social shaping logic would dictate, existing institutions have little incentive to render themselves obsolete, and are much more likely to adapt new technologies to existing practices than to allow technology to shape practice. It is clear that in neither the United States nor the United Kingdom has the government moved to the extreme of direct democracy highlighted in Table 3.1. The findings discussed in this chapter suggest that governments are positioned midway along the scale. They have made a commitment to full online service delivery; a large amount of information is now online; many of the offline consultation processes have some online component. Electronic government has not moved beyond this point, however, to stimulate institutional innovation or democratic transformation. In this sense, governments' online presence mirrors its offline role in maintaining a form of representative democracy that provides limited opportunities for citizens to make representations to government. It has not propelled governments in the direction of more direct forms of democracy.

There are some indications that governments in both countries may now be giving greater consideration to the democratising potential of the Internet, and repositioning their e-government strategies to encourage greater citizen participation. If online consultation does develop it could have important consequences not only for the government–citizen relationship, but also for the balance of power between institutions. Direct consultation of citizens can be a resource for the executive branch of government, used to sideline the representative claims of the legislature by giving the executive an independent channel to public opinion. In this scenario, consultation could contribute to existing trends for the executive to accrue power at the expense of the legislature. Alternatively, if legislative bodies are innovative in their use of consultation at committee stage this may strengthen pre-legislative scrutiny of bills and be a tool in the armoury of legislators. In Britain, particularly, where parliamentary scrutiny of bills has tended to be a formality in the past, the willingness of committees to be experimental in the use of online consultation may signal a new assertiveness.

If governments do move in this direction, it will be a slow and incremental shift. Surrendering their own control over policy-making is unlikely to be a priority for politicians. Recent interest in expanding citizen involvement may reflect a desire to maintain governments' relevance, in an age when declining turnout and new forms of Internet-based campaigning are threatening to sideline mainstream politics. If governments feel that they must harness new forms of participation to maintain their own legitimacy, the emphasis of electronic government may shift slightly towards consultation and involvement. Without these incentives, it is likely that the government will engage in dialogue with the citizen-consumer, but leave the active citizen silenced.

Notes

1 'Electronic' (or 'e-') is used in preference to the many alternative prefixes – digital, virtual, cyber – as this term has become the most widely used by governments themselves and in analyses of online activity. The term government, as used here, refers to both executive and legislative institutions, except where otherwise specified.

2 Interview conducted 21 November 2000.

3 On a visit to the site on 6 November 2001, there were 451 consultations listed, 61 of which were open.

4 This was downloaded from <http://www.ukonline.gov.uk/online/citizenspace/consultation/default.asp> on 14 February 2001, but has now been removed from the site.

5 Clift was a founder of the Minnesota E-democracy programme in 1994. The programme aimed to provide political information and online discussion forums for local users. It is now widely held to be one of the most successful local electronic democracy initiatives. See <http://www.e-democracy.org>

6 The Council for Excellence in Government is a non-partisan, non-profit organisation undertaking research to further the goal of better government performance. The fieldwork for the survey was done during 14–16 August 2000 by the research firms of

Peter D. Hart and Robert M. Teeter. It was a three-part study that included surveys of: 150 government officials; 155 business and non-profit leaders; and 1,003 members of the general public. The margin of error for the survey is +/− 4 per cent.

7 The Hansard Society for Parliamentary Government is an independent non-partisan educational charity, whose president is the Speaker of the House of Commons. See <http://www.hansard-society.org.uk>

Bibliography

Alexander, C. and Pal, L. (eds) (1998) *Digital Democracy*, Oxford: Oxford University Press.

Alexander, D. (2001a) Interview, *Guardian Unlimited*, 22 June <http://www.guardian.co.uk/Archive/Article/0,4273,4208681,00.html>, accessed on 8 October 2001.

Alexander, D. (2001b) Speech to Conference on Democracy in the Information Age, 25 October <http://www.dti.gov.uk/ministers/speeches/alexander251001.html>, first accessed 11 November 2001.

Allan, A. (2000) 'E-democracy', Lecture to the Hansard Society, 22 May.

Barber, B. (1999) 'Three Scenarios for the Future of Technology and Strong Democracy', *Political Science Quarterly*, 113, 573–90.

Blair, T. (2000) 'Foreword: Draft Code on Written Consultation', London: Cabinet Office, 12 April.

Bush, G. (2001) *A Blueprint for New Beginnings* <http://www.whitehouse.gov/news/usbudget/blueprint/budix.html>, first accessed 7 December 2001.

Cabinet Office (1996) *Government Direct: The Electronic Delivery of Government Services*, London: HMSO, <http://www.citu.gov.uk/greenpaper.htm>, first accessed 12 January 2001.

Cabinet Office (1999) *Modernising Government*, Cm 4310, London: HMSO <http://citu.gov.uk/moderngov/whitepaper/4310.htm>, first accessed 10 November 2000.

Cabinet Office (2000a) *E-Government* <http://www.iagchampions.gov.uk/iagc/strategy.htm>, first accessed 12 January 2001.

Cabinet Office (2000b) 'UK Online Citizen Portal Goes Live', Press Release, 4 December.

Cabinet Office (2000c) 'New Approach to Public Consultation Will Give People Bigger Say in Government – Mowlam', Press Release, 27 November.

Cabinet Office (2000d) 'Code of Practice on Written Consultation', 27 November <http://www.cabinet-office.gov.uk/servicefirst/index/consultation.htm>, first accessed 12 February 2001.

Carr-Brown, J. (2001) 'No 10 Spins Its Own News on "Pravda.com"', *Sunday Times*, 18 February.

Chadwick, A. and May, C. (2001a) 'Interaction Between States and Citizens in the Age of the Internet', paper presented to the American Political Science Association, San Francisco, August, <http://pro.harvard.edu/abstracts/040/040004ChadwickAn.htm>, first accessed 16 September 2001.

Chadwick, A. and May, C. (2001b) 'Interaction Between States and Citizens in the Age of the Internet', paper presented to the European Consortium of Political Research Joint Workshops, Grenoble, April, <www.essex.ac.uk/ecpr/jointsessions/grenoble/papers/ws3/chadwick_may.pdf>, first accessed 21 March 2001.

Clift, S. (2001a) 'UK Government's Major E-Democracy Push', Online. Email: clift@ publicus.net (26 October).

Clift, S. (2001b) 'UK Gov E-Democracy Efforts – Ministerial Committee on E-Democracy', Online. Email: clift@publicus.net (5 December).

Clift, S. (2001c) 'Engaging Citizens in Policy-Making', Online. Email: clift@publicus.net (19 February).

Clinton, W. (1999) 'Memorandum for the Heads of Executive Departments and Agencies', 17 December <http://ec.fed.gov/wh_egov.htm>, first accessed 12 February 2001.

Coleman, S. (1999) 'Cutting Out the Middle-Man: From Virtual Representation to Direct Deliberation', in Hague, B. and Loader, B. (eds), *Digital Democracy*, London: Routledge.

Coleman, S. (2000) Director of Studies, Hansard Society, Interview with the author, 21 November.

Coleman, S. (2001) *Democracy Online*, London: Hansard Society, <http://www.hansard-society.org.uk/MPWEB.pdf>, first accessed 30 October 2001.

Coleman, S. and Normann, E. (2000) *New Media and Social Inclusion*, London: Hansard Society.

Congress Online Project (2001) 'E-mail overload in Congress' <http://www.congressonlineproject.org/email.html>, first accessed 6 November 2001.

Council for Excellence in Government (2001) *E-Government: The Next American Revolution* <http://www.excelgov.org/>, first accessed 16 March 2001.

Cunningham, J. (1999) 'Introduction', *Modernising Government*, London: HMSO.

Davis, R. (1999) *The Web of Politics*, New York: Oxford University Press.

Deloitte Consulting and Deloitte & Touche (2000) *At the Dawn of E-Government* <http://www.us.deloitte.com/PUB/egovt/egovt.htm>, first accessed 12 February 2001.

Department for Trade and Industry (2001) 'Alexander: Opportunities for Democracy in the Information Age', News Release, 25 October <http://www.nds.coi.gov.uk/coi/coipress.nsf/2b45e1e3ffe090ac802567350059d840/eca70dbb4d8645f380256af00037cba1?OpenDocument>, first accessed 7 December 2001.

Electronic Government Act 2001 (2001) <http://lieberman.senate.gov/newsite/egov.pdf>, first accessed 6 November 2001.

Elshtain, J. (1982) 'Democracy and the QUBE Tube', *The Nation*, 7–14 August.

Environmental Protection Agency (2001) 'Public Involvement in EPA decisions' <http://www.network-democracy.org/epa-pip/>, first accessed 6 November 2001.

Finney, C. (1999) 'Extending Public Consultation via the Internet', *Science and Public Policy*, 26(5), 361–73.

Firstgov (2001) 'Firstgov: Your First Click to the US Government' <http://www.firstgov.gov/>, first accessed 7 December 2001.

Grossman, L. (1995) *The Electronic Republic*, New York: Viking.

Gyford, J. (1991) *Citizens, Consumers and Councils*, London: Macmillan.

Hagen, M. (1997) 'A Typology of Electronic Democracy' <www.uni-giessen.de/fb03/vinci/labore/netz/hag_en.htm>, first accessed 8 October 2001.

Hague, B. and Loader, B. (eds) (1999) *Digital Democracy*, London: Routledge.

Hill, K. and Hughes, J. (1998) *Cyberpolitics*, Lanham, Md: Rowman and Littlefield.

Katzen, S. (2000) Testimony to the Committee on Government Reform, Subcommittee on Government Management, Information and Technology, US House of Representatives, 11 October, <http://www.whitehouse.gov/omb/legislative/testimony/october_2_2000.html>, first accessed 7 December 2001.

Kennedy, Jane (2000) Parliamentary Secretary – Lord Chancellor's Department, *Hansard*, 7 June: Column 113WH, <http://www.parliament.the-stationery-office.co.uk/>, first accessed 15 March 2001.

Leslie, C. (2001) *Hansard*, 29 November: Column 353WH, <http://www.publications.parliament.uk/pa/cm200102/cmhansrd/cm011129/halltext/11129h01.htm#11129h01_spmin0>, first accessed 12 December 2001.

Lieberman, J. (2000) 'E-Government Project Launched to Improve Citizen Access to Government', News Release, 18 May, <http://www.senate.gov/~lieberman/press/00/05/051800a.html>, first accessed 16 August 2001.

Lieberman, J. (2001) 'Electronic Government Act of 2001', News Release, 1 May, <http://www.senate.gov/~lieberman/press/01/05/2001501810.html>, first accessed 16 August 2001.

Lieberman, J. and Thompson, F. (2000) 'E-Government' <http://www.senate.gov/~gov_affairs/egov/index.cfm>, first accessed 16 August 2001.

Livesey, P. (2001) Assistant Director, E-Government Policy & Best Practice Team, Interview with the author, 23 February.

Malina, A. (1999) 'Perspectives on Citizen Democratisation and Alienation in the Virtual Public Sphere', in Hague, B. and Loader, B. (eds), *Digital Democracy*, London: Routledge.

Margolis, M. and Resnick, D. (2000) *Politics as Usual*, Thousand Oaks, CA: Sage.

Martinson, J. (2001) 'Microsoft Comes to Aid of e-Envoy', *Guardian*, 27 March.

Moran, Margaret (2000) *Hansard*, 7 June: Column 112WH, <http://www.parliament.the-stationery-office.co.uk/>, first accessed 15 March 2001.

National Audit Office (1999) *Government on the Web*, London: HMSO.

National Partnership for Reinventing Government (1997) 'Introduction by Al Gore', *Access America Initiatives* <http://www.accessamerica.gov/docs/intro.html>, first accessed 12 February 2001.

National Partnership for Reinventing Government (2001) 'Electronic Government' <http://govinfo.library.unt.edu/npr/initiati/it/>, first accessed 12 February 2001.

Neill Committee on Standards in Public Life (2000) *Sixth Report* <http://www.official-documents.co.uk/document/cm45/4557/4557.htm>, first accessed 15 March 2001.

Norris, P. and Jones, D. (1998) 'Virtual Democracy', *The Harvard International Journal of Press and Politics*, 3(3), 1–4.

Noveck, B. (2000) 'Paradoxical partners', *Democratization*, Spring, 7(1), 18–35.

O'Keefe, S. (2001) Testimony to the Senate Committee on Governmental Affairs, 11 July <http://www.whitehouse.gov/omb/legislative/testimony/20010710-1.html>, first accessed 7 December 2001.

Office of the e-Envoy, Cabinet Office (2000) *UK Online Annual Report*, London: HMSO, <http://www.e-envoy.gov.uk/2000/progress/anrep1/text/default.htm>, first accessed 6 April 2001.

Office of the e-Envoy, Cabinet Office (2001a) 'Things You Can Now Do Online' <http://www.e-envoy.gov.uk/online_now.htm>, first accessed 7 December 2001.

Office of the e-Envoy, Cabinet Office (2001b) 'E-Communications Group' <http://www.e-envoy.gov.uk/ecomms_index.htm>, first accessed 14 October 2001.

Office of Management and Budget (2001) 'Mark Forman Named Associate Director for Information Technology and E-Government', News Release, 14 June, <http://www.whitehouse.gov/omb/pubpress/2001-13.html>, first accessed 7 December 2001.

Owen, D., Davis, R. and Strickler, V. (1999) 'Congress and the Internet', *Harvard International Journal of Press and Politics*, 4(2), 10–29.

Parliamentary Office of Science and Technology (1998) 'E-1, December 1998, Data Protection – On-line Discussion', December <http://www.parliament.uk/post/report.htm>, 12 February 2001.

Schumpeter, J. (1965) *Capitalism, Socialism and Democracy*, London: Allen & Unwin.

Scobbie, Moira (2000) 'Responses to Digital Scotland Task Force Report', June <www.scotland.gov.uk/digitalscotland/responses/moiras.pdf>, first accessed 12 February 2001.

Shulman, S. (2000) 'Citizen Agenda-Setting, Digital Government and the National Organic Program', paper presented to the American Political Science Association, Washington, DC, August.

Silcock, R. (2001) 'What is E-Government?', *Parliamentary Affairs*, 54, 88–101.

Smart, V. (2001) 'The Shambles of E-Whitehall', *Guardian*, 16 August.

Steinberg, T. (2000) 'Parliamentary IT briefing', *Institute for Economic Affairs*, November.

Stringer, G. (2001) 'Putting Government Online, Bring Citizens Online', Speech to the Global Forum conference, Naples, Italy, 15 March.

Ten Downing Street Press Office (2001) 'Opportunities for Democracy in the Information Age', Press Release, 25 October, <http://www.number-10.gov.uk/news.asp?NewsId=2840&SectionId=30>, first accessed 6 November 2001.

UK Online (2000) 'Future Plans' <http://www.ukonline.gov.uk/futureplans/>, first accessed 15 February 2001.

UK Online (2001) 'How Government Consults' <http://www.ukonline.gov.uk/online/citizenspace/default.asp?url=/online/citizenspace/consultation/how_govt_consults.asp>, first accessed 14 October 2001.

Vasishtha, P. (2001) 'Citizen Communication Will Nourish e-gov', *Government Computer News*, 30 July 2001, 20, 21 <http://www.gcn.com/vol20_no21/news/4755-1.html>, first accessed 7 December 2001.

Waller, P., Livesey, P. and Edin, K. (2001) 'E-Government in the Service of Democracy', *International Council for Information Technology in Government Administration*, 74, June <www.ieg.ibm.com/thought_leadership/issue74-waller.pdf>, first accessed 10 October 2001.

West, D. (2001) 'E-Government and the Transformation of Public Service Delivery', paper presented to the American Political Science Association, San Francisco, August, <http://pro.harvard.edu/papers/024/024007WestDarrel.pdf>, first accessed 16 September 2001.

White, M. (2000) 'Blair Sets Earlier Target Date for Online Whitehall', *Guardian*, 31 March.

4 Digital parliaments and electronic democracy

A comparison between the US House, the Swedish Riksdag and the German Bundestag[1]

Thomas Zittel

Parliaments on the net

As in many areas of social life, computer networks along with other kinds of new digital information and communication technology have entered the parliamentary sphere. This is the conclusion of a volume edited by Stephen Coleman, John Taylor and Wim van de Donk, which collects in-depth case studies on the digitalization of modern parliaments such as the British House of Commons, the Danish Folketinget and the Australian Parliament (Coleman *et al.* 1999). A comparative survey on new information technology among members of eleven legislative assemblies provides further comparative evidence on this trend towards digital parliaments. The respondents to this survey report the general availability of personal computers as well as widespread access to the Internet across all cases.[2] Intranets, videoconferencing technology, mobile phones and notebooks belong to the standard equipment of most of the respondents to this survey. These kinds of empirical data stress the efforts that have been made on the part of legislative assemblies to catch up with the most recent developments in telecommunication technology.

To many students of media and political communication the proliferation of computer networks heralds the coming of an electronic democracy, which opens up new avenues for political participation. According to former chairman of NBC Lawrence Grossman, a new political system is already taking shape in the United States. He argues that new digital media are turning America into an electronic republic, which vastly increases the people's day-to-day influence on political decisions (Grossman 1995: 3). Journalist Wayne Rash concludes his empirical study on digital politics in the United States with the observation that the Net is already giving voters a voice that reaches directly to the highest levels of government (Rash 1997: 181).

From a theoretical point of view, these so called 'cyberoptimists' point towards the vast technological potential of the Internet for decentralized and interactive mass communication. They subscribe to the notion of technological determinism that assumes a causal relationship between major technological breakthroughs such as computer networks on the one hand and social structure on the other.

According to this perspective, the social diffusion of new digital media will trigger far-reaching social change in almost automatic ways (Toffler 1980; Naisbitt 1982; Street 1992: chapter 2; Hoff 2000). From an empirical point of view, cyberoptimists emphasize new strategies of digitalized political communication in the parliamentary realm to argue their case.

Parliamentary websites are one of the most visible indicators for these changing strategies in political communication. In her book, Pippa Norris reviews on the Digital Divide the whole universe of parliamentary websites around the world. Her numbers indicate that legislative Websites have become a universal trend throughout Scandinavia, North America and western Europe with the exception of Cyprus (Norris 2001: 132–3). A count by the Inter-Parliamentary Union found out that 87 per cent of all national parliaments in Europe have established a presence on the web by April 2000 (Inter-Parliamentary Union 2000). A variety of case studies offer more in-depth analyses on the history and the content of particular parliamentary websites. Some of these studies emphasize the fact that these digital publications have been launched during the mid-1990s in an attempt to increase the transparency of the parliamentary process and to exploit new opportunities for interactive communication. To achieve this goal, legislative websites allow among others easy access to the full text of plenary transcripts and to information on the progress of legislation. Interactive elements such as email addresses or discussion fora are designed to foster interactive communication with citizens (Casey 1996; Coleman *et al.* 1999; Fühles-Ubach and Neumann 1999; Mambrey *et al.* 1999; Coleman 2000).

In contrast to cyberoptimism, some students of electronic democracy are sceptical regarding the significance of digital parliaments for democratic government and political participation. These so called 'cybersceptics' claim that digitalized political institutions do not live up to the standard of electronic democracy and thus represent examples of technological modernization rather than political transformation. A substantial number of students of digital parliaments, for example, voices concern about the suboptimal uses of the Internet in many parliaments that have been subject to research (Coleman *et al.* 1999: 369–70). According to Michael Margolis and David Resnick, legislative websites can be expected to reinforce support for the dominant political attitudes and established political parties rather than to transform current systems of interest representation (Margolis and Resnick 2000: 93–4). While cyberscepticism should be applauded to reintroduce a more realistic tone to the debate on electronic democracy, it nevertheless shares two important shortcomings with its counterpart.

First, many empirical studies on electronic democracy raise the question of relevance. They suffer from a lack of political theory in failing to define and explain a standard or a theoretical frame that could be used to identify relevant empirical phenomena from the perspective of democratic theory. Most of these studies take conceptual shortcuts by drawing far-reaching conclusions on democracy that are based upon the analysis of political communication. These analyses take strategies of political communication and the implementation of interactive mass communication on the Net as a vantage point to evaluate progress towards electronic democracy. However, while the use of new technological opportunities for the purpose of political communication is an important prerequisite of political impact, it is not a sufficient one. In this chapter we argue that we have to take the procedural and structural implications of a specific act of political communication into account in order to be able to draw conclusions regarding its larger impact on democracy. We thus need a standard that identifies relevant acts of digital communication from the perspective of democratic theory. This standard has to be based upon technology as well as upon structural and procedural considerations.

A second shortcoming concerns the lack of general evidence regarding the impact of new digital media such as computer networks on democracy. Most of the available empirical analyses are impressionistic or in a case study format. The explorative nature of most of these case studies and the lack of a common relevant theoretical focus does not allow for cumulative knowledge and for general conclusions regarding the impact of new digital media on democracy (Lijphart 1971; Peters 1998: chapter 6). In order to produce more general conclusions on this question, we need more case studies based upon a relevant common theoretical frame. A second strategy of empirical research on electronic democracy should be based upon the comparative method in order to unveil the current political ramifications of new digital media in general and to understand the impact of digital parliaments in particular.

This chapter touches upon both problems to shed light on the political ramifications of digital parliaments. It will proceed in three distinct steps: In a first step, it will sketch an ideal model of electronic democracy. The aim is to define a meaningful standard that takes into account the procedural and structural dimension of politics in order to assess the relevance of digital parliaments for democracy. In a second empirical section, we will analyze different digital parliaments on the basis of this model in order to test the two hypotheses sketched here. In this empirical section we compare the US House, the German Bundestag and the Swedish Riksdag. This empirical analysis draws from a quantitative content analysis of personal websites in these three parliaments and from qualitative case studies on institutional reform in digital parliaments. A third section takes the result of this analysis as a vantage point to reconsider the link between technological change in telecommunications and political change and to speculate about prerequisites of electronic democracy beyond technological change in telecommunication.

The rational for the selection of our cases is based upon the magnitude of technological change in telecommunication. Each of the three parliaments in our sample experienced change in telecommunication infrastructure at a similar level. The German Bundestag, for example, started in the mid-1980s to equip its members with personal computers (Lange 1988; Einemann 1991; Mambrey *et al.* 1991). By 1989, forty-seven German MPs had access to this new technology either directly in their own office or indirectly via committees or parliamentary party organization (Einemann 1991: 11–14). Today, almost every single workplace in the German parliament is equipped with state-of-the-art desktops, which run on the basis of the most recent software. Along with this proliferation of personal computers, the Bundestag built up a powerful network infrastructure. In 1995, when the World Wide Web (WWW) took off, only very few members had access via modems and commercial online-providers, sometimes at their own expenses. With the move to Berlin, the Bundestag implemented a Local Area Network that connects all computers internally as well as externally.

A quite similar development took place in the Swedish Riksdag. According to a Swedish MP, thirty years ago, his predecessors were restricted to only two telephone booths in the lobby to enter into contact with the media or their constituents (Gylling 2000). Today, there are mobile phones, fax machines and personal computers all around the place. The number of personal computers in parliamentary buildings increased, for example, from 10 in 1987 to 1,800 in October 2000.[3] Moreover, an increasing number of Swedish members use portable notebook computers to connect via a 128 Kbit line to a Local Area Network with a 100 Mbit Backbone and a 2 Mbit connection to the Internet. A mobile videoconferencing system with cameras, screens and a sound system that can be used at various studios within the buildings of the Riksdag supplements this new communication infrastructure in the Swedish Riksdag (Ulfhielm 1998).

Similar developments in the US House are summarized by a story published in the *Washington Times* in 1999. This story reported the tremendous investments made over a time span of five years to equip the US House with the most recent communications technology. In the course of these efforts, the US House provided congressmen and their staffers with new personal computers and software, renovated congressional office buildings with new fibre optic cables and provided at least one T1 Internet connection line to each office with an access rate of 1.5 million bits per second (Archibald 1999; see also Casey 1996). Apart from internal technological change, each of the three parliaments we selected experienced far-reaching external technological change in telecommunication as well. In Sweden, Germany and the United States significant numbers of the population own personal computers and have access to the Internet. According to survey research, by early 2000, almost half of the population in the United States and Sweden was online while in Germany, about 20 per cent of the population had access to the Internet at this point in time (NUA 2001).

In this chapter we ask whether our three digital parliaments use the Internet along the lines of our model of electronic democracy or rather whether these three digitalized legislative assemblies are falling behind this standard. While the first observation would support the claim of cyberoptimists, the second finding would stress the cybersceptics point of view. Our comparative design furthermore allows testing for differences between the three cases under study regarding the implementation of electronic democracy in the process of technological change. This outcome would point towards the impact of intervening contextual variables.

What is electronic democracy?

The term democracy has been linked to many adjectives during the course of its history: direct democracy, representative democracy or parliamentary democracy are some of the most widely known combinations. The term electronic democracy marks a more recent version. Adjectives are analytical tools to empirical theorists of democracy to specify and clarify this very broad concept. They are a means to characterize specific forms of democracy and to distinguish between different basic types of this form of government (Collier and Levitsky 1997). This observation raises questions regarding the meaning of electronic democracy and the specific form of democracy it signifies.

In the debate on electronic democracy this term is frequently used as a catch-all concept. It combines different empirical phenomena such as the websites of political parties or parliaments, electronically mediated debates on political topics, community networks, electronic voting or even the provision of administrative services via new digital media (Leggewie and Maar 1998; Kamps 1999). We argue that this type of usage is too unspecific and not suited to foster a clear understanding of electronic democracy. More important, its most serious shortcoming lies in the tendency to take conceptual shortcuts by drawing conclusions on democracy on the basis of the study of political communication and communication technology. This general usage of the term ignores the fact that democracy cannot be reduced to communication but rather that it is also about institutions. A definition of electronic democracy has to take these defining elements of democracy into account.

There have been some efforts to conceptualize electronic democracy in a more explicit and comprehensive manner (see e.g. Arterton 1987; Hagen 1997; Bellamy 2000). These mainly theoretical undertakings chose to model this concept in terms of a real type on the basis of empirical developments and discourses regarding the use of new digital media in the political realm. While these analyses give way to a more sophisticated understanding of the phenomenon at hand, they still suffer from major shortcomings. We argue that at this early stage of technological developments one cannot assume to capture relevant phenomena with this kind of method. Real types simply do not provide analytical lenses that are sharp enough to distinguish the relevant from the irrelevant and to detect small and so far hardly visible trends in the transformation of democracy. As a consequence, most of the available models of electronic democracy are somewhat fuzzy and hardly able to give us a clear idea what electronic democracy is all about and how to distinguish it from other types of democracy. They also do not put their finger on the general problem of conceptual shortcuts in the debate on electronic democracy. Most theoretical models of electronic democracy are therefore ill-suited to guide systematic empirical research on the political impact of new digital media.

In contrast to these earlier theoretical analyses we model electronic democracy as an ideal type that is based upon basic ideas of democracy and is structured along three different levels of political analysis. By using this method, we aim to forego the problem of conceptual shortcuts and to sharpen our analytical lenses in the study of electronic democracy. We define electronic democracy, as outlined in Figure 4.1, as a three-layered concept that emphasizes political participation as a core value in the process of decision-making (conception of democracy),

	Participatory democracy		Liberal democracy
Conception of democracy	• Individual as part of the political community		• Antagonism between individual and political community
Democratic design	• Direct democracy via electronic means • Direct, participatory system of representation via electronic means • Foster civil society via new media		• Strictly representative system • Indirect system of representation • Protect private sphere
Participatory behaviour	• Taking decisions via electronic means • Deliberate via electronic means to prepare political decisions • Getting political information via electronic means to learn about political decisions and decision-making process		• Voting

Figure 4.1 Electronic democracy: a three-layered concept.

sketches three different strategies for institutional/structural reform to make democracy more participatory via new digital media (democratic design) and aims at influencing individual behaviour by increasing all types of political participation via the use of new digital media (participatory behaviour).

This definition marks a sharp distinction between political communication on the one hand and electronic democracy on the other. At the level of participatory behaviour, it excludes individual acts of digital communication that are not aimed at influencing political decision-making such as exchanging ideas in a USENET group or retrieving information on community services (see e.g. Barnes *et al.* 1979: 42). At the level of democratic design our model emphasizes the need for digitalized communication and interaction to be integrated into the decision-making process in order to count as an element of electronic democracy. We do not consider acts of digitalized public relations such as discussion fora run by the parliamentary bureaucracy as an element of electronic democracy per se.

Our definition of electronic democracy also makes a strong statement regarding our third level, which focuses on different conceptions of democracy. At this level, we do not consider electronic democracy as a distinct type of democracy. We argue instead that most of the discourse on electronic democracy closely resembles the debate on participatory democracy and that electronic democracy rather becomes a distinct phenomenon at the other two levels of our model.

Conceptions of democracy focus on the level of ideas and primarily ask about the nature of citizenship (Rawls 1971). At this most general level, we distinguish between two basic ideas (conceptions) of democracy: participatory and liberal democracy. Participatory democracy perceives the self as part of the political community. It therefore strives to involve individuals as much as possible into the political process. From this point of view, democracy becomes a way of life (Pateman 1970; Barber 1984; Fishkin 1991; Habermas 1992). This perspective is in stark contrast to a liberal conception of democracy, which perceives individuals as autonomous entities independent from the political community and which assumes a basic antagonism between individuals and their social environment. Individuals are perceived as consumers and private beings who do not care much about political involvement, who develop interests apart from the political community and who are sometimes in conflict with the political community. Liberal theory emphasizes the legitimacy of these interests and aims at protecting the private lives of citizens. From this point of view, democracy merely becomes a process of collective decision-making (Schumpeter 1950; Sartori 1987).

The liberal conception of democracy is considered the dominant paradigm of modern democracy. It owes part of this dominance to the problems of its counterpart to design a participatory scheme of democracy under conditions of the modern nation state. Theorists of participatory democracy are ardent critics of the liberal model. They perceive liberal democracy as 'thin democracy' that threatens the stability of democracy, creates negative policies and leads individuals to live isolated and estranged lives. But a community of millions of citizens and an area of hundreds of thousands of square miles silenced many protagonists of participatory democracy when it came to questions of designing participatory democracy in terms of specific political institutions (Schmidt 2000: 175).

This is where electronic democracy comes in. Electronic democracy shares with the participatory model its general conception of democracy. Its goal is to make democracy more participatory, to involve citizens more into the political process and to strengthen political community (Hagen 1997; Kleinsteuber and Hagen 1998). Theorists of electronic democracy perceive new digital media as means to implement their ideal under the conditions of the nation state and to overcome most of the technical obstacles to participatory democracy (Krauch 1971; Etzioni *et al.* 1975; Becker 1981; Slaton 1992). This definition provides a standard at the level of ideas and motivations to evaluate current developments regarding the use of new digital media in general and regarding digital parliaments in particular. We should assume that digital parliaments matter to democracy in cases where this kind of motivation prevails among political actors.

Apart from this macro-analytical perspective, most critics of participatory democracy focus on the micro-analytical level while arguing against this conception of democracy. They emphasize low rates of political participation and the lack of political interest among ordinary citizens as an indicator that speaks against the feasibility of participatory democracy (Berelson *et al.* 1954; Campbell *et al.* 1960). According to these critics, individuals have more important things in their mind than politics, and voting should be considered the only type of political participation citizens might be able to squeeze into their busy schedules. As a reaction to these claims, early theorists of electronic democracy stressed digital media as a tool to foster various types of individual participation beyond voting such as retrieving political information to learn about political decisions, entering into political debates to deliberate political decisions and registering political opinions on policy issues (Krauch 1971; Etzioni *et al.* 1975; Becker 1981; Slaton 1992).

These theorists used the vehicle of experiments in order to demonstrate that citizens are ready to take advantage of new digital means of political participation. This was the conclusion German teledemocrat Helmut Krauch drew from an early project he organized in cooperation with German TV in 1971. In this experiment on teledemocracy, a representative panel of citizens was given the opportunity to follow a televised debate on problems of environmental protection and to register opinions on several questions that were raised in the course of this debate via a digital phone system. The votes were registered by a mainframe computer, electronically processed and turned into graphs, which were immediately displayed to the discussants (Krauch 1971). American teledemocrats Ted Becker and Christa Slaton used digital phone lines in 1981 to poll citizens in New Zealand in order to involve the public in long-range strategic political planning (Becker 1981; Ryan and Becker 1983). According to Becker, New Zealanders were excited about the new participatory tools and took to teledemocracy like birds to trees. As a consequence, Becker perceives advances in interactive cable TV and in home computer systems as prerequisites for a bright future in political participation (Becker 1981: 8).

Political Philosopher Amitai Etzioni took a different path towards electronic democracy by emphasizing deliberation in his experiments with telecommunications media. In the mid-1970s he and his collaborators organized a series of telephone conferences to study this medium as a means to foster political dialogue. The purpose of this experiment was to demonstrate that '[...] the technological means exist through which millions of people can enter into dialogue with one another and with their representatives and can form the authentic consensus essential for democracy'. Etzioni concluded his studies with the observation that phone conferences are well suited to increase the quantity as well as the quality of political participation (Etzioni *et al.* 1975).

These kinds of experiments were designed to demonstrate the interest of ordinary citizens in digital political participation beyond voting. They suggest another standard to evaluate the impact of new digital media in general and digital parliaments in particular. On the basis of this standard we have to ask whether citizens are using parliamentary websites to retrieve information on the parliamentary process or whether they take advantage of interactive features to communicate with the parliamentary sphere. This understanding of electronic democracy is focused on the behavioural level of political analysis.

Original theorists of participatory democracy argue for a close link between participatory behaviour and participatory institutions or designs. Unfortunately, students of electronic democracy have been much less specific regarding this third element of electronic democracy. There has been little interest to link the idea of participatory democracy via digital means to specific institutional designs. Having reviewed the literature on electronic democracy we have to conclude that current concepts of electronic democracy are under-complex in institutional terms – to say the least. However, the discourse on electronic democracy as well as available models of electronic democracy include general considerations that are pointing towards three broad strategies of democratic design via new digital media.

The first two strategies are only of passing interest in the context of our argument. The first argues that new electronic media should be used to implement measures of direct democracy such as electronic referenda or initiatives (Budge 1996). This perspective does not advocate to completely abolish representative types of democracy and to shift from a representative mode towards a direct mode of decision-making. It only proposes to take some decisions by means of direct democracy while others should be taken by elected representatives. In recent years there have been several experiments and pilot projects that aim to solve not only technological problems related to electronic referenda but which also aim to answer questions regarding necessary procedural and structural problems in the process of implementation (Muralt Müller 2000; Buchstein 2001; Mutter 2002).

The second strategy of democratic design via new digital media highlights cyberspace as a new type of public space, which could be organized as an autonomous self-regulatory social sphere. Theorists of cyberdemocracy assume that this new type of social sphere will strengthen civic engagement and social cooperation (Rheingold 1993; Schuler 1996; Katz 1997). There are no elaborate institutional designs available so far to put more flesh on this general concept of cyberdemocracy as a means for democratic decision-making. However, some students of the Internet point towards the history and the organization of the Internet as an example for a self-regulatory and decentralized political sphere based upon new digital media (Hofmann 1998). From this perspective, the Internet ought to be free from any type of state intervention and state regulation in order to be able to emerge as a new type of civil space.

A third strategy of institutional reform is most consequential for our initial question regarding the relevance of digital parliaments for democracy. It stresses the function of political representation as the main target of political reform. It advocates a shift from an indirect system of interest representation towards a direct and participatory system of political representation. The current system of political representation stresses intermediate organizations such as political parties, interest groups or mass media as major linkages between citizens and the state. Political parties are of crucial importance in this current system of interest representation. Modern democratic theory perceives political parties as mass organizations that mobilize citizens, aggregate and articulate political interests and link these interests to the decision-making process. Elections are in the core of this process. Parties compete in political elections on the basis of manifestos, the party who wins a majority forms a government and implements its manifesto. It is crucial to this system that parties impose a rigid discipline on the MPs to secure the implementation of their manifesto (Katz 1987; Weber 1990; Gallagher *et al.* 2001).

This current system of interest representation has been criticized for its trend towards oligarchy (Michels 1911), for being systematically selective regarding the type of social interest that could gain representation (Schattschneider 1975) and for being biased towards a certain type of information that is being communicated particularly via the mass media (Sarcinelli 1998). According to these critics, this system of indirect representation establishes weak links between citizens and the state. Citizens remain in the role of voters who have the opportunity to decide upon government policies during subsequent elections, while many cannot gain access to crucial information, cannot take the political initiative to voice their interests or cannot influence policy-making according to their interests.

The alternative system of direct, participatory political representation is structured in very different ways. In this system, intermediary organizations such as political parties are weak and direct communication and interaction function as the main linkage between the public and the state. Theorists of electronic democracy assume that new digital media such as the Internet can be used to redesign prevailing indirect systems of interest representation and to close the gap between citizens and parliaments in twofold ways.

The first approach perceives new digital media as a way to link individual representatives closer to particular constituents (Arterton 1987; see e.g. McLean 1987; Snider 1994). According to this approach, the bandwidth and the decentralized structure of computer networks allow each individual member easy and efficient access to mass communication in order to enter into a constant dialogue with his constituents, to disseminate information on his policy views and to learn about the policy views of the constituents. Moreover, the merging of communications technology with data processing technology allows even individual MPs to constantly poll citizens on specific policy issues. The Internet thereby functions as a direct link between individual members and citizens and enables MPs to bypass traditional linkage structures such as mass media, political parties or interest groups. With this infrastructure in place, single representatives can become delegates of particular constituents (Pitkin 1967).

Another type of participatory representative system by electronic means stresses the possibility to draw citizens closer to the parliamentary process. Electronic consultations, for example, allow a more representative sample of citizens to voice their opinions on pending legislation and to deliberate with each other as well as with policy-makers in the wake of political decisions (Coleman 1999, 2000; Needham 2001). Parliaments could also decide to adjust established principles of public access to the technological potential of the Internet to open up the parliamentary process to public scrutiny and to use new digital media to publicize public information in far-reaching ways.

While both schemes of participatory political representation presuppose the implementation of new digital media technology as well as new patterns of political communication, they also stress the need for institutional and structural adjustments. The first scheme of participatory political representation presupposes a decentralized pattern of digital communication and interaction between citizens and legislative assemblies rather than a centralized one. It thus suggests strengthening the autonomy of individual MPs in relation to their party. The second scheme of interest representation via digital media suggests a close link between digital communication and the parliamentary process in institutional terms. In the context of this scheme the integration of digital communication in the decision-making process becomes a crucial question.

The following empirical analysis focuses on the US House, the German Bundestag and the Swedish Riksdag. It asks whether the technological developments in telecommunication within these digital parliaments are in line with the models of participatory representative design sketched here. In our analysis we focus on the structural level in order to evaluate the technological developments in modern parliaments and to determine whether digital parliaments matter to democracy. We neither ask about the motivation and ideas that drive the digitalization of parliaments nor do we ask whether citizens are using the new opportunities to communicate and interact with parliaments. In a first section, we focus on the media strategies of individual representatives. We ask whether individual representatives are using the Internet and whether they are using this medium in ways to enter into closer relationships with constituents. Next we focus on institutional policies and ask whether digital parliaments trigger institutional reforms that are designed to open up the parliamentary process and to allow for direct citizen participation. Due to restrictions in space, we will only be able to sketch some preliminary findings from a more comprehensive study on political representation in the networked society.

Digital parliaments and individual representatives on the net

Each of the three parliaments established a presence on the WWW between 1995 and 1996 by introducing an official parliamentary website. However, there are striking differences between these parliaments regarding the degree to which parliamentary subunits are using the WWW for external communication. This finding results from a count of all links at the main website of these three parliaments on a specific day in January 2000. This count displays a clear difference between the US House on the one hand and the German Bundestag and the Swedish Riksdag on the other hand. Figure 4.2 demonstrates that in the US House, websites are used at all parliamentary levels to almost 100 percent. Contrary to this, in the German Bundestag and the Swedish Riksdag, committees are not using websites at all and MPs are still a minority on the net. In the Swedish Riksdag, even the parliamentary party organization does not have a presence on the web. Therefore, in both European national parliaments, digital communication is much less decentralized than it is in the US House of Representatives.

Unfortunately, we do not have quantitative data on the development of personal websites in the US House, the Riksdag and the Bundestag. A comparison between the US House and the German Bundestag, which is displayed in Figure 4.3, demonstrates individual initiatives within a similar time frame in mid-1995. But while in the US House members rapidly started to use websites as a means of communication, there was much less enthusiasm in the German Bundestag until mid-1998. It was only after mid-1998 that more and more

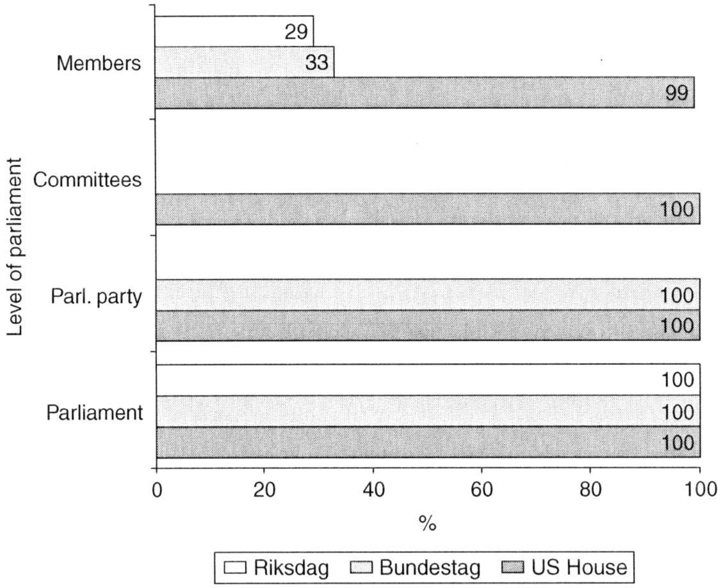

Figure 4.2 Websites per parliamentary unit in the US House, German Bundestag and Swedish Riksdag, January 2000.

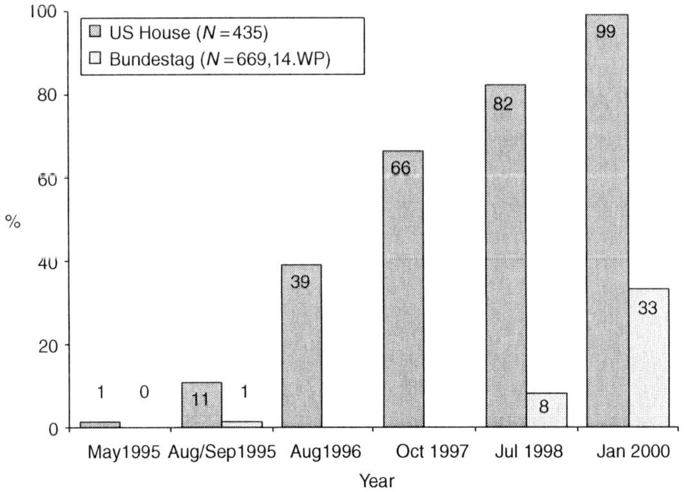

Figure 4.3 Personal websites in the US House and the German Bundestag, 1995–2000.

members of the German Bundestag were starting to use this medium. But still, in January 2000, there were considerable differences between the German Bundestag on the one hand and the US House on the other.

Apart from the act of using personal websites, the decentralization of political representation is also dependent upon the way that personal websites are being used: Do these Websites foster access to crucial information on the parliamentary process? Do they stimulate direct dialogue between MPs and citizens? Do they increase members' knowledge about the policy views of their constituents? To answer these questions, we downloaded the personal websites we have identified and performed a quantitative content analysis.

This analysis produces two main findings. First, in all three parliaments, personal websites are not used in a way to consequently implement the model of a direct, participatory system of political representation. Only a minority of members uses their websites to increase public dialogue and to learn more about the policy positions of their constituents. Furthermore, only a minority of members increases access to crucial information on the parliamentary process via their websites; second, there are important differences between the three cases under study. Members in the US House provide more access to crucial parliamentary information via their websites as well as more opportunities to register opinions than their European counterparts. Contrary to this, Swedish and German websites are aiming more towards public dialogue than the American websites. We will illustrate these general findings in greater detail in the remainder of this section.

Almost all of the websites we analyzed provide basic interactive elements such as email addresses or webmail forms. However, this kind of interactivity is of a private nature and means little progress compared to traditional forms of one-to-one communication such as constituency letters or phone calls. Discussion fora or public guestbooks are more progressive forms of public communication on the WWW because they involve representatives in public dialogues. Our analysis demonstrates that in all three parliaments, only a very small minority of members uses these kinds of applications on their websites. Apart from these similarities, there are obvious differences regarding the dominant type of interactivity between the US House on the one hand and the Swedish Riksdag as well as the German Bundestag on the other. Figure 4.4 demonstrates that compared to the US House more members use sophisticated interactive applications in the Riksdag and the Bundestag. We also observe a slightly greater interest in the use of email and webmail forms among Swedish and German MPs.

Another characteristic of a participatory and individualized scheme of representation is the congruence between the policy views of constituents and the decisions taken by their representative. This presupposes a clear understanding of the constituents' positions on specific policies on the part of the individual representative. So far, national opinion polls did not provide individual representatives with information of that nature. At best, they gave guidance to national parties and the party leadership on how their followers feel regarding crucial issues of national importance. They did not inform single representatives on how

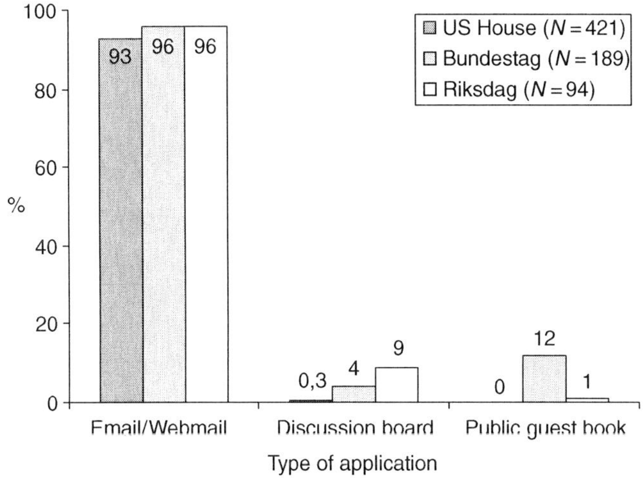

Figure 4.4 Interactivity of personal websites in the US House, German Bundestag and Swedish Riksdag, January 2000.

particular constituents think of issues they care most about. Online surveys offer an easy and very cost-efficient means to change this situation. This Internet application allows constituents to register their opinions on political issues with a single mouse click and thus enables representatives to learn about their policy views. As Figure 4.5 demonstrates, in all three parliaments only tiny minorities were using this application in January 2000 on their personal websites. But again, Figure 4.5 also demonstrates differences between these different cases. While 6 per cent of the US representatives with websites use online surveys, basically none in the two European parliaments use the surveys.

In-depth information on the parliamentary agenda and the policies that are up for decision is a crucial prerequisite for the formation of policy views. In a next step of our analysis, we asked whether personal websites in the US House, the German Bundestag and the Swedish Riksdag foster access to this type of information. A first indicator for this is the quantity of textual content on personal websites. A website with little or no textual information can hardly be regarded as a means to more relevant political information. Although a website with a lot of textual content does not guarantee access to crucial information, it increases the probability that it is serving exactly this kind of function. We calculated the quantity of textual information per single website in standard letter size to compare the member websites in the three parliaments regarding the quantity of textual information they provide. Figure 4.6 demonstrates that across all three parliaments only a minority of personal websites exploit the opportunity to provide large amounts of text. However, there are considerable differences between the US House on the one hand and the two European national parliaments on the other.

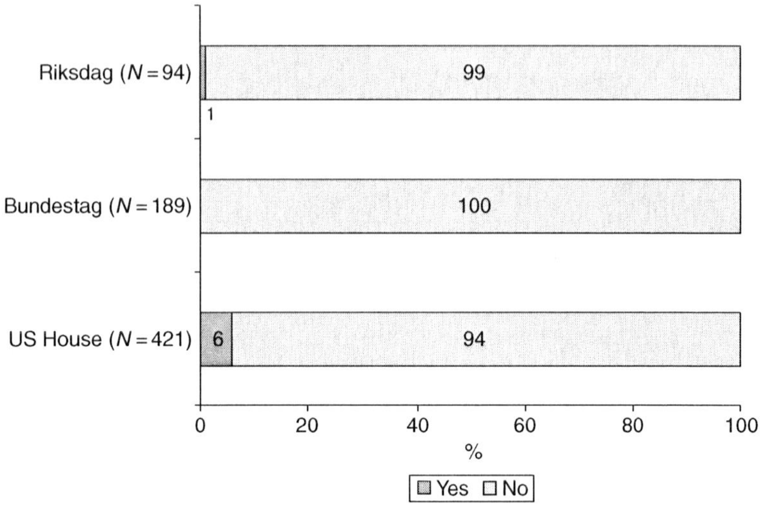

Figure 4.5 Online surveys on personal websites in the US House, German Bundestag and Swedish Riksdag, January 2000.

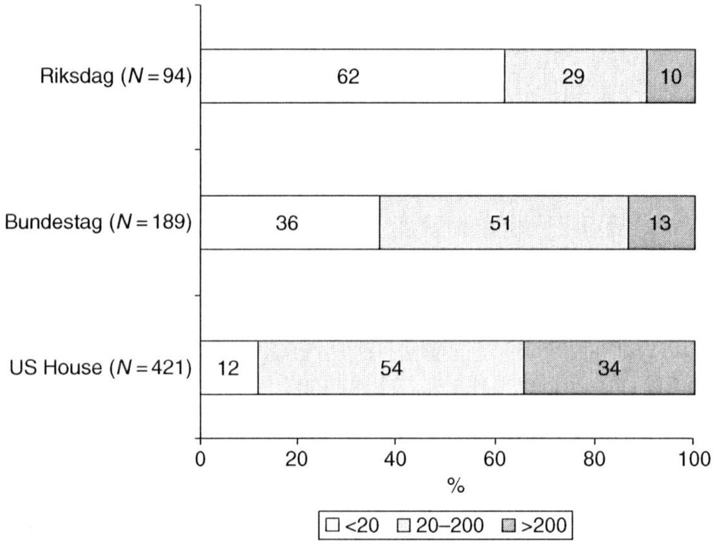

Figure 4.6 The quantity of textual information on personal websites in the US House, German Bundestag and Swedish Riksdag, January 2000.

A large majority of personal websites in the Swedish Riksdag and a significant minority in the German Bundestag fall below twenty pages of textual information. This type of digital brochure contains only a welcome page with the picture of the member, a biography and some basic information such as a postal address or his committee assignments. Contrary to this, digital brochures are less widespread in the US House of Representatives. The median is even more illuminating in this respect: it is 133 for the US House compared to 24 for the German Bundestag and 1 for the Swedish Riksdag.

A high quantity of textual information is not an equivalent for the availability of relevant political information, which helps constituents to understand the policy position of their representative and to screen his legislative behaviour. To study the quality of content, we analyzed the type of information that could be found on personal websites in the three parliaments. Figure 4.7 demonstrates again similarities and differences between the US House, the German Bundestag and the Swedish Riksdag.

Across these three parliaments, many personal websites lack crucial information on the parliamentary process. As Figure 4.7 demonstrates, press releases are the kind of information that is most likely to be found on the websites of individual representatives. The function of press releases is to provide news to the mass media in a suitable format that is short and to the point. Press releases do not aim at the ordinary citizen and do not provide comprehensive access to information on the parliamentary process. Therefore, they do not increase the transparency of the parliamentary process. This function could be performed, for example, by a comprehensive selection of issue-position papers of a member, an in-depth analysis of the issues a member cares about most and a comprehensive documentation of his legislative behaviour. As we can see in Figure 4.7, across the three parliaments under study, many personal websites lack these types of information.

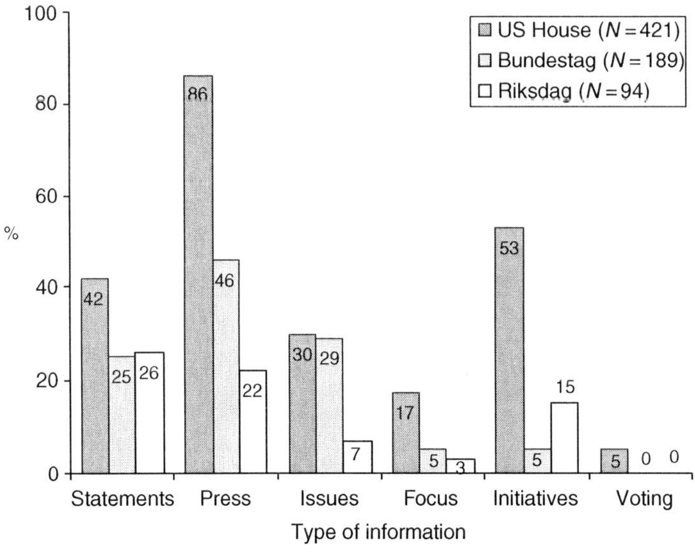

Figure 4.7 The type of information at personal websites in the US House, German Bundestag and Swedish Riksdag, January 2000.

However, besides this similarity, again there are stark differences between the US House of Representatives on the one hand and the German Bundestag and the Swedish Riksdag on the other. In each of the categories displayed in Figure 4.7, the US House is in the lead regarding the number of personal websites in line with our model of direct, participatory representation. The differences are particularly striking with regard to information on the parliamentary initiatives of single MPs.

Digital parliaments and institutional reform

Another scheme of direct, participatory representation presupposes the integration of digital communication into the decision-making process. Parliaments might decide to reconsider their policies regarding public access to parliamentary information because of new technological opportunity structures. They might also take decisions to use the Internet as a means to increase public participation in the parliamentary process. In this section we ask about debates regarding institutional reforms that aim towards this direction. The subsequent remarks will provide a very brief summary of three case studies on this topic, which cover the period until January 2000.

In the German and the Swedish cases, there has been little open debate on whether to use the Internet to make legislative assemblies more participatory. One of the main arenas regarding debates on the institutional ramifications of the Internet in the German Bundestag has been the special commission (Enquete), 'Zukunft der Medien in der Informationsgesellschaft'. This commission dealt among others with the issue of public participation via the Internet. Yet, the public hearing the commission held in September 1997 mainly focused on the local level and on administrative reform while only a few questions to the witnesses touched upon the national level and the issue of participation via electronic media. Member of the Bundestag, Michael Meister, asked a representative of the administration about the government's concept for providing legislative information on the Net (Deutscher Bundestag 1997: 50), and Social Democrat Jörg Tauss questioned Claus Leggewie, professor of political science at the University of Gießen, about the necessity of legislative initiatives (Deutscher Bundestag 1997: 63). Neither of these questions stimulated any debate on specific institutional reforms towards participatory democracy. This stresses the general point, made by one of the witnesses during the hearing, that in the German case the relationship between models of electronic democracy and existing democratic institutions is unresolved (Deutscher Bundestag 1997: 49). Models of electronic democracy have not yet been translated into specific programmes of institutional reform. At the same time, the political use of the Internet within the Bundestag has not raised open controversies on institutional issues as well.

The final report of the special commission on 'Zukunft der Medien in der Informationsgesellschaft' underscores the perception of an unresolved relationship between models of electronic democracy and existing democratic institutions. It contains a chapter on 'citizens and government' including sections on access to information and new types of participation. The latter section sketches new opportunities for political participation via the Internet such as electronic dialogues and electronic voting without relating these new technological options to existing political institutions and without raising questions regarding necessary institutional adjustments. The section on access to information simply points to existing legislative information on the Internet without raising the issue of the information's quality and quantity and without debating the types of information that could and should be published on the Internet (Deutscher Bundestag 1998: 78–9).

In the Swedish Riksdag, the new digital communications infrastructure triggered administrative policies to increase staff for parties and members. According to one high-level administrative official, the administration of the parliament assumes that the Internet will increase communication between members and citizens and that the members need help in dealing with this new situation. Apart from this, there have been two main institutional arenas where members of the Swedish Riksdag debated the institutional ramifications of the Internet. The IT group in the Swedish Riksdag consisted of one representative of each party as well as representatives of the administration of the Riksdag. Its purpose was to link parties and the administration regarding questions of communication technology. According to several participants, this group was mainly focused on the development of the technical infrastructure of the parliament and did not take up the issue of possible institutional ramifications of the new communication infrastructure. The IT group was dissolved in 2000 in the course of an administrative reform in the Riksdag.

The commission on democracy was a parliamentary commission that assembled an unusually large number of MPs under the chairmanship of a former minister of education. It was created in 1998 for a period of two years to study the current state of democracy in Sweden, to discuss means to revitalize Swedish democracy and to make proposals in this respect. In early 2000, the commission submitted a final report that emphasized the need for more public dialogue and deliberation in Swedish politics. It did acknowledge the potential of new information technology for 'widening the opportunities for citizens to participate in and influence problem formulations and discussions before decisions are made by elected assemblies' (Swedish Ministry of Justice 2000: 7). However, the commissions' report has not produced specific policy recommendations. It has been under review ('remis') during the course of the year 2000 and it will now be the task of the newly established department of democracy to come forward with specific policy recommendations. According to an official of this department, this process is in a very early stage so far. Therefore, we can conclude, that, as in the German case, there have been no specific open policy debates on more participatory schemes of representation via new digital media.

This is different in the case of the US House of Representatives. We identified several controversies indicating that House rules regulating access are in a state of flux because of the proliferation of Internet technology. These controversies touch upon two specific questions: first, should the US House change existing rules to make public documents more accessible via the Net and to increase the publicity of the process; second, should the US House change existing rules to make public information that has not been public before.

The first question touches upon the difference between the notions of 'to make public' and 'to publicize'. Many important proceedings in the US House, such as committee hearings, are public in the sense that one can attend. But they are not heavily publicized. In this case as in any other cases concerning information on the committee process, the decision on publication in printed format rests solely with each committee chair. Yet, even in cases of publication, the number of copies is limited, publication in hard copy takes up to a year and copies are not free of charge. Thus, timely and easy access, even to public documents, is heavily restricted. Parliamentary television has brought about some changes since its introduction in 1979 but the carrying capacity of C-SPAN I, which broadcasts proceedings of the US House, is limited and thus C-SPAN has to be selective, though to a lesser degree than commercial news outlets.

Then designated Speaker of the House, Newt Gingrich, touched upon this issue when he promised in November 1994 to require that 'all documents and all conference reports be filed electronically as well as in writing [...] so that information is available to every citizen in the country at the same moment that it is available to the highest paid Washington lobbyist' (Gillespie and Schellhas 1994: 188). The issue of public access to congressional documents was put on the agenda of a Task Force on Committee Review, established by the House Republican organizing conference in December 1994 with a mandate to review the committee structure of the House and make recommendations. In July 1996, the Task Force recommended changes in House Rules that would force House committees to facilitate access to a variety of specified committee documents via the Internet (US House of Representatives 1996a). Representative Rick White, a member of the Task Force, subsequently introduced legislation aimed at implementing these recommendations.[4]

These efforts went nowhere in the 104th Congress. The Resolution introduced by Representative White was referred to the House committees on Rules and Oversight. Neither committee took action, and the legislation was never brought to the floor. Subsequently, a much weaker provision was inserted in the Rules of the House at the beginning of the 105th Congress. This provision required that each committee 'shall to the maximum extent feasible, make its publication available in electronic form' (US House of Representatives 1997: 12), which still leaves much discretion to committee chairs.

The House floor became the arena where members debated the second question, whether previously non-public documents should be made public via the Internet. The focus of this debate was on material prepared by the Congressional Research Service (CRS), a congressional support agency that is part of the Library of Congress and whose mission is to provide non-partisan policy advice to members. Up to then, CRS material was only available in hard copy and in electronic form via the House Intranet to congressional staffers. Citizens could obtain material via their representative, but would not know what material was available, would have to depend on the willingness of their representative to release material on a specific question and would have to bear costs in terms of time and effort to get hold of this material. In 1998, Representative Christopher Shays and Senator John McCain simultaneously introduced a bill in the House of Representatives and the US Senate to make CRS material publicly available over the Internet on a CRS website[5] (Fasman 1998: 16; Friedly 1998; *Washington Post* 1998: A12). Both bills did not receive a necessary majority in a final floor vote.

Apart from these debates on public access, some slight attention was given to possible reforms to foster dialogue between members and their constituents. When the Subcommittee on Rules and Organization conducted a hearing in May 1996 on the possible legislative impact of new communications technologies, one of the committee's members, participated via videoconference. The option to allow MPs to participate in parliamentary proceedings via the Internet became an important subject to debate in the course of this hearing (US House of Representatives 1996b). Since then, committees have extensively used this infrastructure to ensure the participation of witnesses who could not be present or to cut down on travel costs to save the taxpayers' money. But the participation of a member via the Internet remained unique.

This technological option would allow members to spend more time in their district and to be closer to their constituents while conducting parliamentary business via the Internet. Technologically, this form of participation need not be restricted to fact-finding hearings as it was the case in the hearing on May 1996. One could also imagine representatives conducting mark up sessions or other kinds of official business via the Internet while being closer to their constituents in the district. However, this presupposes changes in House rules that demand representatives to be physically present while conducting official business. According to several staffers, these kinds of institutional changes are subject to informal considerations but they have not stimulated serious and open policy debates so far. Figure 4.8 provides a comparative summary of debates on institutional reform, which aim at a more participatory system of political representation via new digital media and which were visible in the three parliaments until early 2000.

Do digital parliaments enhance electronic democracy?

The preceding analysis reveals trends towards more participatory schemes of political representation in the process of putting parliaments on the Net. However, these trends are of a very moderate nature and hardly revolutionary in scope. While many MPs already take advantage of the Internet, their way of using personal websites is not suited to strengthen schemes of direct, individualized representation. And while we were able to identify some visible debates aimed at using the Internet to make the parliamentary process more transparent and participatory, the outcome is far from revolutionary as well.

At first glance, this conclusion supports a cybersceptic point of view that decries visions of electronic democracy as utopian driven by the enthusiasm and

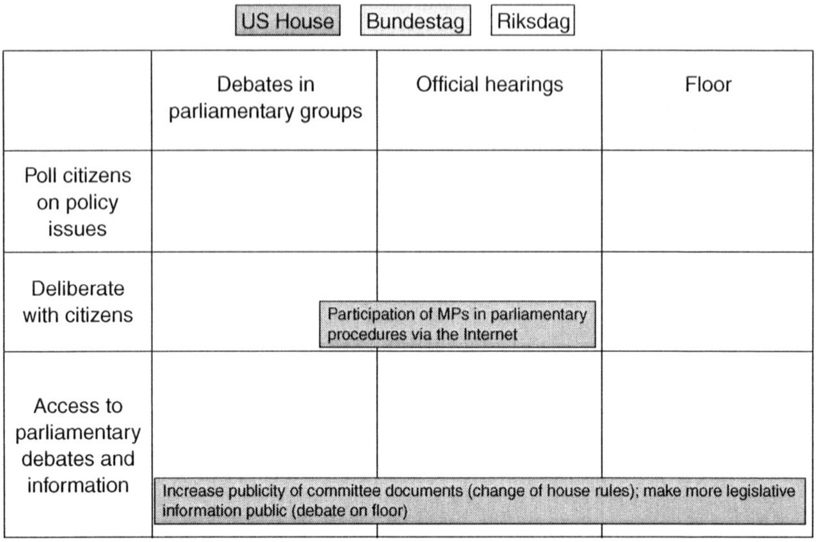

Figure 4.8 Digital parliaments and institutional reform in the US House, German Bundestag and Swedish Riksdag, January 2000.

the excitement about new technologies in telecommunication. From this perspective, electronic democracy is in line with a multitude of promises and visions that were related to past technological changes in telecommunication and which never materialized in the end (Kubicek *et al.* 1997; Jarren 1998). Cybersceptics perceive digital parliaments as indicators for technological modernization rather than political transformation. However, a more cautious interpretation of our analysis suggests two important reservations regarding this line of reasoning.

First, we have to remember that the findings of our analysis are nothing more than a snapshot taken at a very early stage of a dynamic technological development. As a consequence we lower our expectations and acknowledge the significance of small effects, which might be first traces of a larger trend towards political transformation. Future progress in telecommunication technology will foster theses early initiatives during the decades to come. With universal access to the Internet, increasing bandwidth, more reliable systems of data-security and new types of hardware such as Web-TV the available digital opportunity-structure will increase in sophistication and will constantly put pressure on systems of political representation to develop into direct and participatory systems of representation. Apart from this general note of caution in response to cyber-scepticism, our analysis suggests a second important objection to both contenders in the debate on electronic democracy.

The preceding analysis emphasizes the fact that trends towards electronic democracy vary with political context. While in some circumstances, the future of electronic democracy appears to be bleak, it obviously is much brighter in other circumstances. This finding contradicts the universalism that characterizes cyberoptimism as well as cyberscepticism. It rather points towards the importance of political context in the process of political change in the networked society. Given the existence of a multitude of political environments we assume that electronic democracy will eventually flourish in many versions, different in scope and design. The crucial research question concerns the existence of systematic relationships between political context, technological change in telecommunication and electronic democracy. The variance in our comparative analysis provides the basis for *ad hoc* explanations, which could give guidance to further more systematic research on this core question in the debate on electronic democracy.

Differences between the Riksdag and the German Bundestag on the one hand and the US House on the other regarding the implementation of electronic democracy are the most visible finding of our comparative analysis. Regarding these differences we have to ask why parliaments that experience technological change at a similar level, implement this technology in different ways. *Ad hoc* speculations on this question point towards a variety of structural factors such as differences in the type of government. The Riksdag and the Bundestag are situated within a parliamentary system that does not provide many incentives and institutional capacities to individual representatives to focus on particular constituents and to structure the representative process in a participatory mode. This is due to the fact that legislative assemblies in parliamentary democracies possess the power to make and break governments. This function imposes a rigid discipline on parliamentary majorities and pushes individual representatives to focus on their party, to concentrate on internal bargaining and to structure the parliamentary process accordingly. Contrary to this, parliaments in presidential systems such as the US House do not possess this function and therefore leave individual representatives much more room to establish a closer relationship to particular constituents. The systematic difference between the US House on the one hand and the Riksdag and the Bundestag on the other could be explained along this line of reasoning. Due to the existing incentive structure, MPs within parliamentary systems should thus not be interested in direct, decentralized schemes of representation no matter what the technological opportunities are. Contrary to this, representatives within presidential systems should be much more open to direct schemes of political representation and thus to technologies that foster the implementation of such schemes.

The preceding analysis stresses that it would be a gross simplification to overemphasize a unicausal relationship between a specific institutional feature such as the type of government on the one hand and the prospects for electronic democracy on the other. The lack of interactivity on the personal websites of American MPs might indicate the impact of additional contextual features. The hesitancy of US Representatives in using discussion fora, which does not fit with the general pattern of our analysis, could reflect the strong first amendment tradition of the United States. While in Germany and Sweden, the principle of freedom of speech is balanced with the principle of fair speech, in the United States we have a clear hierarchy of values that prevents any kind of censorship, regardless of content. The rulings of the Supreme Court demonstrate this tradition in a very obvious manner. The risks of using public discussion fora can only be controlled in the American case by not using them at all. Contrary to this, in Sweden and Germany, improper contributions to public discussion fora can be censored on the basis of the principle of fair speech.

The differences between Swedish and German MPs serve as another example against the assumption of a clear unicausal relationship between a specific institutional feature on the one hand and electronic democracy on the other. German MPs are more eager to utilize the new digital opportunity structure compared to their Swedish colleagues despite the fact that Swedish as well as German MPs operate in the context of a parliamentary system. This variance might be based upon differences regarding the electoral connection. The German electoral system allows for a higher degree of personalization compared to the Swedish electoral system. Half of the German MPs are elected in single-member districts by a majority vote while the other half is elected via a party list in a proportional vote. Many of the latter were also candidates in one of the district races. Contrary to this, the Swedish electoral system is characterized by a much lower degree of personalization. It has been reformed in 1998 to give voters the opportunity to either elect a party list or a single candidate and thus increased the systems, potential for a personal vote. But according to students of Swedish electoral law, these new opportunities are not well established in the hearts and minds of Swedish voters so far (Möller 1999). In general, the Swedish electoral system is still a list-based system that emphasizes parties rather than individual candidates. On the basis of this observation one might argue that the degree of personalization of electoral systems affects the incentives among individual representatives to take advantage of the new digital opportunity structure in order to cultivate a decentralized and direct system of political representation.

By way of conclusion, we have to stress that technological modernization in general and digital parliaments in particular will not automatically push towards new forms of democracy. We rather have to emphasize the impact of political context on the future of political representation in the networked society. Contrary to cyberscepticism we perceive the glass as half full rather than half empty in this respect. While some contextual environments act as an obstacle to electronic democracy, others might also work to its advantage. It remains a crucial task to future theoretical as well as empirical research to study this interrelationship between political context, technological change and electronic democracy (Zittel 2002a,b). This type of research should be seen as a prerequisite in the attempt to understand the political significance of digital parliaments and technological modernization.

Notes

1 This essay is part of a larger study on the relationship between new digital communications media and representative government. I am indebted to many staffers and members in

the US House, the German Bundestag and the Swedish Riksdag who gave large portions of their time to support my research. I am particularly grateful to representative Johnny Gylling. I am also grateful to the Fritz-Thyssen-Foundation, which has supported, my research with a generous grant, and to the Department of Government of the University of Uppsala, which provided a hospitable research environment during my field research in Sweden.

2 This survey was taken during a two-day European conference of Members of National Parliaments on Communication Technologies, which took place in Helsinki and Tallinn on 11–12 September 2001 <www.epri.org/main/static_main_1_131_ENG.htm> June 2002.

3 Numbers compiled by the Swedish Riksdag.

4 See H.Res. 478, July 1996; Congressional Record H 7658.

5 See US House of Representatives, 105th Congress, 2nd Session, H.R. 3131; US Senate, 105th Congress, 2nd Session, S. 1578.

Bibliography

Archibald, G. (1999) 'Congress spends $ 1billion on Computers', *Washington Times*, 12 September 1999, C 1.

Arterton, C. F. (1987) *Teledemocracy*, Newbury Park: Sage.

Barber, B. (1984) *Strong Democracy*, Berkeley, Calif.: University of California Press.

Barnes, S., Kaase, M. *et al.* (1979) *Political Action*, Beverly Hills: Sage.

Becker, T. L. (1981) 'Teledemocracy', *The Futurist*, 15, 6–9.

Bellamy, C. (2000) 'Modeling Electronic Democracy', in Hoff, J., Horrocks I. and Tops, P. (eds), *Democratic Governance and New Technology*, London/New York: Routledge.

Berelson, B., Lazarsfeld, P. and McPhee, W. (1954) *Voting*, Chicago: University of Chicago Press.

Buchstein, H. (2001) 'Modernisierung der Demokratie durch E-Voting', *Leviathan*, 29 (2), 147–55.

Budge, I. (1996) *The New Challenge of Direct Democracy*, Cambridge: Polity Press.

Campbell, A., Converse, P. E., Miller, W. E. and Stokes, D. E. (1960) *The American Voter*, Chicago: University of Chicago Press.

Casey, C. (1996) *The Hill on the Net*, Boston: AP Professional.

Coleman, S. (1999) 'Cutting out the Middle Man', in Hague, B. N. and Loader, B. D. (eds), *Digital Democracy*, London/New York: Routledge.

Coleman, S. (2000) 'Parliament in the Information Age', in Gibson, R. K. and Ward, S. (eds), *Reinvigorating Democracy?* Aldershot: Ashgate.

Coleman, S., Taylor, J. and van de Donk, W. (eds) (1999) *Parliament in the Age of the Internet*, Oxford: Oxford University Press.

Collier, D. and Levitsky, S. (1997) 'Democracy with Adjectives', in *World Politics*, April, 430–51.

Deutscher Bundestag (1997) Enquete – Kommission Zukunft der Medien in Wirtschaft und Gesellschaft, Öffentliche Anhörung zum Thema 'Nutzung von Informations- und Kommunikationstechniken in der öffentlichen Verwaltung. Auswirkungen auf die staatliche Souveränität und das politische System', Wortprotokoll, 22 September 1997.

Deutscher Bundestag (1998) Enquete-Kommission 'Zukunft der Medien in Wirtschaft und Gesellschaft', *Drucksache* 13/11004, Schlussbericht, Bonn.

Einemann, E. (1991) *Computer für die Volksvertreter*, Marburg: Schüren.

Etzioni, A., Laudon, K. and Lipson, S. (1975) 'Participatory Technology', *Journal of Communication*, 25, 64–74.

Fasman, J. E. (1998) 'States Find Little Difficulty with On-Line Research', *The Hill*, 18 March, 16.

Fishkin, J. S. (1991) *Democracy and Deliberation*, New Haven/London: Yale University Press.

Friedly, J. (1998) 'Members Introduce Bills to Publicize CRS Research', *The Hill*, 4 February.

Fühles-Ubach, S. and Neumann, H.-P. (1998) 'Zwei Jahre Deutscher Bundestag im Internet', *Nachrichten für Dokumentation (NfD): Information – Wissenschaft und Praxis*, 4.

Gallagher, M., Laver, M. and Mair, P. (2001) *Representative Government in Modern Europe*, Boston, MA: McGraw Hill.

Gillespie, E. and Schellhas, B. (eds) (1994) *Contract With America*, New York, 188 (Newt Gingrich, Remarks before the Washington Research Group Symposium).

Grossman, L. K. (1995) *The Electronic Republic*, New York: Viking.

Gylling, J. (2000) 'A Swedish Perspective', in *Hansard Society E-Guide for Parliamentarians*, London: Hansard-Society.

Habermas, J. (1992) 'Drei normative Modelle der Demokratie', in Münkler, H. (ed.), *Die Chancen der Freiheit*, München: Piper.

Hagen, M. (1997) *Elektronische Demokratie*, Hamburg: Lit Verlag.

Hoff, J. (2000) 'Technology and Social Change', in Hoff, J., Horrocks, I. and Tops, P. (eds), *Democratic Governance and New Technology*, London: Routledge.

Hofmann, J. (1998) 'Am Herz der Dinge – Regierungsmacht im Internet', in Gellner, W. and von Korff, F. (eds), *Demokratie und Internet*, Baden-Baden: Nomos.

Inter-Parliamentary Union (2000) 'Guidelines for the Content and Structure of Parliamentary Websites', approved by the *Inter-Parliamentary Council at the 166th Session*, Amman, 6 May.

Jarren, O. (1998) 'Demokratie durch Internet?' in Eisel, S. and Scholl, M. (eds), *Internet und Politik*, Konrad-Adenauer-Stiftung, Interne Studie 164/1998.

Kamps, K. (ed.) (1999) *Elektronische Demokratie?* Opladen/Wiesbaden: Westdeutscher Verlag.

Katz, J. (1997) Birth of a Digital Nation, *WIRED*, 5 April.

Katz, R. S. (1987) *Party Governments*, Berlin: de Gruyter.

Kleinsteuber, H. J. and Hagen, M. (1998) 'Was bedeutet "elektronische Demokratie"?' *Zeitschrift für Parlamentsfragen*, 1, 128–43.

Krauch, H. (1972) *Computer Demokratie*, Düsseldorf: VDI-Verlag.

Kubicek, H., Schmid, U. and Wagner, H. (1997) *Bürgerinformation durch 'neue' Medien?*, Opladen: Westdeutscher Verlag.

Lange, H.-J. (1988) *Bonn am Draht*, Marburg: SP-Verlag.

Leggewie, K. and Maar, C. (eds) (1998) *Internet Politik*, Köln: Bollmann.

Lijphart, A. (1971) 'Comparative Politics and the Comparative Method', *American Political Science Review*, 65, 682–93.

Mambrey, P., Vorwerk, E. and Wurch, G. (1991) *Computer im Deutschen Bundestag*, Opladen: Westdeutscher Verlag.

Mambrey, P., Neumann, H.-P. and Sieverdingbeck, K. (1999) 'Bridging the Gap Between Parliament and Citizens – The Internet Services of the German Bundestag', in Coleman, S., Taylor, J. and van de Donk, W. (eds), *Parliament in the Age of the Internet*, Oxford: Oxford University Press.

Marschall, S. (1999) *Öffentlichkeit und Volksvertretung*, Opladen/Wiesbaden: Westdeutscher Verlag.

McLean, I. (1987) *Democracy and New Technology*, Cambridge: Polity Press.

Michels, R. (1911) *Zur Soziologie des Parteiwesens in der modernen Demokratie*, Leipzig: Klinkharot.

Möller, T. (1999) 'The Swedish Election 1998', *Scandinavian Political Studies*, 22, 261–76.

Muralt Müller, H. (2000) 'E-Government – Herausforderung für Behörden', *Neue Züricher Zeitung*, 14 April <http://www.parlament.ch/E/Egovernment/nzz14042000_e.htm?servlet_get_content>, first accessed 5 January 2001.

Mutter, C. (2002) 'Das Rubbelfeld auf dem Stimmzettel', *Die Weltwoche*, 3 January, 1, 15.

Naisbitt, J. (1982) *Megatrends*, New York: Warner Books.

Needham, C. (2001) 'Electronic Consultation in the UK and the USA', paper for presentation at the 2001 Joint Workshops session, Grenoble, 6–11 April.

Norris, P. (2001) *Digital Divide*, Cambridge, MA: Cambridge University Press.

NUA (2001) 'How Many Online ?' <www.nua.ie/surveys/how_many_online>, first accessed 7 January 2002.

Pateman, C. (1970) *Participation and Democratic Theory*, Cambridge, MA: Cambridge University Press.

Peters, G. (1998) *Comparative Politics*, New York: New York University Press.

Pitkin, H. F. (1967) *The Concept of Representation*, Berkeley, CA: University of California Press.

Rash Jr. W. (1997) *Politics on the Nets*, New York: Freeman.

Rawls, J. (1971) *A Theory of Justice*, Cambridge, MA: Cambridge University Press.

Rheingold, H. (1993) *The Virtual Community*, Reading, MA: Addison-Wesley.

Ryan, D. and Becker, T. (1983) 'The Commission for the Future and the New Zealand Televote', *World Futures*, 18, 309–15.

Sarcinelli, U. (ed.) (1998) *Politikvermittlung und Demokratie in der Mediengesellschaft*, Opladen: Westdeutscher Verlag.

Sartori, G. (1987) *The Theory of Democracy Revisited*, Vols 1 and 2, Chatham, NJ: Chatham House.

Schattschneider, E. E. (1975) *The Semisovereign People*, Hinsdale, Ill: Dryden Press.

Schmidt, M. G. (2000) *Demokratietheorien*, Opladen: Leske & Budrich.

Schuler, D. (1996) *New Community Networks*, Reading, MA: Addison-Wesley.

Schumpeter, J. A. (1950), *Kapitalismus, Sozialismus und Demokratie*, Bern: Francke.

Slaton, C. D. (1992) *Televote*, New York. Praeger.

Snider, J. H. (1994) 'Democracy On-Line', *The Futurist*, September/October.

Street, J. (1992) *Politics and Technology*, Basingstoke: Macmillan.

Swedish Ministry of Justice (2000) Sustainable Democracy. English Translation of the Recommendations made by the Government Commission on Swedish Democracy in their Final Report, 12 September, Stockholm.

Toffler, A. (1980) *The Third Wave*, New York: Bantam Books.

Ulfhielm, C. G. (1998) *Information Technology in the Swedish Parliament*, unpublished manuscript, Stockholm.

US House of Representatives (1996a) 'Task Force on Committee Review', *Report of Reforming Committee Operations, Procedures and Staffing*, Washington, DC, 16 July.

US House of Representatives (1996b) *Committee on Rules, Public Hearing on Legislating in the 21st Century*, Washington, DC, May.

US House of Representatives (1997) *Rules of the U.S. House of Representatives. Effective for 105th Congress*, Washington, DC

The Washington Post (1998) 'Whose Research is it?' 7 July, A 12.

Weber, M. (1990) 'The Advent of Plebiscitarian Democracy', in Mair, P. (ed.), *The West European Party System*, Oxford: Oxford University Press.

Zittel, T. (2002a) 'Wither Responsible Party Government?' Revised paper presented to the *Joint Sessions of Workshops of the European Consortium of Political Research*, Turin, 22–27 March.

Zittel, T. (2002b) 'Political Representation in the Network Society', paper presented to the Workshop on the Cross-National Study of Legislatures at the 2002 Annual Meeting of the American Political Science Association, Boston, 29 August–1 September.

5 Digital democracy

Ideas, intentions and initiatives in Swedish local governments

Joachim Åström

Introduction

It has commonly been suggested that the public in post-industrial societies has become increasingly disenchanted with the traditional institutions of representative government, detached from political parties and disillusioned with older forms of participatory activity. The political parties – the most important intermediary link between the people and the centre of government – seem to have lost their hold on the voters. Fewer voters are able to identify with a single party, the voting behaviour becomes more and more flexible and the number of party members decreases (Gidlund and Möller 1999). In addition to this, there is an increase in the general distrust felt towards parties and politicians. Field surveys indicate that confidence in politicians and parties during the last decades has been undermined in almost all countries where time series surveys have been conducted (Norris 1999a). In Sweden, formal studies are available since the 1960s, and they all indicate that confidence in politicians has been undermined, slowly but constantly (Holmberg 1999). Due to this evidence, there is a 'crisis of democracy' debate running.

While the trends are evident, the explanation for, and interpretations of, these phenomena have proved more controversial. Among other things, the interpretation depends on how one judges citizens' dissatisfaction with the possibilities for political participation and with the outcomes of political decision-making. According to one line of argument the problems are output related, rather than input related. Decline in identification of citizens with political parties does not necessarily mean that the legitimacy of the central institutions of representative democracy is eroding. Citizens can use other non-institutional forms of action for attaining political goals. Instead, low trust is considered as being due to weakened government performance. People who are critical of the various services they receive tend to be less trusting than people who are satisfied. Following this line of reasoning, the policy prescription should be to enhance the effectiveness of problem-solving rather than democratic responsiveness to the demands of citizens (Klingemann and Fuchs 1995).

The opposite line of argument implies that we are facing a crisis of political communication. The diagnoses claim a challenge to representative democracies has arisen, which can be met only by decisive reform. Declining voter turnout and lack of attendance at public meetings are heralded as evidence of citizen apathy and a fundamental disconnection between citizens and their government. Citizen apathy and a general culture of indifference to politics calls into question both the extent to which councils can claim to represent their communities and their broader legitimacy to govern. Social science literature has advanced numerous hypotheses to explain citizen apathy. Political economists, for example, argue that citizen non-action is actually the result of a rational calculus comparing the costs and benefits of participation. Given that any single individual's effort is unlikely to make a difference and that the costs of participation are high, most citizens will choose not to take part in political activities (Downs 1957). The policy prescriptions for reducing citizen apathy usually involve a set of proposals to simplify public participation in government by encouraging authorities to become more transparent and to develop a range of consultation and participation techniques.

More recently, new information and communication technologies (ICTs) have been put forward as one possible solution to the perceived problems of communication. According to Gibson and Ward (1998), the Internet has the potential to increase internal party democracy and intensify interparty competition. Hague and Loader (1999) suggest that ICTs could potentially promote government accountability, create a better-informed citizenry and facilitate public deliberation and participation in the decision-making process in state and civil society. Budge (1996) believes that the development of the Internet makes direct democracy feasible in a mass society for the first time. In many different ways then, the Internet offers opportunities to reconnect people to the political process.

Will hopes for a digital democracy be realized? In Sweden, prospects for a digital democracy might be considered better than in many other countries. The rapid expansion of the Internet, combined with the ongoing broadband expansion, imply that a technological platform now exists in order to develop applications that in different ways are considered to strengthen democracy. According to statistics during the second half of the year 2000, 76 per cent of the Swedish population between 16 and 79 years of age had access to a computer at home, and 65 per cent had access to the Internet at home (SCB 2001). As use of the Internet and World Wide Web by citizens has increased, many have touted the web as a means to increase citizens' political involvement. According to several state-backed studies in later years, the Internet should be used to promote government accountability and to increase public participation in politics (SOU 2000: 1; 2001: 48).

Still, changes in political behaviour are far from certain. Technological change must be translated into political change through decisions made by the members affected. They must decide whether they want to adapt to a new communications environment, and if so, in what ways (Zittel 1999). This chapter examines the relationship among ideas, intentions and initiatives in the process of wiring Swedish local governments. The first part reviews the normative theoretical argument in favour of digital democracy, while the second draws on evidence from a survey examining how local politicians in Sweden relate to these new ideas.

Do they believe in the use of the Internet in the political process? Are some opportunities via the Net more supported than others? The third part of the chapter, moving from formal norms to active norms, focuses on the role and function of local government websites. How far do these sites provide comprehensive information and opportunities for interactive communication? What factors help to explain the patterns that we find? The conclusion summarizes the core findings and considers some implications for understanding the role of the Internet in a Swedish context.

Theories of digital democracy

In many countries there are programmes for 'democratic renewal' these days. Renewal does not, however, take the same form everywhere, and the direction of development is frequently being contested. 'Digital democracy' is often used as a title for programmes of democratic renewal based on new ICTs. As such it captures both the perceived problems with the existing institutions of local government and the ambitions of the current reform process. It suggests that local democracy is failing and that new ICTs can help to address these failings in order to revitalize democratic practice. In this way digital democracy has a precise meaning: it is about adjusting the institutions of local government to make them more democratic. On the other hand, the concept of democracy, and equally its digital manifestations, is inherently ambiguous (Held 1987). Programmes of digital democracy are grounded in different notions of democracy and connect different democratic values to technological change. In this respect it might be fruitful to distinguish between different models of digital democracy. In this part of the chapter three different models will be presented: direct, interactive and indirect. The direct model is basically about providing more effective means for direct registrations of citizens' opinions on current issues. The essence of the interactive model is to strengthen civic engagement and political activism through online discussion and deliberation. The indirect model of democracy refers to opportunities to strengthen the core institutions of representative democracy through dissemination of information and transparency. By sketching these models, it is possible to see in what direction digital technologies are pulling local democracy. Are intentions and initiatives in local governments in line with the indirect model of democracy, or are they part of a move towards a more direct or interactive democracy?

Direct democracy

One common point of view in the debate on digital democracy is the recommendation of citizens' direct participation in political decision-making. In this argument, citizens are, or at least can be, adequately informed in most issues and they know their interests better than anyone else. If each person is the best judge of his/her best interests and the object of policy is as far as possible to advance these, this makes a strong case for every citizen to participate in the making of public choices.

It is of utmost importance that the will of the majority is allowed to directly influence decisions in all areas of society. Accordingly, representation can be seen as a practical necessity in some situations, but must generally be regarded as a necessary evil that could and should be avoided in different ways (Premfors 2000).

Use of ICTs is seen as one such way. The core of the direct democratic claim rests on the idea that communication capacity is a kind of rate-limiting factor in political engagement and influence. At present, political professionals, interest groups and other elites dominate the comparatively limited resources for effective political communication. The Net can decentralize access to communication and information, increasing citizens' political resources. As a consequence individuals' engagement in politics will increase, as will their influence. In this vision not only will a mass audience be able to follow politics and express its views to government, but it will also be fundamentally less dependent on linkage organizations and group politics (Bimber 1998).

The more radical proponents of this model see ICTs as the decisive means by which direct democracy Athenian style can be implemented in today's society. In their proposed model professional politicians and political parties become more or less redundant. Instead a new kind of public rule will emerge. Through computer networks, individuals' views and opinions can be solicited, registered, stored and communicated, enabling direct democracy to be implemented not only at a local level but nationally and even internationally. With ICTs, effective political participation does not have to diminish with scale (Dahl and Tufte 1973). At all levels, representation can be substituted by independent cyber citizens who act in a responsible manner at the electronic agora, without any professional politician acting as an intermediary and guardian (Ilshammar 1997).

Less radical proponents do not want to abolish the representative system altogether, but combine it – 'revitalize it' – with direct elements. In Budge's (1996) vision there would still be an elected party-based government. This government would put important bills and other political decisions to popular votes, just as it does with legislative votes under representative democracy. The function of the Net is to facilitate this running public referenda. Another possibility often referred to is a more frequent use of advisory opinion polls, by way of new technology, making sure that the parliament really knows what the people want. McLean (1989), for example, argues that the new media can do much to make governments more responsive to the wishes of the public by linking members more closely to their constituents.

Interactive democracy

While the most important participatory activity in the direct model of democracy is tied to the moment of casting a vote into the ballot box, interactive democracy pays more attention to public debate as a political tool. An interactive democracy can be described as a group of citizens whose matters of common concern are dealt with through ongoing discussions, debates and deliberations.

The great value of the discussion is due to the fact that one believes that people let themselves be convinced by rational argumentation. The primary driving force of humans is personal autonomy, that is, a strife to realize the projects they rate the highest, however the individuals' perceived interests and wishes are decided in the dialectic process of social interaction. The source of legitimacy is, consequently, not the predetermined will of individuals, but rather the process of its formation, that is, deliberation (Barber 1984; Bohman 1996; Elster 1998).

Similar to direct democracy, interactive democracy wants and indeed requires active citizens. Real democracy is realized only to the extent that ordinary people are given opportunities to carry on a dialogue and act on matters of common interest. Unlike direct democracy that trusts that people would learn if we only bring power to them, interactive democracy emphasizes the need to involve people in discussion and deliberation processes. Following the proponents of this model, it is an illusion to believe that qualified standpoints in complex societal issues are 'out there' automatically and can be caught easily in polls or referendums in accordance with the principle of majority (Fishkin 1991). Participation is seen not only as a means to give people power, but also to provide education and an opportunity to develop an opinion among fellow citizens. Whereas previously the role of participation was mainly to make the representative system more representative by active dialogue between politicians and citizens, today much attention is paid to the benefits of horizontal communication among citizens: when people discuss societal issues, a platform is created for respect, confidence, tolerance and openness, crucial ingredients of an interactive democracy (Friedland 1996). Following this line of reasoning, Barber (1984) recommends that the capabilities of the new technology should be used to strengthen civic education, guarantee equal access to information and tie individuals and institutions into networks that will make real participatory discussion and debate possible.

In practice, this kind of interactivity could be facilitated in many different ways. Schuler (1996) stresses in particular the possibility to create interactive information systems that support information exchange and communication within a geographically defined area, known as community networks. Others emphasize the possibility for communication within groups that need to bridge geographical distances, for example, parties and interest organizations (Gibson and Ward 1998). A third group of authors stress the possibility to use ICTs in deliberative processes among a representative sample of citizens (Etzioni 1972; Dahl 1989).

Indirect democracy

In the model of indirect democracy it is only the members of the political elite who fully participate in the political process. This is because the ordinary citizen is considered as being not that interested in politics or for that matter qualified to participate. Instead, the basic idea is having several elites competing for citizens' votes. Elections are about choosing leaders based on a general account of the programmes they represent. The elites must then have sufficient room to manoeuvre, to revise and detail their political programmes. The ground for legitimacy is the

Table 5.1 Three models of digital democracy

	Direct democracy	*Interactive democracy*	*Indirect democracy*
Aim	Sovereignty/equality	Autonomy	Individual freedom
Ground for legitimacy	Principle of majority	Public debate	Accountability
Citizens' role	Decision-maker	Opinion former	Voter
Mandate of the elected	Bound	Interactive	Open
ICT-use focusing	Decisions	Discussion	Information

accountability of the elites – the public in free elections should be able to decide whom they want to govern their common affairs (Schumpeter 1976).

The new technology is not seriously considered to be able to have an influence on the characteristics that make the representative system the best solution; citizens will not be any wiser, nor less partial or more willing to really get into political issues (Sartori 1987). Instead, the democratizing potential of the new technology is regarded as being related to politicians' possibilities to spread information and gather support. The display of politics in the media is sometimes said to have caused a crisis in political communication (Blumler and Gurevitch 1995) and is often stated as the main reason for the growing distrust towards politicians (Möller 2000). Today, politicians are given an opportunity to communicate directly with citizens without interference from the media. In this way, the Internet might make it easier for the representatives to justify their policy with restored confidence.

When it comes to technical development, there are also hopes that citizens will be able to make their electoral choices and predict the consequences of casting their ballot more easily. Government websites can provide particularly effective mechanisms for providing the public with detailed and comprehensive information about the legislative procedures and activities, allowing public scrutiny of the policy process and promoting the accountability of elected members to their constituents (Norris 2000a). Moreover, the new technology is believed to have an equalizing effect on parties, and intensify interparty competition. Since the cost of starting a home page is quite low, small as well as large parties can be given the opportunity to spread their messages and introduce themselves to the voters (Gibson and Ward 1998). Competition strengthens indirect democracy since it forces the parties to produce products that citizens really want. Table 5.1 summarizes the underlying concepts of the three models of digital democracy.

Attitudes towards digital democracy

Many scholars have devoted attention to ICTs, and the literature provides a broad range of ideas on how the Internet may revive democracy. But how do local policy-makers relate and respond to these ideas? To influence policy choices, ideas must reach and convince decision-makers whose roles include evaluating the overall goals and tools of policy, initiating policy change and overseeing implementations of new policies. We now examine (1) whether Swedish politicians in general are optimistic or pessimistic about the democratic potential of the Internet, and (2) which opportunities via the Internet they find attractive. The data is based upon a survey questionnaire sent to the Swedish chairmen of the municipal executive boards. The survey, conducted during the spring of 2000, was returned by 80 per cent of the 289 chairmen.

Cyberoptimism or pessimism?

The debate on digital democracy has been a lively one, altering between ominous pessimism and exuberant optimism. Cyberoptimists, as we have seen, express hopes that the Internet may provide new opportunities for democracy as governments go online, facilitating communications between citizens and the state. Cyberpessimists are more sceptical, suggesting that new technology cannot be expected to transform existing power structures, make political decision-making more transparent or revive public participation. The first question aims at positioning the Swedish politicians along this optimism–pessimism continuum. How do they view the democratic potential of the Internet and other computer networks? (See Table 5.2.)

The conclusion to be drawn from Table 5.2, is that there is a general positive opinion about the democratic potential of ICTs among the Swedish chairmen of municipal executive boards. More than 80 per cent of the respondents agree that the technology has the potential to enhance the quality of democracy today or in the future. But even if the majority of politicians seems to be optimistic about the possibilities of the new technology, this does not necessarily mean that they are prepared to experiment with digital democracy. Concerns are often expressed about the gap between technology haves and have-nots (the so-called 'digital divide'), and that digital democracy will exacerbate inequalities among citizens. Tambini (1998) distinguishes two fundamentally different attitudes towards this problem: conservative and radical. The conservative attitude implies that key functions in the democratic process are kept offline in order not to treat unfairly persons with no access to the new technology. Following this line of reasoning the

Table 5.2 The politicians' views on the democratic potential of ICTs

	Percentage	*No. of politicians*
New ICTs have the potential to enhance the quality of local democracy even at this time	28	62
New ICTs are important new mediums that can enhance the quality of local democracy in the long run	53	124
New ICTs can enhance the quality of local democracy to some extent, but its alleged significance is exaggerated	16	35
New ICTs will not have any real significance for the quality of local democracy	2	4
Total	99	225

Internet will not be allowed any greater importance until it is made available for everyone on the same conditions. The alternative, the radical solution, implies that you try to keep everything online regardless of whether everybody has access to the medium or not. Democratization for a few is considered better than no democratization at all. What are the Swedish politicians' attitudes towards this dilemma – are they radical or conservative? (See Table 5.3.)

In previous studies it has been shown that there is a strong awareness of the limited nature of the audience among politicians. Many politicians interviewed refer directly to the unrepresentative nature of the socio-economic profiles of Internet users, frequently noting the inequalities involved in giving undue weight to the information haves, at the expense of those without the means to access technology (Åström 1999; Magarey 1999; Gidlund and Möller 1999). In the light of these studies, the figures in Table 5.3 are quite surprising. Table 5.3 says that almost 50 per cent of the Swedish chairmen of the municipal executive boards do not think that unequal access among citizens give cause for a limited use of ICTs in the democratic process. Of course, this radical view might be a reflection of the rapid diffusion of computers and the Internet among citizens; as the electorates constituents are relying more heavily on Internet communications, it becomes more and more difficult for politicians not to use the Internet themselves. But the result also indicates that we are brought up against different interpretations of the potential of the Net to create political equality. For those who consider the activity on the Net to be a complementary addition to other political activities and that gives former peripheral groups access to information and political arenas, the technology does not need to be generally available for the political landscape to be levelled out. For those who believe that the activities on the Net threaten to further widen the existing gaps in society, the technology should be available to everyone in order to experiment with digital democracy.

Following this line of reasoning, we can distinguish between politicians who affiliate with the *mobilization perspective* within the literature and those who affiliate with the *reinforcement perspective* (see Bellamy and Taylor 1998; Norris 2000b). The concept of mobilization is based upon the assumption that the activity on the Net represents a distinct form of political participation, which in several ways differs from conventional activities, such as working in political parties or lobbying against elected representatives. By facilitating participation and increasing the availability of political information, the Net is considered to be able to reduce

Table 5.3 Does unequal access among citizens give cause for just a limited use of ICTs in the democratic process?

	Percentage	*No. of politicians*
Agree completely	11	25
Basically agree	40	89
Basically disagree	33	74
Disagree completely	15	33
Total	99	221

the imbalance of public social life. From the more sceptical reinforcement perspective, technology is considered to be shaped by the already influential and it also becomes a tool in the process by which power structures are reinforced. This means that the social imbalance one can find in traditional political activities will be found on the Net as well.

So far the empirical studies of the social and political characteristics of net activities tend to support the reinforcement theses. Those who are politically active also use the Internet, and those who do not engage in politics, also do not use the Internet (Norris 1999b; Martinsson 2001). However, politicians' interpretations of the democratic potential and ability of the technology to create political equality can be assumed to be of importance when it comes to their will to experiment with new methods and techniques based on ICTs. A pessimistic interpretation of the technology in combination with a reinforcement perspective would, if we are right, result in a lack of interest and a limited use of it, while a general optimism combined with a mobilization perspective would result in commitment and active initiatives. If we put these two issues in relation to one another, we can thus create four categories of politicians: radical optimists, conservative optimists, radical pessimists and conservative pessimists. The pessimists, as we can see in Table 5.4, clearly belong in the reinforcement camp, while the optimists are split in two relatively equal groups. Also, it becomes evident that the radical optimists constitute the largest category.

Direct, interactive or indirect democracy?

In order to get an idea of the political representatives' course of ambition, they were asked to show their attitudes towards five proposals that occur in the debate on how to use ICTs in the democratic process. Could it be that some proposals to use the new technology, more than others, are attractive to Swedish politicians?

For citizens to be able to make their choices at general elections, they need the information that makes it possible to form an opinion of the parties and candidates competing for their votes. Only if they can study political programmes and form an opinion of how those in authority have been acting, will they be able to make choices reflecting their political preferences. This kind of reasoning constitutes the core of the indirect model of democracy. Information is a determining factor when it comes to citizens being able to scrutinize those in authority and hold them responsible for their actions, collectively as well as individually. This

Table 5.4 Four categories of politicians (in percentage)

	Mobilization	*Reinforcement*	*Total percentage*
Cyberoptimism	Radical optimists 46	Conservative optimists 36	82
Cyberpessimism	Radical pessimists 3	Conservative pessimists 15	18
Total percentage	49	51	100

kind of information may come, and most often does come, from several different sources. Usually, information is provided through media, but sometimes also through political campaigns and discussions with individual politicians. The local government websites may be a complementary addition to these sources, not just by providing the same information, but also by providing a more detailed and easily accessible information, such as records from various meetings. The first question aims at reflecting this accountability-enhancing aspect of Internet usage: how do politicians view the proposal to publish online political records of the city council and committees?

A further kind of information is that which may underlie political standpoints and decisions. In order to make democracy more participatory, citizens must get the chance to study the political issues before the decisions are made. This argument constitutes an important part of the direct as well as the interactive model of democracy. Access to decision data is not just considered a determining factor when it comes to informed participants but for political commitment as well. Earlier, the access to decision data was very limited. Today, an effective website may offer extensive and detailed policy-relevant information and a chance to study the most obscure and difficult propositions and reports. Our second question is whether the Swedish politicians are willing to invite citizens to the political process by publishing decision data on the Internet before city council and committee meetings take place.

The third question deals with the possibility of creating new public arenas where citizens can participate in political discussions. The occurrence of such arenas is particularly important in interactive democracy, which above all gains legitimacy and stability out of active public dialogue: horizontally, so that citizens can decide on their preferences, and vertically, so that citizens can express their wishes "upwards" to parties and representatives. From this perspective, it is a public concern to create these arenas, and they should be supported by public means (Cohen 1997). The municipalities can, for instance, offer online discussion forums and chat pages on their websites, and thereby try to encourage an active citizenship, stimulate public debate and provide new channels to citizens in order to make them more influential. What are the local politicians' views on using online discussion forums that include the public?

In the direct model of democracy it is not just considered important that citizens get the opportunity of keeping up with politics and expressing their wishes to those in authority, it is also considered important that they can do this without being dependent on intermediate links. The Net can, from this point of view, enable continuous online polls and create immediate electronic feedback from voters to the elected (Bimber 1998). The use of opinion polls enables the representatives to get an idea of the preferences of their voters in a way that makes citizens less dependent on media, interest groups, parties and other intermediate organizations for their participation. The question is whether politicians consider it good or bad to conduct online polls in local issues of current interest?

Internet voting can be seen as a way of making the election procedure simpler, more flexible and cheaper from the perspective of increasing participation in general elections and thereby strengthening the legitimacy of the representative system. The disabled, the elderly, travellers and people under stress would not have to go to a voting place to cast their votes. But Internet voting is also an important part of the direct model of democracy, since this method, together with a more well-informed and competent electorate, offers a chance of making direct participation more frequent (Solop 2000). Finally, we query politicians' attitudes towards conducting online referendums.

Table 5.5 summarizes politicians' views on the different proposals for changing democracy by using ICTs. The proposals are placed in order of preference; the most favoured proposals are found on top of the table, and the least favoured at the bottom. The results reveal that there is a majority of positive attitudes towards four out of five proposals. Thus, the majority of the proposals for change seem to appeal to most politicians. However, the number of positive opinions becomes fewer when moving from proposals that concern dissemination of information to proposals that concern two-way communication. It is also worth noting that politicians' opinions on the democratic potential of the Internet, and its chance to create political equality, have an impact on the very issues that deal with communication. When it comes to the proposals that concern the dissemination of information, there are no big differences between the various categories of politicians. They have, however, relatively different attitudes towards the proposals that concern the discussion forums, public opinion surveys and Internet voting.

The most attractive proposal when it comes to communication concerns the possibility to create a discussion forum on the Internet, which indicates that politicians

Table 5.5 Attitudes towards a number of proposals for using ICTs in the democratic process

Proposals	*Percentage of politicians favourably disposed to the proposal*				
	Radical optimists	*Conservative optimists*	*Radical pessimists*	*Conservative pessimists*	*All*
Publish political records online	91 (99)	91 (79)	83 (6)	88 (33)	91 (226)
Publish documents before meetings online	89 (102)	82 (79)	67 (6)	79 (33)	85 (228)
Use online discussion forums	89 (102)	75 (77)	50 (6)	39 (31)	76 (224)
Conduct online polls	78 (102)	57 (76)	50 (6)	38 (32)	65 (223)
Conduct online referendums	44 (99)	19 (78)	17 (6)	9 (33)	29 (222)

Note

The politicians could choose between the following alternatives when answering the questions: 'a very good proposal', 'a fairly good proposal', 'a neither good nor bad proposal', 'a rather bad proposal', 'a very bad proposal' and 'no opinion'. The percentage favourably disposed refers to those whose answers were 'very good proposal' or 'a fairly good proposal'.

are more positive to proposals that lean towards interactive democracy, rather than direct democracy. This impression is confirmed by the fact that the only proposal that receives more negative votes than positive ones, is the proposal to conduct popular votes on the Internet. To be sure, the issue of Internet voting has been racing up the political agenda in Sweden, due to, among other things, the declining participation in general elections. A parliamentary assembled commission has proposed that Internet voting should be given a trial run (SOU 2000: 1), the majority of the political parties has claimed to be positive towards Internet voting (Vision 01-02-04), and according to a recent public opinion survey, 55 per cent of the voters would prefer the Internet to the traditional voting place if there was a choice (SCB 2001). But the proposal for more frequent elections by conducting popular votes in specific factual issues, implies a more pronounced ideological dimension, which is also suggested by the answers in Table 5.5. A common view is that having more frequent voting between elections runs the risk of making politics too populist. Numerous politicians might then not risk making unpopular though important decisions with an election always at hand. The fact that twice as many radical optimists as conservative optimists have a positive attitude towards this, also suggests that the view on equality is particularly important when it comes to electronic voting. This is not surprising, since one of the most serious charges against Internet voting involves the question about the discriminatory impact it may have for specific groups in the population. According to Davis (1999), electronic voting, as a supplement to traditional voting, would not disenfranchise others, but it would still disadvantage them vis-à-vis the more active. And exclusive Internet voting certainly shifts the bias toward the middle and upper classes: the already politically active.

To sum up, it seems as if the ideas to develop democracy by using the Internet have reached and convinced the Swedish chairmen of the municipal executive boards. They are not just optimistic about the potential of the technology in order to strengthen democracy, many of them are also positive towards the more participatory orientated reform proposals. Only the proposal for conducting popular votes on the Internet receives more negative votes than positive ones. It is now time to study if politicians' positive opinions about ICT are being put into action on the local political arena. Is there a connection between word and deed, between formal and active norms?

Assessing the online conditions

The most direct method of studying how local governments are using the Internet, is a systematic examination of their Internet products, that is, their websites. A content analysis of 289 Swedish local government websites was conducted during January and February in the year 2001. Of course, this examination can only provide a snapshot of websites at one point in time. The exercise needs to be repeated in future years to monitor how far local government websites adapt to the new technological developments. Also, we need to do more in-depth analysis of sites. Still, this study can provide a first indication of how far the municipalities have gone when it comes to offering citizens information and possibilities for interactive communication on their websites.

Today, all Swedish municipalities are represented on the Internet, but there are wide variations in quality and activity. The first thing we examined was the various information features that local government websites have online. More precisely, we studied citizens' possibilities to receive information in connection with the meetings of the municipal council and the municipal executive board. It was demanded that the municipality provide all information, and not only selected parts thereof, both when it comes to minutes or other documents from meetings. A greater insight presupposes that both parties in the communications process are equal, that is, that the citizen has the possibility to get hold of the document he or she wants from the municipal machinery.

From Figure 5.1 it becomes apparent that many local governments have put online accountability-enhancing material such as minutes. Also, the vast majority of sites provide the meeting schedules for municipal council (75 per cent) and municipal executive board (65 per cent). Considerably fewer municipalities present the issues that will be discussed during the next meeting on the Internet. One can also note that it is more common to publish the agendas before the open municipal council meetings (45 per cent) than before the closed municipal executive board meetings (32 per cent). In order to really give citizens a possibility to study the issues on the agenda and encourage participation on equal conditions, one has to climb further up on 'the ladder of information' (Bellamy and Raab 1999), by letting them study the documents that underlie decisions before the decisions are made. Figure 5.2 shows that, today, only 4 per cent of the municipalities do this before the municipal council meetings, and 3 per cent do it before municipal executive board meetings.

In our examination of the websites, we also looked for several key features within each site that would facilitate the interactive connection between government and citizens. The first of these features was email capability. Here we studied, among

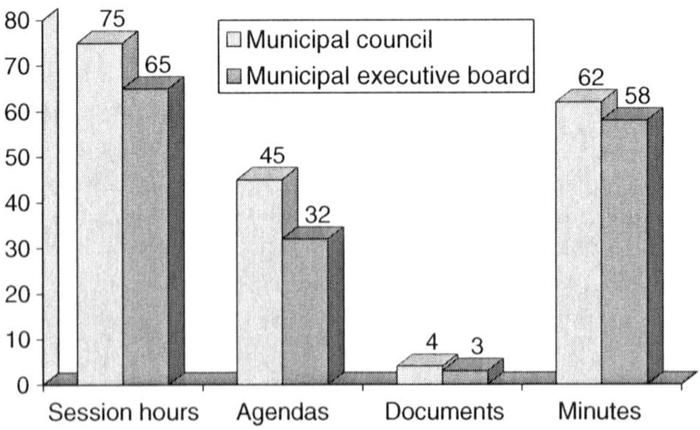

Figure 5.1 Online provision of information (in percentage).

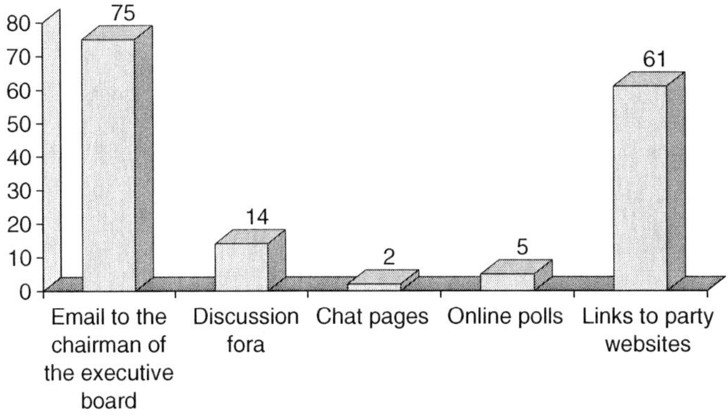

Figure 5.2 Opportunities for interactive communication (in percentage).

other things, whether a website visitor could email the chairman of the municipal executive board. If a person can merely look at information on a government website without being able to contact at least one politician, the potential for two-way interaction is thwarted. On the majority of the websites this technology was available; 75 per cent had the email address to the chairman of the municipal executive board.

While email certainly is the easiest method of contact, there are other methods that government websites can employ to facilitate democratic conversation. These include opportunities for public participation in online polls, regular online discussion forums and chat pages. These technologies were nowhere near as prevalent as email; only 14 per cent of the websites offered discussion forums, 2 per cent offered regular chat pages or recurrent chats with politicians and 5 per cent used online polls. The access offered to the parties was somewhat limited as well. The parties or their representatives were very seldom given the opportunity to comment on the pursued policy or to present their own policy on the local government websites, and only six out of ten municipalities facilitated citizens' contacts with the parties by providing links to their own websites. Even if this, to some extent, has to do with the fact that local parties do not have working websites, these findings also suggest that local governments are not trying very hard to use the Internet to promote interparty competition.

Although politicians have a positive attitude towards the opportunities offered by the Internet, it is easy to conclude that they fail to exploit these opportunities on their websites. For instance, 85 per cent of politicians claim to be positive towards publishing documents on the Internet before meetings and 75 per cent claim to be positive towards using discussion forums, as against only 4 and 14 per cent respectively of the municipalities. This means that there is an interesting discrepancy between what politicians say they want and what they really do. To analyze further this relationship we need to compare municipalities more systematically. Experience shows that some organizations are not as open to new ideas as others. While some municipalities always tend to adopt them, others allow themselves to be influenced only on rare occasions. There are wide variations in openness, and there seems to be a pattern. This has been described in terms of some municipalities being pioneers while others are followers or standbys (Schmidt 1986), or that some municipalities are active while others are passive (Henning 1996). The innovation research is, however, characterized by considerable disagreement about the factors that have an influence on the tendency to innovate. Factors found to be important for innovation in one study are found to be considerably less important, not important at all or even inversely important in another study (Downs and Mohr 1976: 700).

In the following step, we examine the relationship between the leading politicians' attitudes and the municipalities' tendency to innovate. This is done with the help of three indexes. The Information Index and the Communication Index were each produced by summing the separate indicators in Figures 5.1 and 5.2, and by standardizing the results to 100-point scales. The indicators of the two indexes were then added together into an overall Total Score (see Table 5.6).

Earlier we made the assumption that politicians' interpretations of the democratic potential and ability of technology to create political equality should be of importance when it comes to their will to experiment with new methods and techniques based on ICTs. We said that a pessimistic interpretation of the technology in combination with a reinforcement perspective, probably would result in a lack of interest and a limited use of it, while a general optimism combined with a mobilization perspective probably would result in commitment and active initiatives. The results in Table 5.6 show that politicians' attitudes towards new ICTs hardly have any significance at all on the information provided and the opportunities for interactive communication offered by the local governments. Local governments in which the chairman of the executive board is a 'conservative pessimist' provide websites that are almost as rich in information, and give almost as many opportunities for interactive communication, as those that have a 'radical optimist' as chairman. While we are not controlling for any municipal-specific factors, the result must be treated with some caution, but the result undeniably confirms the impression that there is a great difference between what politicians claim they are aiming at, and what they actually do.

Table 5.6 Local government websites and attitudes towards digital democracy

	Mean information index	*Mean communication index*	*Mean total score*	*Number of municipalities*
All	46	31	38	289
Radical optimists	49	34	40	97
Conservative optimists	45	30	37	79
Radical pessimists	42	33	37	6
Conservative pessimists	47	30	37	32

Conclusions

In this chapter we have examined the relationship among ideas, intentions and initiatives in the process of wiring Swedish local governments. We started off by reviewing some of the normative theoretical arguments in favour of digital democracy, and by examining how the Swedish chairmen of municipal executive boards relate to these new ideas. We found, on the whole, optimistic views and positive attitudes not only to the proposals supporting the indirect model of democracy, but also to proposals aiming at developing more participatory forms of democracy. The most significant finding, however, came up in the third part of the chapter and concerns the lack of causality between politicians' expressed intentions and the local government initiatives.

In light of the four basic scenarios listed in the introduction of this volume, only a few local governments have tried to develop a new mode of democracy in which different components of indirect, direct and interactive democracy are combined to create a more open, participative and responsive polity at the local level. Two good examples of this is the use of online referendums in the cities of Kalix and Nyköping as the basis of local decision-making on some important issues. Other examples include more interactive, or deliberative, forms of participation as in Bollnäs and Älvsjö. Digital democracy activities in these cities contain a number of innovations in the democratic procedures, for example, open dialogue forums, citizen panels, video broadcasting from the council and opportunities for citizen proposals. As the analysis shows, most local governments do, however, use the Internet for modernization rather than radical regeneration. Although politicians have a positive attitude towards the interactive opportunities offered by the Internet, it is easy to conclude that they fail to exploit these opportunities on their websites. Instead the websites serve as information archives for the press and public, and email may sometimes function as a replacement for telephone or postal queries.

The stability of political forms demonstrates the importance of an institutional perspective in a terrain that remains dominated by the assumption that information technology determines structure. At the core of the so-called new institutionalism is the notion that institutions do not necessarily change due to a changing technological environment, or that preferences alone shape politics. Institutional theories provide accounts of the constraints that institutions impose on action. Following the institutionalist line of reasoning, the effects of the Internet on government will be played out in unexpected ways, profoundly influenced by organizational, political and institutional logic. Technologies themselves influence choice, but the relationship is indirect, sometimes subtle, and exercised in combination with other economic, cultural, political and social influences. This is why the Internet does not always lead to institutional transformation but sometimes is enacted to strengthen the status quo (Fountain 2001). Even if this chapter is not the place to discuss the whole range of factors that might influence how local governments shape new ICTs it is possible to outline a few characteristic features of the Swedish local ICT policy that might be of importance for the discrepancy between politicians' expressed intentions and local government initiatives.

First, it seems like the municipalities have entered the world of new technology almost without any predefined, explicit strategies. The most manifest evidence of this is that only 20 per cent of the municipalities have agreed on a policy on ICT and democracy (Kommunaktuellt 2000: no. 16). This, and claims from spokesmen of the municipalities that there has been some resistance within the organizations towards the implementation of the new ICTs, imply that new technology is still not a very well-integrated part of the municipalities' activities. In many cases, the initiative to adopt new ICTs comes from individuals without any prior discussions within the organization, mainly as a result of other municipalities' adoption of websites as well as the general public rhetoric on the information society. Consequently, decision-making proceeds by successive limited comparison and learning by trial-and-error. This achieves simplification through limiting the number of alternatives considered to those that differ in small degrees from existing policies.

Second, it is evident that politicians' access to and knowledge of the Internet have received scant attention. It is rather common that politicians themselves, and laymen politicians in particular, do not have access to the basic requirement (computer, email and the Internet) that are necessary in order to take an active part in the political activities on the Net (Ranerup 1999). If ICT is to be used to a greater extent in the democratic processes, it is, however, necessary that politicians generally have the ICT easily accessible in their political work. This means that politicians need to not only decide upon communication strategies, but also to decide whether to give themselves hardware and software, as well as the expertise to connect to and use the Internet in the ways suggested by these strategies (Zittel 1999). So far, few municipalities seem to have accepted this challenge; only 10 per cent of the municipalities offer home computers to their politicians, and usually this offer only applies to members of the municipal executive board and its working committee (Kommunaktuellt 2000: no. 16).

A third distinctive trait of the local ICT policies is that the power of social production lies within the bureaucracy. Instead of moving the development forward, politicians have relied on ICT experts to create solutions. This means that the municipalities' Internet usage, to a great extent, is dependent on the fact that there are motivated actors within the organization, who have the will and ability to organize ideas and activities so that the process can be driven forward (Wihlborg 2000). Municipal officers often have an active interest in using the advantages of the new media, but at the same time they also find it difficult to develop new democracy functions if they do not have politicians' active consent; with the result that the same functions as earlier are conveyed, but on the Net, and that ICTs in themselves become the solution to the problems of democracy.

On the basis of these characteristic features of the Swedish local ICT policy, it is possible to argue that the loose connection between politicians' attitudes and the municipalities' web activities, at least partly, might be due to the fact that (a) politicians have not yet set up a distinct policy on how to use the new technology within the municipality; (b) that there is still no working ICT support for elected politicians and (c) that the development of digital democracy is driven more by municipal officers than by politicians. This does not, however, mean that it should be only a matter of time for digital democracy to arrive. It is also possible that local ICT policies rest on symbolic or image-reasons rather than rational decision-making. The current interest in reforming democracy in Sweden as well as the general Internet hype indicates that there is certain pressure by the institutional environment to incorporate modern and legitimate ideas about digital democracy. Local governments are more or less forced to adapt to the new technological environment with regard to its profile, legitimacy and identity in relation to other organizations and their citizens. This does not, however, mean that there is always a true desire to bring in citizens and give them opportunities to participate in decision-making processes. If local governments use ICTs for image-reasons and not in the first place to expand and make easier communication between citizens and politicians, ideas will stay 'disengaged' and not have any real impact on the organizations' activities (Brunsson 1989; Rövik 1998).

The discrepancy between what politicians claim they are aiming at and what they actually do certainly leaves questions to be dealt with in future research: What are the mechanisms translating technological change into political change? How do media and media changes relate to political change and different concepts of democracy? How does the Internet affect culture and practices? To answer these questions we need to examine in-depth why the technology is translated, how it is translated and by whom. Above all, it seems important to link ideas more closely to institutions for political innovations are often blocked or hampered by the present political institutions, which are orientated towards and structured according to a different political public. There is a time lag between the new developing public, which tries to reorganize institutions, and the present public that has formed the present institutions. This tension between stability and change makes the future role of ICTs with regard to democracy an open question.

References

Åström, Joachim (1999) 'Digital demokrati?' in *IT i demokratins tjänst*, SOU 1999: 117, Stockholm: Fritzes.

Barber, B. (1984) *Strong Democracy*, Berkeley: University of California Press.

Bellamy, C. and Taylor, J. A. (1998) *Governing in the Information Age*, Buckingham: Open University Press.

Bellamy, C. and Raab, C. D. (1999) 'Wiring-up the Deck-Chairs?' in Coleman, S., Taylor, J. and van de Donk, W. (eds), *Parliament in the Age of the Internet*, Oxford: Oxford University Press.

Bimber, B. (1998) 'The Internet and Political Transformation', *Polity*, XXXI (1): 133–60.

Blumler, J. G. and Gurevitch, M. (1995) *The Crisis of Public Communication*, London: Routledge.

Bohman, J. (1996) *Public Deliberation. Pluralism*, Cambridge/London: MIT Press.

Brunsson, N. (1989) *The Organization of Hypocracy*, New York: John Wiley.

Budge, I. (1996) *The New Challenge of Direct Democracy*, Cambridge: Polity Press.

Cohen, J. (1997) 'Deliberation and Democratic Legitimacy', in Hamlin, A. and Petit, P. (eds), *The Good Polity*, New York: Basil Blackwell.

Dahl, R. A. (1989) *Democracy and Its Critics*, New Haven/London: Yale University Press.

Dahl, R. A. and Tufte, E. (1973) *Size and Democracy*, Stanford: Stanford University Press.

Davis, R. (1999) *The Web of Politics*, Oxford: Oxford University Press.

Downs, A. (1957) *An Economic Theory of Democracy*, New York: Harper & Row.

Downs, G. W. and Mohr, L. B. (1976) 'Conceptual Issues in the Study of Innovation', *Administrative Science Quarterly*, 21, 700–14.

Elster, J. (1998) *Deliberative Democracy*, Cambridge: Cambridge University Press.

Etzioni, A. (1972) 'Minerva', *Policy Sciences*, 3, 457–74.

Fishkin, J. S. (1991) *Democracy and Deliberation*, New Haven/London: Yale University Press.

Fountain, J. E. (2001) *Building the Virtual State*, Washington, DC: Brookings Institution Press.

Friedland, L. A. (1996) 'Electronic Democracy and the New Citizenship', *Media, Culture & Society*, 18 (2), 4–16.

Gibson, R. K. and Ward, S. J. (1998) 'U.K. Political Parties and the Internet', *Harvard International Journal of Press/Politics*, 3 (3).

Gidlund, G. and Möller, T. (1999) *Demokratins trotjänare*, SOU 1999: 130, Stockholm: Fritzes.

Hague, B. N. and Loader, B. D. (1999) *Digital Democracy*, London: Routledge.

Held, D. (1987) *Models of Democracy*, Cambridge: Polity Press.

Henning, R. (1996) *Att följa trenden – aktiva och passiva kommuner*, Stockholm: Nerenius & Santérus förlag.

Holmberg, S. (1999) *Representativ demokrati*. SOU 1999: 64, Stockholm: Fritzes.

Ilshammar, L. (1997) *Demokr@i. Det elektroniska folkstyrets möjligheter och problem*, SOU 1997: 56, Stockholm: Fritzes.

Klingemann, H.-D. and Fuchs, D. (1995) *Citizens and the State*, Oxford: Oxford University Press.

Kommunaktuellt 2000, no. 16, *Snigelfart när demokratin ska ut på nätet.*

Magarey, K. (1999) 'The Internet and Australian Parliamentary Democracy', in Coleman, S., Taylor, J. and van de Donk, W. (eds), *Parliament in the Age of the Internet*, Oxford: Oxford University Press.

Martinsson, J. (2001) 'Den svenska nätopinionen', in Holmberg, S. and Weibull, L. (eds), *Land, du välsignade?* Göteborg: SOM-institutet.

McLean, I. (1989) *Democracy and New Technology*, Cambridge: Polity Press.

Möller, T. (2000) *Politikens meningslöshet*, Malmö: Lieber.

Norris, P. (1999a) *Critical Citizens*, Oxford: Oxford University Press.

Norris, P. (1999b) *Who Surfs Café Europa?* paper presented at the Annual Meeting of the American Political Science Association, Atlanta, 1–5 September 1999.

Norris, P. (2000a) *Democratic Divide?* paper presented at the American Political Science Association annual meeting in Washington, DC

Norris, P. (2000b) *A Virtuous Circle*, Cambridge: Cambridge University Press.

Petersson, O. (2000) *Demokrati utan partier?* Stockholm: SNS förlag.

Premfors, R. (2000) *Den starka demokratin*, Stockholm: Atlas.

Ranerup, A. (1999) 'Elektronisk debatt i kommunal politik', in *IT i demokratins tjänst*, SOU 1999: 117, Stockholm: Fritzes.

Rövik, K. A. (1998) *Moderne organisasjoner*, Bergen-Sandviken: Fagboksforlaget.

Sartori, G. (1987) *The Theory of Democracy Revisited*, New Jersey: Chatham House Publishers.

SCB (2001) *IT i hem och företag*, Örebro: SCB.

Schmidt, S. (1986) *Pionjärer, efterföljare och avaktare*, Lund: Kommunfakta förlag.

Schuler, D. (1996) *New Community Networks*, New York: ACM Press.

Schumpeter, J. A. (1976) *Capitalism, Socialism and Democracy*, London: Allen and Unwin.

Solop, F. I (2000) *Digital Democracy Comes of Age in Arizona*, paper presented at the American Political Science Association national conference, Washington, DC.

SOU 2000: 1, *En uthållig demokrati*, Stockholm: Fritzes.

SOU 2001: 48, *Att vara med på riktigt*, Stockholm: Fritzes.

Tambini, D. (1998) 'Civic Networking and Universal Rights to Connectivity: Bologna', in Tsagarousianou, R., Tambini, D. and Bryan, C. (eds), *Cyberdemocracy*, London/ New York: Routledge.

Vision 01-02-04, *Politikerna vill ha e-val 2006.*

Wihlborg, E. (2000) *En lösning som söker problem*, Linköping: Linköping Studies in Arts and Science.

Zittel, T. (1999) *The Internet and U.S. Representatives*, paper presented at the International Conference on Parliaments in the Information Age, Paris, 18–20 November 1999.

6 Cyber-campaigning grows up

A comparative content analysis of websites for US Senate and gubernatorial races, 1998–2000

Jennifer D. Greer and Mark E. LaPointe

Introduction

This chapter focuses on one of the key supports of representative democracy – current and prospective elected representatives. Specifically, we examine individual candidates' use of the new information and communication technologies (ICTs) in the race for state executive and national legislative office in the United States. While politicians are vital parts of the representative institutions they serve, during their battles for voter sympathy one might expect them to opt for more individualistic and direct channels of communication with the electorate. This may especially be the case in the United States with its more candidate-centered form of election campaigning and governance. Such a system offers a more flexible and diverse platform for candidates to experiment and innovate in how to engage voters. The goal of this chapter is to assess how far candidates' use of web communication during the 1998 and 2000 US Senate and gubernatorial elections actually reflected these more direct and experimental possibilities. Specifically, did candidates tend to follow offline campaign trends and adopt a largely symbolic and image-based message that took an attacking stance toward opponents? Or, did they opt for more participatory features and seek to present policy-rich information in positive and inviting ways? We also ask whether the communication style on the sites changed very much between the two election cycles. And finally, we assess the role of various structural factors, such as the level of office sought, and individual characteristics of the candidate, such as gender or incumbency status, in influencing candidates' online communication style. In addressing these questions, the chapter presents an alternative perspective on the response of executive and legislative institutions to the challenge of new ICTs from that offered by Catherine Needham and Thomas Zittel in Chapters 3 and 4 in this volume. While their work revealed these bodies as a whole to be cautious in increasing their openness and public access via new ICTs, it might be that the elected individuals comprising them take a somewhat bolder stance.

The Internet was first used by US presidential candidates in 1992 (Davis and Owen 1998), although according to most accounts, 1996 marked the real beginnings of cyberpolitics with most major and minor party presidential candidates establishing sites in that year. Two years later, media observers were calling the

1998 election "the most wired in history" (Miller and Schrader 1998: A1). Indeed, D'Alessio (2000) found that 43 percent of the 1,296 US Senate, House of Representatives, and gubernatorial candidates had established websites in 1998, up from 18.7 percent in 1996. The website put up by former wrestler Jesse Ventura in his bid for the governorship of Minnesota in particular, gained headlines for its simple text-based approach. The site was credited with generating a strong surge of support from younger voters and securing his surprise victory (Fineman 1999). Overall, however, cyber-campaigning was not expected to make a widespread impact on real-world politics until at least the 2000 electoral cycle, when people were predicted to become more familiar with the Internet as a mass medium (Corrado 1996). Some rather less-optimistic verdicts on the impact of cyber-campaigning were also delivered during this period. One congressional campaign manager, for instance, lamented in 1996 that his site had been visited just 26 times, and that half of those visits were by the candidate checking on the number of hits (Dulio *et al.* 1999). During the 1990s, therefore, the web was generally seen as having exhibited more potential than impact as a campaign tool (Just 1997: 100).

By 2000, almost every contender for a major office in the United States had a campaign-specific website, as did contenders for most minor offices. Anecdotes at all levels of politics suggested that sites were becoming an integral part of campaigns. The day after Republican presidential candidate John McCain's decisive win in the New Hampshire primary, $415,000 reportedly poured into his campaign via his site, up sharply from the $10,000 daily trickle into the site prior to the victory (Kornblut and Abraham 2000). Within a week, it was estimated that the site had raised 2 million dollars and recruited 22,000 new volunteers (Birnbaum 2000). Signs of the Internet's significance also emerged at the local level in the race for mayor in Snellville, Georgia in 2000. Challenger Brett Harrell credited his site with bringing in 500 votes, a yield that allowed him to unseat the 26 year incumbent. Harrell commented afterward, "I think there will not be another election – local to the White House – that won't be affected by the Internet" (Shelton 2000: 1JJ). The popular press noted a distinct change in candidates' orientation toward the Internet as news media prepared for elections in 2000. "E-campaigning has gone from a novelty to a necessity in less than a year… The Internet is fast becoming a Virtual New Hampshire: a quirky but pivotal place where campaigns are launched or scuttled" (Fineman 1999: 50). Evidence of this growing commitment can be seen in terms of the financial resources being channeled toward online campaigning. In the lead-up to the 2000 presidential election, contenders from the major parties had full-time web teams and consultants, and at least 16 percent of the sites for all congressional and gubernatorial campaigns in 1998 were run by professional consultants (McManus 1999a). By late 1999, *Campaigns & Elections* magazine listed about thirty companies specializing in online politics and political websites were estimated to be a $2.5 billion a year industry (McManus 1999b: 76).

US Internet users, on the whole, treated candidates' sites with a modicum of interest. While almost one in five or 18 percent of Americans used the Internet for campaign news in 2000 (a dramatic rise from the 4 percent who did so in 1996) only 8 percent of online users visited a candidate or campaign site. This compares with just over half of online campaign-news users relying on the online versions of traditional news outlets (Pew Research Center 2000). In addition, when asked about the value of the experience, only a third of those who visited campaign sites rated them as "very useful," compared to the 57 percent of online news users who gave CNN.com this high rating (Pew Research Center 2000). This rather muted reception led one commentator to point out, "Despite considerable hype, perhaps the Internet has yet to become a player on par with TV" (Lynch 2001: 24). Certainly visitors to campaign sites may have been turned off by what some analysts have termed "cyber-fluff" (Greer and LaPointe 1999) and "brochureware" (Miller and Schrader 1998: A1) masquerading as content. Sites were generally seen as thin on content and interactivity and offering little more than glossy photographs and rosy biographies of candidates and their families (Kamarck 1998).

The question being investigated in this chapter is how far such impressions are justified. Are sites really stuck in existing and largely static forms of campaigning or have candidates begun to exploit the web's dynamic and interactive capabilities? In addition, if changes are taking place, how can we explain them? Is it simply a function of time, or a particular party taking the lead? To answer these questions we conduct a systematic content analysis of Senate and gubernatorial candidates' websites in 1998 and 2000. Specifically we focus on three main aspects of website content:

- To what extent are candidates infusing their sites with a wider variety of information graphics and interactivity as the web evolves?
- Do candidates offer positive or negative messages on their sites and how far they emphasize image-oriented messages versus issue-oriented politics?
- To what extent are those variables that play a role in traditional campaign communication, such as gender and party and candidate standing, also related to these features of online communication?

This study investigates these topics by examining the content and communication style of campaign sites in two recent US election cycles for two distinct levels of office: state gubernatorial and federal Senate races in 1998 and 2000. In doing so, this chapter moves forward the study of cyber-campaigning in a number of ways. First, it adds a longitudinal component to such analyses; to date, most analyses have examined sites for one type of candidate in one election cycle (Epstein 1996; Klotz 1998; Greer and LaPointe 1999). In addition, comparative analyses of candidates' and parties' campaign sites have focused on the content and overall design of the sites rather than their general tone or style of communication. In systematically examining the tone of the messages being delivered on the sites, we can more rigorously investigate the idea that the web serves as a less hostile and more positively oriented forum for political campaigning.

In examining these questions, the chapter can also address broader debates in the literature about the transformation taking place in political campaigning in what has been termed the postmodern (Norris 2000) or professionalized era (Gibson and Römmele 2001) that began to emerge in the United States in 1988 (Farrell and Webb 2000). As these authors have pointed out, previous shifts in campaign eras, namely from the premodern to the modern, have been intimately linked with changes in communication technology. While newspapers were tied to the premodern campaign era, television ushered in the modern era. The arrival of the Internet and other new digital means of communication are now leading to a fresh set of possibilities and challenges for political actors. These new technologies are producing a fragmentation, proliferation, and blurring of information and entertainment sources and a 24-hour news cycle. As such, campaign communications are increasingly marked by narrowcasting and adapting messages to the audience (Farrell and Webb 2000). "Such trends," as Norris points out, lead to a "postmodern conceptualization [that] sees politicians as essentially lagging behind technological and economic changes and running hard just to stay in place by adopting the techniques of political marketing in the struggle to cope with the more complex news environment" (Norris 2000: 149).

Inevitably, therefore, the postmodern era has seen an increasing role for professional media advisors, advertising, and polling, and a heightened emphasis on "spin" and image. Such trends are clearly observable in the American "candidate-centered" context, which has significantly fewer limitations on how to campaign than other countries (Farrell and Webb 2000: 108). However, as Norris (2000) has argued, the "new channels of communication also allow for greater interactivity between voters and politicians" akin to that which characterized the premodern era (p. 140). This is a point echoed by Wring and Horrocks (2001), who argue that while the new media may fragment and distil the political process into sound bites, it also presents the chance to encourage more interactive citizen practices (pp. 191–200). Thus, in examining the questions regarding candidates' emphasis on style versus substance and negative campaigning, we can address some of these broader questions about the direction that postmodern campaigning is taking under the influence of the Internet.

Campaigning online: the story so far

Empirical studies of campaign websites

Although virtually all parties across the world had established websites by 2002, they have probably been used most intensively for campaigning in the United States (Farrell and Webb 2000: 111). Such exploitation has no doubt followed from the fact that the US, along with the Scandinavian democracies have led the way in terms of public access and use of the net with rates of 59 percent and higher as of late 2002 (NUA 2002).

Early analysis of US election sites revealed that for the most part, candidates were content to simply migrate their offline publicity material to the online environment.

Websites were filled with speeches and position papers. Homepages for the 1996 US Senate elections typically included a photo of the candidate, biographical information, a position statement, and contact information – the traditional fare for campaign information (Meadow 1989; Bryant 1995; Johnson-Cartee and Copeland 1997). A few sites in 1996 featured virtual postcards, screen savers, video clips, and trivia, however, most were fairly unadventurous (Epstein 1996; Hall 1997; Klotz 1997). Presidential sites in 1996 were equally predictable (Reavy and Perlmutter 1996). McKeown and Plowman (1998) concluded that while the Dole and Clinton sites in 1996 allowed the candidates to provide more in-depth information than they were able to convey on television, neither candidate was effective in using the technology to increase interactivity with voters.

The picture did not appear much different in 1998. While Davis and Owen (1998) did note that a few sites used the interactive nature of the medium to solicit opinion, collect money, and identify supporters, most studies pointed to a less than aggressive use of the participatory features of the Net. LaPointe (1999) found that standard campaign information and photographs dominated Senate websites in the 1998 election. This pattern was replicated on gubernatorial candidates' sites in 1998 with interaction outside of E-mail being sporadic (Greer and LaPointe 1999). Kamarck's study of sites for US Senate, House, and governors' races in the 1998 elections underscored this picture of websites as static electronic brochures, where "pictures of the family, text of speeches and issue papers are all standard fare... Many campaign sites seek to get you to volunteer or contribute money – although few allow you to volunteer in cyberspace or make campaign contributions over the Web" (Kamarck 1998: B4). Dulio *et al.* (1999) found that while 73 percent of congressional candidates in 1998 solicited contributions on their sites, just less than one-third of that group allowed visitors to make contributions online. Others simply gave out a campaign address or asked for contributors to enter their addresses. Finally, questionnaire data collected by Faucheux from 270 candidates in local, state, and federal elections in 1998 revealed that while nearly all campaigns (97 percent) reported biographical information on their sites and 90 percent reported policy positions, just over half (52 percent) reported offering opportunities for any feedback. Faucheux remained hopeful, however, that "more creative Internet strategies will be hatched and more 'bells and whistles' will be explored and employed over time" (Faucheux 1998: 25).

Overall, in terms of the sheer volume of websites, more US candidates used the web in the 2000 elections. Kamarck (2002) found that although website use by gubernatorial candidates did not increase between the two election cycles, use by Senate candidates increased slightly and among House of Representatives' candidates, use of the web nearly doubled, from 35 to 66 percent. Kamarck also found that by 2000 more incumbents were using websites in their campaigns and candidates in very competitive races were more likely to use the Internet as a campaign tool. In 2000, a survey by Netelection.org found that 78 percent of incumbent congressional candidates in competitive districts established sites, compared with 50 percent in secure districts (Lynch 2001).

Analyses of US election sites after 1998 did suggest some areas of content improvement among presidential candidates. The Democratic nominee for president in 2000, Al Gore, developed an interactive children's area and live streaming of his Nashville headquarters via a webcam. The site also featured downloadable computer wallpaper with the Gore logo, an interactive information generator on states' voter registration rules, and a place where visitors could create their own issue-oriented web page (Fineman 1999; Tillett 2000). Online fundraising also attracted more attention in 2000. Kamarck (2002) reports that the majority of major party candidates were using their websites for fundraising. This was no doubt due to the fact that a year earlier the US Federal Elections Commission decided online credit-card donations were eligible for matching federal funds. This was a "very important symbol...that legitimizes the Web as a real part of American politics" (von Sternberg 1999: 6A).

While some work has been done on tone or style of the political message being delivered by candidate sites in the United States, this aspect of online campaigning has not been investigated as frequently and in as much depth as the functional aspects discussed here. What evidence has been collected has concentrated on the use of negative campaigning and has shown the web to be something of a neutral to upbeat zone. Klotz (1997), for instance, found that only seventeen of fifty US Senate candidates mentioned their opponent in an unfavorable light on their sites in 1996. Other studies have shown that both Senate and gubernatorial candidates in 1998 had highly positive homepages and saved the rare attack for pages deep within the sites (Kamarck 1998; LaPointe 1999; Greer and LaPointe 1999).

Finally, as well as building a picture of what is being offered by candidates on the web, a very limited amount of work has been done to identify the individual and environmental factors that may determine the differences discovered in site content and communication style. Gender differences, for instance, have been observed as important for online campaign style. Women candidates in the US Senate races of 2000 were found to have used a greater percentage of the web's interactive capabilities than male candidates (Puopolo 2001). Incumbency has been found to be an important factor in shaping website content. LaPointe (1999) found that Senate incumbents had significantly more interactive sites and were significantly more positive in their message than challengers. This is not too surprising since as Fenno has pointed out, office holders need to establish a positive reputation for their on-the-job performance (Fenno 1996). However, research has shown also that congressional and gubernatorial incumbents were also more likely to rely on official government sites instead of putting up their own campaign sites (Klotz 1998; D'Alessio 2000). Incumbents in jeopardy, however, proved to be more likely to establish an independent website (Kamarck 1998).

Party has also been argued to influence online campaign communication since minor parties and independents may see the web as a way to combat the "freezing out" they receive from the traditional media (Gibson and Ward 1998). Recent research by Gibson *et al.* (2003) on the German party system has also lent support to the idea that parties' primary goals (i.e. vote maximization, office seeking, etc.) may play a role in determining how far they emphasize the participatory features of the web as opposed to its electioneering and information-provision capabilities. In the United States, Republican sites were found to outperform Democrats in 1996, in terms of the information offered on candidate's policy stances, and facilities for making financial contributions as well as signing up for mailing lists (Tedesco *et al.* 1999). D'Alessio (2000) later found Democrats to be slower adopters than Republicans in US House, Senate, and gubernatorial contests. Analysis of the 2000 Senate races in the United States, however, showed that 61 percent of Democrats' sites had a mission statement, compared to 47 percent of Republican sites. Democrats were also found to be more likely to discuss education than Republicans, but Republicans were more "web savvy," because they were more likely to include volunteer options, voter registration information, a market place, audio, video, motion graphics, links, pop-up features, and several other features (Puopolo 2001). Major party candidates were also found to be more likely than minor party candidates to use the Internet as a campaign tool. Most minor party candidates' sites are basic and tend to be associated with the Reform Party, Libertarian Party, or the Green Party (Kamarck 2002).

This review makes it clear that cyber-campaigning and our understanding of it is evolving. There is evidence of innovation but also of a bias toward controlled dissemination of information, rather than more radical strategies to promote participation. The primary goal of this chapter is to investigate these impressions through systematic empirical analysis of Senate and gubernatorial candidates' websites in the 1998 and 2000 elections. The sites are content analyzed with regard to the information, graphics, and interactivity that they contain as well as their overall tone in terms of attacks on opponents. The differences that emerge are then explored with a range of variables that have been associated with variance in offline campaigning such as candidates' gender, outsider status, and party affiliation, in addition to election year (1998 versus 2000) and type of office sought. The findings are then discussed in terms of what they reveal about the overall direction in which candidates' sites are moving, and finally what those changes say about the move toward a more postmodern style of campaigning.

Data and methods

The population studied in this research is gubernatorial and Senate candidates' websites in the 1998 and 2000 US elections. In 1998, gubernatorial races were ongoing in thirty-five states, and Senate races were being fought in thirty-four states. In 2000, thirteen states were choosing a governor, and thirty-four Senate seats were up for grabs. The campaign websites were found from state-by-state listings published online by Politics One (www.politics1.com) and Election Net (www.electnet.org). In addition, the Yahoo Internet directory (www.yahoo.com), the Excite search engine (www.excite.com), and, in 2000, the Google search engine (www.google.com) were used to find any other campaign sites the directories might not have included. Any candidate having a homepage on the web, whether sponsored by the campaign or the candidate's party, was included in this study. Candidates who had web pages but had lost their party primary were excluded unless they continued to run as an independent for another party after the primary. Incumbents that had only a government-sponsored site as their web presence were also included. The web sources consulted proved very comprehensive with only four sites added to the dataset that were not found using the directories.

In terms of research design, Senate and gubernatorial candidates' sites were examined for several reasons. First, there are relatively few studies of them, with most US analysts tending to look mainly at presidential sites. Second, Senate and gubernatorial contests provide a large number of sites for analysis but not so many that the entire population cannot be studied. Finally, because these contests are alike in a number of key ways – both have statewide constituencies, require large budgets, and attract candidates at about the same stage in their political careers – it is possible, following the most similar systems design logic, to pool the data and create a larger sample, from which the impact of the varying political and demographic influences can be more readily detected.

Methodologically, following the practice of previous studies of parties online, coders collected basic website data on the presence or absence of certain types of information items (i.e. candidate biography, stand on issues, constituent help), types of visual elements (pictures, video, animation), and interactive features (i.e. E-mail address, guestbook, bulletin board). If the items were present, the website scored one and if absent zero was assigned. The number of items present within each category was then summed to create total information, graphical element, and interactivity scores for each candidate (further information on the items scored can be seen in Tables 6.1–6.4 in the results section). Higher numbers on each score indicated that more of the types of information, graphical elements, and interactivity were present.

In addition to types of content available, researchers examined the focus and tone of the sites. Only the first page of the site was examined for these variables because homepages mark the entry to the sites. Also, examining the entire content of the site for focus and tone would have proven prohibitive. Focus was measured by a seven-point scale whereby "1" indicated a homepage devoted solely to candidate image and "7" was selected for a homepage devoted solely to campaign issues. A score of "4" represented a mixed image/issue focus. Tone of the site was measured by a five-point scale whereby "1" indicated a homepage that was 100 percent positive and "5", one that was 100 percent negative. A score of "3" represented an even mix of positive and negative. A neutral option was included (e.g. for sites that only had a directory on the homepage), however, no sites were found to be neutral in tone. Attacking was measured on a seven-point scale with '1' indicating no attacking present on the homepage and "7" indicating the entire homepage was devoted to attacking. The attacking measure was designed to measure a narrow subset of negative communication beyond that measure by the tone variable. Specifically, negative communication referred to content that was directly aimed at attacking another candidate or party. Unlike the content measures, therefore, these measures of style and tone were assigned according to coders overall judgment of a site, rather than counts of items present or absent. In order to ensure coder consistency, two different sets of trained coders examined the sites in each election. Their scores were fairly consistent on the tone measures, with intercoder reliability averaging 84.7 percent. This was slightly lower than the overall reliability for the entire instrument (see later).

Finally, data was collected about candidates including gender, party affiliation, and candidate standing (challenger or incumbent). Type of site used by the candidate also was noted. Some candidates were incumbents and only used their official governmental site. Others, typically minor party candidates, had only a page or a brief mention on a party site, while other candidates' only web presence was on a business, citizens group, or other type of site. Sites specifically focused on one candidate's bid for a given office were coded as candidate-specific election sites.

Data was collected from the Monday to the Sunday immediately preceding the Tuesday general elections in each election cycle (from October 26 until November 1 in 1998 and from October 30 to November 5 in 2000). This time frame was chosen because, as Election Day nears, candidates and campaign communicators are most engaged in trying to win votes (Fenno 1996). Candidates establishing sites, therefore, would have to have done so by this time. Sites not accessible during the first check were rechecked up to the Sunday before the election. If still not accessible on that day, demographic information on the candidates was collected using the Politics One site but site information was recorded as missing data. In 1998, 129 sites were identified for active gubernatorial candidates and 93 for Senate candidates (222 sites analyzed in total). In 2000, 46 sites for gubernatorial candidates were identified and 125 for Senate races were found (171 in all). In total, 393 sites were analyzed. In both years, two coders collected data, with 10 percent of the sites coded by both coders. Intercoder reliability for the entire coding instrument (i.e. both content and tone measures) on the 40 sites ranged from 74.3 to 98.1 percent for an average of 91.3 percent.

Findings

First, descriptive statistics are presented about the sites across the two time periods being studied, based on the characteristics of the candidates running them in terms of office sought, gender, party, and incumbency status. Then, the content and tone of the 393 sites are discussed and compared by election year and finally, we present a more rigorous statistical analysis that examines the impact of election year on site content and tone, along with other important candidate and election variables.

Overall profile of websites

The distribution of sites according to individual candidate characteristics is reported in Table 6.1, according to year. Overall, there were more senatorial sites than gubernatorial, reflecting the fact that the former outnumbered the latter in total number of races during the period studied. In terms of demographics, websites were much more likely to be run by male candidates than female in both election years. Again this was reflective of the overall campaign environment,

Table 6.1 Distribution of Senate and gubernatorial sites in the 1998 and 2000 elections according to selected election and candidate-specific variables

Background variable	*1998*	*2000*	*Total*
Office sought			
Senator	93 (41.9)	125 (73.1)	218
Governor	129 (58.1)	46 (29.9)	175
Gender			
Male	189 (85.1)	149 (87.1)	338
Female	33 (14.9)	22 (12.9)	55
Type of site			
Govt.	20 (9.0)	9 (5.3)	29
Party	31 (14.0)	7 (4.1)	38
Candidate	155 (70.1)	151 (88.8)	306
Other	15 (6.8)	3 (1.3)	18
Party			
Republican	67 (30.2)	49 (28.1)	115
Democrat	68 (30.6)	43 (25.1)	111
Minor/independent	87 (39.2)	80 (46.8)	167
Standing			
Insider	118 (53.2)	85 (49.7)	203
Outsider	104 (46.8)	86 (50.3)	190
Race type			
Open	56 (25.2)	49 (28.7)	105
Incumbent running	166 (74.8)	122 (71.3)	288
Total for election cycle	222	171	393

Notes

Figures are raw '*n*' followed by percentages in parentheses. Percentages are calculated from the column totals for each variable by year. For example, in 1998, 41.9 percent of the sites analyzed were those of Senate candidates and 58.1 percent those of gubernatorial candidates.

rather than any inherent bias in the technology since major parties put forward only eleven female nominees in the races for Senate or governor in 2000. Indeed, our findings show that ten of those eleven nominees ran websites indicating that women candidates actually had a highly proactive stance toward cyber-campaigning. Most sites were candidate-specific campaign sites, rather than official government sites or party sites, particularly by 2000. In terms of party, Republicans and Democrats operated most sites, but a significant number of minor party and independent candidates also ran sites in both election years. In addition, almost half of the sites that were put up belonged to candidates who had never held any elective office, indicating outsiders were keen to use the medium. Finally, websites were more common in those races where an incumbent was running compared with those vying for an open seat. This distribution can also be seen to reflect offline campaign dynamics to a large degree in that Senate and gubernatorial races with incumbents outweighed open races by a factor of about four to one in 1998 and 2000.

After examining the distribution of the sites in terms of their "background" features, the sites were then scrutinized in terms of their content and overall style.

Table 6.2 Mean scores for content, style, and tone of candidates homepage by year

Style and tone measures	*1998*	*2000*
Information	4.18	6.33***
Graphics	1.49	1.88***
Interactivity	1.97	3.96***
Focus	3.77	4.20*
Tone	1.70	1.76
Attacking	1.50	2.36***

Notes
Independent sample t-tests for significant increases or decreases in scores between 1998 and 2000. A p value <0.05 is indicated by *; *** indicates $p<0.001$.

Information dissemination, graphics, and interactivity

Information was measured using a 0–11 scale, in which candidates scored one point for each information item present on their sites. While every site scored at least 1, no site scored maximum points, and only two sites scored 10. On average, candidates scored 5. The range of information presented increased significantly from 1998, when candidates scored an average of 4.2, to 2000, when this rose to 6.3, a statistically significant increase ($t=11.74$, df $=384$, $p<0.001$).

As Table 6.2 also shows, the emphasis on graphics rose between the two election cycles. Within a range of 0–3, the average graphical element score increased from 1.5 in 1998 to 1.9 in 2000, a jump that proved statistically significant ($t=4.89$, df $=386$, $p<0.001$). Finally, for interactivity, sites were awarded 1 point for each of 12 elements coded. As many as 36 sites scored 0 points on this index, offering no interactivity at all, not even an E-mail address. The two most interactive sites scored 10, while the average score was a low 2.8. As with the previous content areas, interactivity showed a significant increase between 1998, when sites had an average score of 2.0, and 2000, when sites averaged 4.0 ($t=9.99$, df $=3.84$, $p<0.001$).

Focus and tone of homepages

Complementing the analysis of content were our measures of the focus and tone of the site's homepage. As Table 6.2 shows, sites were evenly balanced between complete focus on image (1) and on issue (7) with a mean score of 4.0 for all 383 sites. Overall, 73 sites (18.6 percent) were considered entirely image-oriented and 17 (4.3 percent) entirely issue-oriented. Interestingly, sites did become significantly more issue-focused between the election cycles, scoring 3.7 in 1998 and 4.2 in 2000 ($t=2.09$, df $=382$, $p<0.04$).

In terms of tone, the results show that overall the sites were very positive, scoring 1.7 on average (where 1 = all positive and 5 = all negative). In fact, 51.4 percent

(202) of the 385 valid homepages were entirely positive. Another 28 percent (111) were mostly positive, and 12 percent (48) had an even mix of positive and negative communication. Only 6 percent (24) were mostly or entirely negative. As Table 6.3 reports no marked differences were observed in the overall tone of the sites according to election cycle. After overall tone was analyzed, a more specific type of negative communication was examined. Attacking indicated the extent of negative communication directed specifically at opponents or their parties (measured on a scale where 1 equaled no attacking and 7 equals all attack). The results confirm that attacking was rare, with an average attack score of 1.9 (indicating that less than 10 percent of the site was devoted to attacking)

Table 6.3 Website content for Senate and gubernatorial candidates by year

Content item	*1998*	*2000*
Information		
Candidate biography	194(89.4)	159 (93.5)
Stand on issues	186 (85.7)	162 (95.9)***
Highlighting achievements	103 (47.5)	114 (85.2)***
News, press releases	139 (64.1)	128 (75.7)*
Voting information	79 (36.4)	154 (91.1)**
Separate links page	56 (25.7)	48 (28.2)
Constituent help information	38 (29.2)	14 (8.3)**
Information about opponent	40 (18.4)	71 (48.6)***
"Other" – novel information	33 (15.2)	70 (41.4)***
General government information	22 (10.1)	29 (17.2)*
Information about family	18 (8.3)	81 (55.0)***
Graphical elements		
Photo/graphic	199 (90.9)	169 (99.4)***
Animation	82 (37.6)	91 (75.8)***
Video/audio	44 (20.2)	60 (35.3)***
Interactivity		
E-mail address	158 (72.8)	154 (91.1)***
"Get involved" CGI form	85 (39.2)	101 (59.8)***
Online contributions accepted	43 (19.8)	104 (61.5)***
Other interactivity	38 (17.5)	43 (25.4)
Subscription service	30 (13.8)	88 (51.7)***
Downloadable content	20 (9.2)	58 (34.3)***
Search capacity	11 (5.1)	17 (10.1)
Guestbook	11 (5.1)	6 (3.6)
Cyber bumper stickers	10 (4.6)	14 (8.3)
Data collection of visitors	8 (3.7)	39 (23.1)***
Voter survey	6 (2.8)	27 (14.4)***
Bulletin board	7 (3.2)	19 (11.2)**

Notes

Figures are raw '*n*' followed by percentages in parentheses. Percentages refer to the overall number of sites containing the specified item in a given year. Chi-square statistics test for significant increases or decreases in numbers of sites containing content items between 1998 and 2000. A p value <0.05 is indicated by *; ** indicates $p<0.01$; and *** $p<0.001$.

and 63 percent of homepages were entirely void of attacks. However, as Table 6.3 shows, sites in 2000 were significantly more attack-oriented than in 1998 (2.4 versus 1.5, $t = 6.25$, $df = 384$, $p < 0.001$). Therefore, while sites were quite positive overall, negative campaigning in the form of attacking opponents did creep into campaign sites in 2000.

By way of expanding on the changes in the mean scores of the content variables reported in Table 6.2, Table 6.3 presents a breakdown of the frequencies for individual items across the two years.

From Table 6.3 it is apparent that although there was an overall increase in information provision over time, some items did appear less frequently in 2000, notably, candidate biographies, links pages, and help to constituents. While the fall in biographical and linkage information is rather puzzling, the drop in the constituent help might be explained by the fact that fewer candidates were relying on government sites by 2000, which arguably, would be more likely to focus on serving constituent needs. In 1998, fifty-one of the sites analyzed were classified as official government and party sites and by 2000 this had dropped to sixteen. Graphical elements featured more heavily on all sites by 2000, with all but one site containing a photo and more than a third carrying audio or video. As Table 6.4 shows, however, it was animation that proved to be the most popular new addition, with almost three-quarters of sites featuring it in 2000 as opposed to just over a third in 1998. In-depth probing of interactivity between the election years reveals that while several types increased significantly over time, the biggest jumps were in tools that allowed visitors to register their support through volunteer forms or online contributions. Opportunities to sign up for news bulletins also increased substantially, as did forms for data collection about users. As Table 6.3 shows, the most commonly available feature, however, remained E-mail contact across both years.

Regression analysis

From these results it would appear that election year or time plays a key role in determining the nature of web campaigning among US candidates. However, these differences might also simply be a function of the larger number of gubernatorial sites analyzed in 1998 compared with 2000. In order to identify the independent impact of these factors, along with a range of other potential influences on candidates' website usage we employ ordinary least squares regression. Thus, the scores for content and tone (as dependent variables) were regressed on a series of dummy variables created to capture the effects of election year and office sought, along with candidate's gender, party affiliation, and status as a political insider, and whether the race was open or included an incumbent. The results are reported in Table 6.4.

The findings, reported in Table 6.4, confirm that election year is indeed the key variable influencing candidates' website production. Senatorial and gubernatorial sites in 2000 were basically far more functional yet also rather more aggressive and negative than had been the case in 1998. In short, the sites were richer and more sophisticated in the three content categories of information, graphics, and interactivity, and overall slightly less image focused, but also more negative in tone.

Table 6.4 Results of regression analyses of content and style measures of candidates' websites

Independent variables	*Information*	*Graphics*	*Interactivity*	*Focus*	*Tone*	*Attack*
Office sought 0 = Sen., 1 = Gov.	−0.004 (0.172)	−0.255** (0.144)	−0.458* (0.199)	0.708** (0.209)	−0.004 (0.098)	−0.449** (0.146)
Standing 0 = insider, 1 = outsider	−0.562* (0.238)	−0.165 (0.118)	−0.316 (0.275)	0.539 (0.290)	0.427** (0.135)	0.449* (0.202)
Party 0 = major, 1 = minor	−1.42*** (0.241)	−0.261* (0.119)	−1.34*** (0.279)	0.779** (0.294)	0.117 (0.137)	0.002 (0.205)
Race type 0 = open, 1 = incumb.	−0.289 (0.181)	−0.127 (0.090)	−0.484* (0.210)	−0.003 (0.219)	0.245* (0.103)	0.267 (0.154)
Year 0 = 1998, 1 = 2000	2.25*** (0.168)	0.335*** (0.083)	1.95*** (0.194)	0.579** (0.204)	0.002 (0.096)	0.701*** (0.143)
Gender 0 = male, 1 = female	0.107 (0.223)	−0.008 (0.111)	0.411 (0.259)	0.168 (0.272)	−0.002 (0.127)	−0.274 (0.190)
Model Adjusted R^2	0.458	0.126	0.343	0.125	0.085	0.149

Notes

Each column indicates a separate regression. Unstandardized betas are reported first, followed by their standard error in parentheses below. A p value <0.05 indicated by *; $p<0.01$ by **; and $p<0.001$ by ***.

After election year, however, the most important influence on websites was type of office being sought and also the party affiliation of the candidate. Specifically, while Senate and gubernatorial candidates offered similar amounts of information on their sites, the former offered significantly more interactivity and graphics and tended to focus more on image rather than issues. Major party candidates offered more of everything in terms of content on their site, although minor party candidates did tend to be less personalized and focus more on the issues. In terms of the impact of other factors, it seems having held office before (being a political insider) led one to provide more information and take a more positive stance. Outsiders were significantly more likely to adopt a more negative tone and attack other candidates. Those races where incumbents were running also tended to see more negativity but also were more focused on interactivity. Gender was notably not important as a predictor of any of the features of campaign websites measured here.

Discussion

So do these findings reveal the new media to be an arena for innovation and change? At first glance one might argue they tell a largely unimpressive story. Sites for major party candidates had more of everything than did those of the minor parties in terms of information, graphics, and interactivity although they did tend to be less focused on policy issues than minor party sites. Political insiders (incumbents and other past or current office holders) also made more information available and tended to be more positive in tone than political outsiders. Although this study didn't examine candidates' financial commitments to the sites, these results support the idea that established political forces are reinforcing their offline dominance (Margolis *et al.* 1997; Norris 2000). One interesting caveat to note here, however, is that while women ran fewer sites than men in both election years, those that did, displayed no significant differences in content and style to their male counterparts, according to the measures used here. While this finding should be treated with some caution given the small number of female candidates included in the analysis, it does raise the interesting possibility of the web as a gender-neutral communications terrain. As such it would clearly differ from previous forms of media advertising where distinct differences have been observed (Trent and Friedenberg 1983; Johnson-Cartee and Copeland 1997).

Despite evidence of a resurfacing of preexisting patterns of political influence, however, these findings also indicative that candidates are becoming more functional and experimental in their approach to the web. Specifically, it seems candidates are becoming savvier in using the web to disseminate news to voters and the media. Certainly journalists are becoming keener to incorporate campaign sites into their election coverage, linking to them directly or telling their audience to visit their sites for more information. In addition, the interactivity of the Internet is clearly being exploited more in elections, with 2000 seeing the proliferation of voter surveys and volunteer forms on offer from candidates. Such initiatives, however, do not necessarily signal the move toward a more participatory democracy. More options for citizen input need to be met by a symmetrical response from elites in order to empower both parties. Indeed, as McKeown and Plowman (1999) have pointed out, much of the political elites' use of new ICTs has tended to take an asymmetrical form, involving voters in ways that are largely beneficial to the campaign.

In terms of how far the Internet is promoting the shift toward a postmodern style of campaigning, these results certainly show that the new technologies are producing a bifurcation in campaign strategy. Campaign websites are becoming both more informative and interactive, but are also using more sophisticated graphics and taking a more negative stance toward opponents. Thus, while websites may be allowing candidates to open up deeper and more direct channels of communication with voters than they had in the "modern" era, they are also being utilized in a flashier, attack-oriented manner. The fact that these changes are related most strongly to election year rather than type of office sought, type of party, or candidate gender, suggests that cyber-campaigning is evolving, to a certain extent on its own steam or according to its own logic, not as a result of a particular type of candidate or party approach.

Any nod to technological determinism here, however, is fleeting. The findings of this chapter essentially return us to the central theme of this volume – the importance of representative democracy as a context for political actors' use of the web. While candidates are showing signs of greater interest in the interactive capabilities of new ICTs, such deployment is generally oriented toward extracting resources from the citizen to aid the campaign, rather than for introducing new forms of direct democracy. Certainly, the reemergence of old habits in the form of negative advertising in the websites of 2000 suggests that candidates' approach to campaigning in the new media is not departing radically from existing practice. The extent to which these emergent trends continue over time, however, is of course a key issue for researchers to explore and one that we shall return to in the US presidential elections of 2004.

Bibliography

Bryant, J. (1995) "Paid Media Advertising," in Thurber, J. A. and Nelson, C. J. (eds), *Campaigns and Elections American Style*, Boulder, Colo.: Westview Press.

Birnbaum, J. (2000) "Politicking on the internet," *Fortune*, March, 84–6.

Corrado, A. (1996) "Elections in Cyberspace," in Corrado, A. and Firestone, C. (eds), *Elections in Cyberspace*, Washington, DC: The Aspen Institute.

D'Alessio, D. (2000) "Adoption of the World Wide Web by American Political Candidates, 1996–1998," *Journal of Broadcasting and Electronic Media*, 44, 556–68.

Davis, R. and Owen, D. (1998) *New Media and American Politics*, New York: Oxford University Press.

Dulio, D. A., Goff, D. L. and Thurber, J. A. (1999) "Untangled web," *PS: Political Science & Politics*, 32 (1), 53–9.

Epstein, E. (1996) "Election '96 Internet Style," *PC World*, May, 174–80.

Faucheux, R. (1998) "How Campaigns Are Using the Internet," *Campaigns & Elections*, September, 22–6.

Fenno, R. F. (1996) *Senators on the Campaign Trail*, Norman, Okla.: University of Oklahoma.

Farrell, D. and Webb, P. (2000) "Political Parties as Campaign Organizations," in Dalton, R. and Wattenberg, M. (eds), *Parties Without Partisans*, Oxford: Oxford University Press, 102–28.

Fineman, H. (1999) "Pressing the Flesh Online," *Newsweek*, September 20, 50–3.

Gibson, R. and Ward, S. (1998) "U.K. Political Parties and the Internet," *Press/Politics*, 3 (3), 14–38.

Gibson, R. and Römmele, A. (2001) "A Party Centered Theory of Professionalized Campaigning," *International Journal of Press Politics*, 6 (4), 31–44.

Gibson, R., Römmele, A. and Ward, S. (2003) "German Parties and Internet Campaigning in the 2002 Federal Election," *German Politics*, 12 (1), 79–104

Greer, J. and LaPointe, M. E. (1999) "Meaningful Discourse or Cyber-Fluff? paper presented at the annual meeting of the International Communication Association, San Francisco, May 1999.

Hall, M. (1997) "One to One Politics in Cyberspace," *Media Studies Journal*, 2, 97–103.

Johnson-Cartee, K. S. and Copeland, G. A. (1997) *Inside Political Campaigns*, Westport, Conn.: Praeger.

Just, M. R. (1997) "Candidate Strategies and the Media Campaign," in Pomper G. M. *et al.* (eds), *The Election of 1996*, Chatham, NJ: Chatham House Publishers.

Kamarck, E. C. (1998) "Stalking the Wild Netizen," *Newsday*, October 25, B4.

Kamarck, E. C. (2002) "Political Campaigning on the Internet" in Kamarck, E. C. and Nye, J. S., Jr (eds), *Governance.com*, Washington, DC: Brookings, 81–103.

Klotz, R. (1997) "Positive Spin," *PS: Political Science & Politics*, 30 (3), 482–6.

Klotz, R. (1998) "Virtual criticism," *Political Communication*, 15, 347–65.

Kornblut, A. E. and Abraham, Y. (2000) "Campaign 2000 / Republicans Touting Conservative Themes, Bush Shifts Tone in SC," *The Boston Globe*, February 3, A28.

LaPointe, M. (1999) "Cyberpolitics and the U.S. Senate," unpublished thesis, University of Nevada-Reno.

Leiter, L. (1995) "Goodbye BBQ and Buttons, Hello Web and Home Page," *Insight on the News*, September 25, 46–8.

Lynch, M. (2001) "E-lection Wrap-Up," *Chief Executive Magazine*, January, 24–8.

Margolis, M., Resnick, D., and Tu, C. (1997) "Campaigning on the Internet," paper presented at the annual meeting of the American Political Science Association, Washington, DC, September 1997.

McKeown, C. A. and Plowman, K. D. (1998) "Reaching Publics on the Web During the 1996 Presidential Campaign," paper presented at the annual meeting of the Association for Education in Journalism and Mass Communication, Baltimore, Md., August 1998.

McManus, T. (1999a) "A Democratic Medium Plays Big 2000 Role," *Advertising Age*, October 11, 62–4.

McManus, T. (1999b) "Political Campaigns Pivot on Web," *Advertising Age*, December 13, 76.

Meadow, R. G. (1989) "Political Campaigns," in Rice, R. and Atkin, C. (eds), *Public Communication Campaigns*, Newbury Park, CA: Sage.

Miller, G. and Schrader, E. (1998) "Internet's Role in Campaigns Still Limited," *Los Angeles Times*, October, 28, A1.

Norris, P. (2000) *A Virtuous Circle*, Cambridge, UK: Cambridge University Press.

NUA (2002) *How Many Online* <http://www.nua.com/surveys/how_many_online/index.html>, first accessed December 12, 2002.

Pew Research Center (2000) *Youth Vote Influenced by Online Information* <http://people-press.org/reports/display.php3?ReportID = 21>, first accessed December 12, 2002.

Puopolo, S. (2001) "The Web and U.S. Senatorial Campaigns 2000," *The American Behavioral Scientist*, 44 (12), 2030–47.

Reavy, M. M. and Perlmutter, D. (1996) "Presidential Websites as Sources of Information," paper presented at the annual meeting of the Association for Education in Journalism and Mass Communication in Los Angeles, June 1996.

Shelton, S. (2000) "Candidates Warming Up to Internet; Plugged In," *The Atlanta Journal and Constitution*, June 4, 1JJ.

Sternberg, B. von (1999) "Cyber Campaign is Getting Crowded," *Star Tribune*, June 3, A6.

Tedesco, J. C. *et al.* (1999) "Presidential Campaigning on the Information Superhighway," in Kaid, L. L. and Bystrom, D. G. (eds), *The Electronic Election: Perspectives on the 1996 Campaign Communication*, Mahwah, NJ: Lawrence Erlbaum Associates.

Tillett, S. (2000) "Getting personal – Campaigns Deliver E-Business Lessons," *Internetweek*, September 25, 128.

Trent, J. S. and Friedenberg, R. V. (1983) *Political Campaign Communication*, New York, NY: Praeger.

Wring, D. and Horrocks, I. (2001) "The Transformation of Political Parties?" in Axford, B. and Huggins, R. (eds), *New Media and Politics*, London: Sage.

7 Global legal pluralism and electronic democracy

Oren Perez

> ... the age of photography corresponds precisely to the explosion of the private into the public, or rather into the creation of a new social value, which is the publicity of the private: the private is consumed as such, publicly.
>
> (Roland Barthes, *Camera Lucida: Reflections on Photography*, 1993: 98)

The emergence of the Internet has transformed the way in which we experience the private and public spheres. On the one hand the Internet has opened new ways for projecting private experiences into the public sphere using various webcast technologies. On the other hand, the Internet promises to reshape the boundaries of the public space. Political communication no longer needs to be centred on face-to-face interactions undertaken in uniquely designed spaces, but can be accessed from the private domain through atomized computer screens and electronically mediated interchanges. What does this blurring of old boundaries mean for the body politic? This chapter seeks to address this broad question with reference to one particular facet of the public sphere: the broadening realm of transnational law.

The increasing encroachment of international legal norms into the previously secluded boundaries of the nation state has raised questions about the legitimacy of this emergent system of governance. This chapter explores how the Internet might be used to address some of these concerns. In doing so, the chapter moves us beyond questions about the Internet's impact on established domestic institutions to examine its role as creator of wholly new representative structures, outside the national context. It is argued that new information and communication technologies (ICTs) do offer significant potential for the development of more inclusive transnational governing structures, but that the realization of such structures depends on focused intervention by civil society and the support of existing national and international bureaucracies. Any theorizing about the possibility of Net-induced democratization at the international level, therefore, must be situated within familiar analytical frameworks about 'collective action' and 'interest mobilization'. Thus, while the focus is on these new, extra-national legal actors, the chapter returns us to a central theme of the book – the understanding that technology alone cannot engineer change. The adoption of new ICTs, even among newly forming representative bodies without a long history or large constituencies, is subject to broader environmental constraints.

The emergence of new forms of global law that operate beyond the traditional geopolitical boundaries of the state system is a key component of the globalization process (Teubner 1997; Perez 2002). This expanding network of global laws is highly diverse, both in terms of its thematic interest and organizational structure. It includes new types of state-oriented systems such as the World Trade Organization (WTO), as well as private regimes covering areas such as technical standardization, governance of the Internet, and transnational commerce.

While many of these systems of transnational law have evolved in the shadow of the new global economy, their impact is not confined to the economic realm. International governance now extends to civic territories such as free speech, art, and the protection of the environment. The legal system of the WTO, for example, has dealt with disputes relating to the risks of synthetic growth hormones in cattle, the industrial use of asbestos, and damage caused to sea turtles from shrimp trawling.[1] International standards setting organizations such as the International Organization for Standardization (ISO) and the Codex Alimentarius Commission have been involved in the production of controversial standards for environmental management (the ISO 14000 series) and foods derived from biotechnology.[2]

The expanding geographic and normative framework of these international organizations has, not surprisingly, led to calls for increasing the openness and transparency of their operations. Coming in for particular scrutiny are the Bretton Woods triad of the WTO, the World Bank and the International Monetary Fund (IMF). The large-scale protests that took place in Seattle in 1998, and Québec, Gothenburg and Genoa in 2001 bear strong testimony to the growing public demand for greater accountability on the part of these organizations and increased awareness of the social and humanitarian consequences of their actions (Ecologist 2000).

The central impetus mobilizing these challenges, one can argue, is a procedural understanding of democratic legitimacy. The right of the transnational regime to govern is established by it allowing the affected community some say in the design and implementation of the ruling norms. In order to be legitimate, some measures need to be in place to ensure that public consent and control is provided.[3] The key issue, therefore, facing these new global legal and political entities, in the light of these challenges, is whether they can devise processes through which these ideals can be realized. Properly responding to this democratic deficit requires the development of inclusive and non-hierarchical decision-making structures, which could break the confines of the current nationalistic order, and offer the public direct access to processes of global norm-production.

This chapter focuses on the possible contribution that the Internet can make, and is making, to the development of these novel decision-making structures. In particular, it examines whether the Internet can offer ways to incorporate the public more meaningfully into the infrastructure of global legal regimes. The capacity of the Internet to short-cut barriers of space and time, make it, at least prima facie, the ideal medium for transnational deliberation. Indeed, this has been shown, somewhat ironically by the fact that the Internet has played a major role in facilitating the protests against these new global regimes. Protestors have used the Internet extensively, both to publicize their critique and, more instrumentally, to coordinate their actions. Websites such as Protest.Net, www.indymedia.org, www.WebActive.com and www.corpwatch.org have turned into 'hubs' of political communication. All of these websites include details of upcoming protests, action alerts and links to other protest websites. This extensive political usage of the Net has even led some commentators to assert that the Internet could revolutionize the face of global politics.[4] However, despite the impressive growth of civic protest over the Internet, the use of the Internet to incorporate the public in transnational governance processes appears to be very limited. The question remains, therefore, whether the Internet has indeed the capacity to foster more inclusive structures of global law-making.

The chapter addresses this question in three stages. First, the traditional conception of transnational governance is reviewed and its weaknesses for understanding and addressing the issues raised by the emerging system of global law are identified. A more contemporary interpretation of international regime formation is then presented that requires a democratic and truly global decision-making forum. Second, the role of the Internet as a means of realizing such ambitions is explored, using the idea of politics as a problem of 'collective action'. The discussion presents a simple game-theoretic model to illustrate the capacity of the Internet to facilitate the emergence of viable transnational communities. In the third and final section, three case studies are presented to show how some international regimes are currently attempting to utilize the Internet to facilitate a more democratic mode of operating. The focus here is on the WTO, the ISO and Internet Corporation for Assigned Names and Numbers (ICANN).

The problem of legitimacy and the Westphalian paradigm

According to the Westphalian, or intergovernmental paradigm of international regime formation, legitimacy rests with state consent – either to a specific set of norms (treaties) or to the establishment of a body with norm-producing powers such as the WTO (Caldwell 1996: 146). The consent of the state is secured through the actions of its authorized agents (state officials), and thus is only indirectly related to the wishes of the state citizenry (Petersmann 1999). This view of the creation and monitoring of international regimes is problematic on a number of grounds. First, from a procedural point of view, the idea that state officials represent and are bound by the preferences of the people is, at best, questionable. The constitutional framework of most states does not provide for any regular, or even sporadic opportunities for public consultation and discussion over transnational issues.

Even if the paradigm could be tweaked to provide for more direct democratic state-based supervision of transnational negotiations, however, it faces a more crucial problem of practical relevance. Essentially, this model has been overtaken by the new realities of norm creation at the international level. According to the Westphalian paradigm, the international organization is a highly controllable entity, which is wholly dependent on the states that created it. This vision of organizational obedience, however, fails to appreciate the increasingly autonomous nature of transnational organizations, as well as the fact that many systems of transnational law rely on bases of support that are located outside the state system. This kind of deep independence characterizes both state-oriented regimes such as the WTO, and global private regimes such as the *lex mercatoria*. To a large extent these legal systems operate as autonomous decision-making structures that are sheltered from the influence of interstate politics. In this sense the Westphalian model of detached polities and fragmented deliberation is wholly inappropriate as the basis for any new model of global cooperation. Indeed one can argue that it forms a barrier to the development of the more internationally oriented communicative processes that are needed by these regimes to enhance their legitimacy.

The legitimacy of these new forms of a-national law, therefore, requires the development of new, cross-border structures of decision-making, which will provide the public with more meaningful forms of participation. The argument of this chapter is that the Internet can provide such novel participatory structures through its ability to deliver 'direct deliberation' on a global scale. Direct deliberation interprets the democratic process as a 'collective decision-making that proceeds through direct participation by and reason-giving between and among free and equal citizens' (Cohen and Sabel 1997: 314). It defines the 'public arena' in which such deliberation takes place as a product of common aims or concerns, and not as a reflection of national identities. This interpretation of democracy as a legitimate way of 'living together' does not rely on the capacity of all-embracing deliberation to produce consensus (and hence, consent). Rather, the legitimizing force of democratic deliberation is postulated to rise from a culturally shared belief in the moral legitimacy of decisions, which were made through a fair and open dialogue. It is the openness of the deliberation process to all those concerned, and its relative fairness, which gives the democratic process its legitimizing power.

A model of electronic participation

This section seeks to assess whether the Internet can be used to construct more inclusive governance structures in the transnational domain. It considers in that context the differences between electronic and non-electronic participatory schemes. These questions are considered through a simple game-theoretic model, which is based on the understanding of politics as a problem of 'collective action'. The goal of using game theory here is to expose the strategic dilemmas that can arise from the introduction of a transnational scheme of e-participation. This exposition brings out more clearly both the various advantages of the Internet as a participatory medium, and its basic limitations.

Constructing a model of e-participation requires a clear definition of 'electronic democracy' or 'electronic participation'. It is possible to distinguish in this context between three different ways in which the Internet can be harnessed to the democratic process. First, the Internet constitutes an efficient means for achieving transparency. Indeed, as one author has put it 'The Internet can make genuinely public what has only been nominally public' (Starr 2000). Transparency is a necessary condition for the evolution of meaningful deliberation. Second, the Internet can be used by the international organization to elicit public comments on its normative output. Here, the Internet is used to facilitate unidirectional communication: the international organization – placed at the receiving end – is responsible for collecting, interpreting and judging the comments of the public. The deliberation process is controlled by the international organization. The Internet is not used here as a medium for conversation but only as a cost-effective delivery service, which carries messages between disassociated individuals and the relevant institution. Finally, the Internet can be used also to facilitate wide-ranging dialogue between the institution and the public and within the public itself. Under this multidirectional model none of the communicators has exclusive control over the timing and content of communications. Only this last option comes near the ideal picture of 'directly-deliberative democracy'.

The model developed in this section is based on a unidirectional participation scheme. This scheme was favoured for several reasons. First, from a pragmatic perspective it is probably a more realistic assessment of the scope of ambition among international institutions for new forms of public dialogue. Second, it is a simpler model but retains the basic collective-action dilemma that participation on an international level encounters, and that the Internet can purportedly help resolve. Thus, heuristically it is preferable. The model, following Olsonian logic, envisages participation as a game whereby 'public (or normative) goods' are secured as benefits that accrue to the (transnational) community as a whole, leaving costs to be borne (exclusively) by the individual participators. I leave the exact nature of the public good undefined. In our context it will usually reflect the possibility of bringing about a change in the content of a proposed transnational norm (hence the term 'normative good').

The structure of the model is as follows.[5] The relevant community (defined as the set of people who could be influenced by a particular transnational norm) consists of N people. Each member of the community faces a binary choice: they can either participate, with a cost of Ci, or not participate, in which Ci is saved (Ci reflects the direct costs of participation). It is assumed that the public good would be provided with probability α only if K people or more participate.[6] This assumption portrays the international organization in largely cynical terms, as responding only to the level of public pressure (modelled here as a function of the number of individual 'reactions'), rather than to the substantive quality of the arguments presented.[7] A successful participatory process yields for each of the N members an expected utility of Vi(Pg). Vi is a function of predetermined individual political/ideological preferences.[8]

From an individual perspective there are two major impediments to collective action. First, because the public good (Pg) could be provided (with probability α) only if the threshold K is achieved, any individual effort that would be made without the presence of additional $K-1$ contributions will be wasted (with probability 1). Thus, a player who believes that there will be, overall, only $K-1$ contributions (including his), will not find it in his interest to participate. Second, a player who believes that there are K participants (beside himself) will have little incentive to participate as his voice will not add to the probability of the public good being provided.[9] This means that – for an individual to contribute – it is not enough that the (expected) value of the public good should be greater than the cost of participation. Rather, a rational individual will make an effort to participate only if he believes that he is the Kth participant, that is, that he has a pivotal role in generating the public good. Before investing resources in the political game the individual would need, then, some assurance that his contribution is indeed critical. This turns the game of transnational deliberation into an 'assurance game'.

A preliminary condition for the emergence of a 'participatory community' is the existence of at least K individuals for whom the participation cost is smaller or equal to the expected value of the public good. The individual rationality condition requires, then, that:

$$\mathrm{Ci} \leq \mathrm{Vi}\ (\mathrm{Pg})^{10} \tag{1}$$

where Ci is the cost of participation and Vi(Pg) measures the expected utility of i from the public good. Assume that N' people (of the total community N) satisfy this basic condition. Under these assumptions the model anticipates two types of Nash equilibrium:[11]

(a) $N'!/(K!(N'-K)!$ that is all the possible combinations of K contributors out of the set N' of potential contributors.[12] We can interpret this number as representing the number of potential coalitions. I will denote the set of these coalitions as B_k (with $X_j \in B_k$ denoting a particular coalition).
(b) Another possible solution is one in which no one contributes.

It is possible to gain some insight into the question of individual criticality by comparing the number of potential solutions at N' and at $N'-1$. This comparison is based on the assumption that each individual evaluates his criticality by considering the influence of his withdrawal from the N' community in terms of the decrease in the number of potential coalitions. The effect of such withdrawal can be appreciated by expressing the number of potential solutions at $N'-1$ contributors (denoted B) in terms of the number at N' (denoted A):

$$B = A \times [(N'-K)/N']^{13} \tag{2}$$

Equation (2) points out two important features of the criticality question. First, when the value of N' (the group of potential contributors) is relatively large compared to K (the threshold community) the importance of each individual contribution decreases (since B approaches A). Second, because the value of A is likely to rise quickly with N', the value of B is likely to remain high even in small ratios of $(N' - K)/N'$; this will contribute again to a diminishing sense of criticality by an individual participant.[14]

It should be noted that the model outlined here does not purport to explain the process by which a particular equilibrium or coalition (out of these multifarious equilibria) is eventually selected. Extensive research on this so-called emergence puzzle, however, has revealed that larger groups exhibit lower levels of cooperation than smaller ones. The main reasons for this are thought to be the decline in perceived efficacy among individuals in a group as it expands. Basically those in larger groups are less likely to believe that their contribution is essential for the provision of the public good. This is consistent with the interpretation offered to equation (2).[15] In addition, the decreasing opportunities for communication in large groups are also seen to adversely influence the sense of solidarity and mutual commitment in these groups (Colman 1995: 218–21).[16] Overall, however, this research has still not resolved the problem of equilibria selection; it has only identified the kind of conditions in which the prospects for cooperation increase – the exact profile of this emerging cooperation remained uncertain (Ostrom 2000).[17]

The results of this research put a pessimistic note on the possibility of a transnational electronic community emerging *spontaneously*. A large and scattered collection of individuals provides a poor basis for the emergence of spontaneous cooperation. To incorporate these difficulties into the model, I have chosen to construct the selection puzzle as a problem of transaction cost, treating the lack of perceived efficacy and appropriate communication opportunities as barriers to the emergence of a threshold community. These costs are denoted C_T.[18] C_T reflects the costs of generating more opportunities for communication (within the relevant community), or of providing the potential participants with some kind of assurance that their 'voice' is critical.[19] C_T could be modelled as a function whose value increases (in a constant or decreasing rate) with the number of participants. It should probably contain also some fixed-cost element. The investment of C_T is treated, then, as a necessary condition for the emergence of a threshold community.

The introduction of the notion of transaction cost adds an additional constraint to the set of feasible equilibria.[20] To be viable any potential coalition should be able to fund the coordination costs; that is, the aggregate (net) value of the public good, within any viable coalition, should be higher than C_T. Formally, this idea could be represented in the following way:

$$\forall X_j \in B_k, X_j: \Sigma_{i=1,k}(\mathrm{Vi(Pg)} - \mathrm{Ci}) \geq C_T \quad (3)$$

This condition could be interpreted in two different ways. A first interpretation assumes that this 'hidden' value will be extracted and utilized by a group leader in order to finance the coordination effort. A second (and less literal) interpretation views this condition as an indicator of social concern rather than a fiscal attribute. This interpretation recognizes the possibility that some (but not all) of the coordination services will be provided and/or funded by external sources (e.g. public agency), without the presence of actual 'extraction' from the community. However, it assumes that for such external intervention to materialize, the external agency should be convinced that there is strong public interest in the provision of the public good.[21]

How will the introduction of electronic participation influence the results of this model? The first influence would be to reduce Ci. The term Ci consists of two main factors: the costs of gathering information on the subject of the political process (e.g. the details of a proposed international standard) and the participation costs (making your voice heard).[22] The introduction of the Internet reduces these costs. Getting information is now much easier, especially as more and more international institutions take seriously the demand for greater transparency (see the discussion in the third section). Further, the costs of responding to the information should decrease since the Internet opens up new and cheaper ways for submission of views. While the introduction of the Internet can also generate new types of costs such as information overload, these costs should be outweighed by the new efficiencies of retrieval and response, especially when users are focused on extracting particular information about a given normative dilemma.

A second, and even more crucial influence, concerns the coordination costs (C_T). The introduction of the Internet should reduce, substantially, the transaction costs associated with organizing a threshold community. In particular, the Internet opens up new and cheaper ways for institutional entrepreneurs to take the lead and organize a particular coalition.[23] Coordinating a threshold community requires the group leader to communicate with each of the group members. Such communication will usually contain information on the issue at hand, and a signal ensuring the criticality of the addressee. The Internet should reduce substantially the costs of this communication, by allowing the leader to use various automated tools for communication. Assuming that the introduction of the Internet has reduced the individual communication costs by a factor of λ, it is reasonable to assume that the coordination costs will be reduced by a factor of $K\lambda$.[24] This reflects the simple intuition that the group leader can use the Internet to interact simultaneously with all the members of the group. In the pre-Net era both Ci and C_T have been (in the transnational context) prohibitively high – blocking, in effect, the evolvement of transnational participatory schemes.

The introduction of Internet could thus turn the project of transnational participation into a truly practical option. The impact of the Net is not limited, however, to the issue of participation/coordination costs. The introduction of the Net could also influence the long-term dynamics of the transnational interaction. So far the participatory process was described as a single-shot process.[25] It was assumed that the participation would take place in the context of a particular discussion (e.g. around a specific transnational norm), and would not form an integral part of the law-making process. The political community would have to be formed anew in each round of participation (with repeated investments of the 'fixed-cost' element of C_T). With the Internet, the transforming of this 'scattered' process into a continuous one becomes much easier (and cheaper).[26] The Internet provides various cost-efficient means, through which an emerging transnational community could be kept alive through time. These include tools such as group lists, e-newsletters, chat-rooms, instant messaging and electronic archives. These different mechanisms enable both the facilitation of continuous conversation and the creation of (enduring) group memory. This kind of time-persistency is an essential element of a true polity.[27] In the pre-Net era, the cost of constructing such infrastructure on a global scale would have made it impossible to implement.

The Internet, then, is more than a cheap participation mechanism. Its extensive global reach and rich repertoire of community-sustaining techniques turn it into an essential tool in the effort to develop meaningful transnational democracy. Shifting the participation process into the electronic domain does not resolve, however, the basic collective-action dilemma that characterizes political action. Indeed, the model that was presented in this section makes clear that the emergence of e-participation cannot be taken for granted, and is strongly dependent on the availability of central direction. By emphasizing the 'enabling' and anarchistic character of the Net, many writers have tended to overlook this dependency (e.g. Hammond and Lash 2000), and its potential implications – in particular, the susceptibility of e-participation to hierarchical manipulation. Thus, one of the challenges facing those seeking to institutionalize mechanisms of e-participation is to find ways to promote coordinated activity yet keep the sponsors of such activity accountable.

Use of the Internet by international institutions

Having outlined, in theory, the usefulness of the Internet for facilitating wider involvement by civic actors in the creation and operation of international regimes, this section examines how far international organizations are meeting these expectations in practice. Three major global regulatory bodies are held up for scrutiny – the WTO, which replaced the General Agreement on Tariffs and Trade (GATT) in 1995; the ISO, which deals with issues of technical standardization; and the ICANN, which regulates the system of domain names on the Internet. These organizations present an interesting mix for analysis in terms of their overall Internet experience and embeddedness in the state system. The WTO and the ISO are both from the pre-Net era. The WTO, as a traditional treaty-based system, is rooted strongly in the Westphalian tradition, while the ISO is more of a hybrid organization in that its members are not governments, but national standardization bodies from some 140 countries. The ISO remains closely linked to the state system, however, in that some members are private bodies, for example, the British Standards Institution, whereas some are governmental agencies, for example, the French Standards Agency, AFNOR (Association française de normalisation).

ICANN, by contrast, is a new, Internet-spawned phenomenon that relies extensively on new technology to carry out its functions. While it relies to a certain degree on the backing of the state system, its jurisdiction and legitimacy are highly dependent on the non-governmental sector. Given its more intimate connection to the Internet, and greater detachment from established national actors, ICANN is anticipated to be more adept in exploiting the innovative and participatory uses of the technology than either the WTO or the ISO.

The chapter turns first to the case of the WTO. The establishment of the WTO was a triumphant culmination of a long institutionalization process that began in 1947 with the establishment of the GATT (Jackson 1997: 31–78). The WTO is concerned, primarily, with the facilitation of transnational commerce and the abolition of trade barriers. The WTO differs from its predecessor, the GATT, in two key respects. First, unlike the weak dispute settlement (DS) system of the GATT, the WTO DS system is highly independent, and is much more immune to political pressures. Its establishment has marked the creation of a new and independent source of normative power in the global arena (Perez 2001: 73–103). Second, the normative setting of the WTO is far more ambitious than that of the GATT. It is not limited to a single trade-sector or to one type of regulatory barrier, but reflects a broad attempt to integrate the global economy. This jurisdictional expansion has resulted in an increased incidence of conflicts between trade and other societal objectives such as environmental protection, and a growing public critique of its legitimacy and accountability (Charnovitz 1996; Esty 1999).

One way in which the WTO has sought to respond to this perception of a democratic deficit has been to increase the transparency of its operations, and to do so it has turned to the web. Almost all of the WTO documents, including secretariat reports, committee protocols and judicial decisions are accessible online – no mean feat especially when one considers the cloak of secrecy that characterized GATT proceedings. In addition, the WTO sought to promote wider public 'engagement' in its affairs, and again the Internet was seen as a crucial part of this strategy. A dedicated community forums section was created on the website that was designed to serve the interests of the media, NGOs and the general public. The goal being to 'provide an opportunity for the public to comment on the WTO, its activities, and the trading system'.[28] In this section participants could post messages, converse with one another in chat rooms and occasionally in WTO-initiated question and answer sessions, with WTO personnel and outside experts.[29] Particular emphasis has been placed on NGOs on the WTO website with special pages set up to brief and interact with NGOs in the months leading up to the fourth Ministerial Conference that took place in Doha, Qatar in November 2001.[30]

While these initiatives are laudable they do not appear to be leading to any great leaps forward in terms of public engagement. As of mid-July 2001 there were less than 250 messages posted on the WTO Forum, a low number by any account and particularly so if one takes into account its growing public profile, especially among the Internet-using segment of the population. While the low level of interest may be due to lack of awareness of the participatory opportunities offered on the website, it may also be due to the lack of formal standing for the community forum within the WTO decision-making structure. The site does not indicate how any feedback will be used by the organization. The opening paragraph to the 'NGO room', for instance states that the WTO 'recognizes the role NGOs can play to increase the awareness of the public in respect of WTO activities' but does not provide details about how NGOs can contribute more meaningfully to the substantive work of the WTO.[31] Overall, therefore, the WTO is linking new communication technologies to an emerging recognition of the legitimate political role of NGOs in its deliberations. However, for practical purposes such groups remain largely outside the decision-making process.

The global push towards standardization has become encapsulated in a wide variety of international organizations governing areas such as electronic engineering and telecommunication, the International Electromechanical Commission (IEC); food standards, the Codex Alimentarius Commission; and technical standards, the ISO. While the products of these organizations are to a large extent voluntary, the globalization process and the new regime of the WTO has in effect upgraded their status, making it much more difficult for both private players and states to disregard them (Perez 1998). Further, despite the apparently specialized and remote nature of their work, such bodies do have far-reaching social implications that merit deeper public scrutiny. Perhaps the strongest example of such societal importance is the ISO and its work in developing a new set of environmental standards – the ISO 14000 series – covering a range of practices relating to management systems, auditing, performance evaluation, labelling and life cycle assessment (Murray 1999: 40–9). Unlike some of ISO's other products, the ISO 14000 series is not really 'technical' – in the sense that it is not composed of detailed technological or emissions protocols. The ISO 14000 series has a broader agenda, which is to teach organizations, in a general and abstract fashion, 'how to think about environmental problems'. Furthermore, this normative agenda is not limited to the corporate realm. The ISO 14000 series seeks, in effect, to provide a comprehensive discourse, which would be used by society as a whole, for judging the environmental behaviour of organizations.

Despite the broad normative implications of this series, however, the project was not subjected to a wide deliberative process (UNCTAD 1996). The standard-making process in the ISO provides overall few opportunities for public participation.[32] The main 'legislative' work is carried out by ISO technical committees and subcommittees; only ISO members have the right to participate in the work of the various committees, that is, to receive drafts, make comments and approve ISO standards.[33] The ISO online presence does little to break the 'closure' of its norm-production process. The ISO website (www.iso.ch) does not offer real opportunities for public involvement. External observers cannot consult existing standards or drafts of future standards but are required to purchase them from the ISO, which retains intellectual property rights to them.

Such practices certainly cast considerable doubt over the ISO claim that 'it shall strive at all times to perfect the application of consensus and transparency principles in standardization, and in this way promote the values of rationality, utility, safety and environmental protection for the benefit of all peoples' (ISO 1999: 3). Internally, however, uses of new communication technologies have been more successfully directed towards opening up decision-making processes. During 2001 a sophisticated system of electronic balloting was introduced, which was designed to speed up the process of voting and securing feedback on ISO draft standards.[34]

The Net – one of the key social domains of the modern society – is also subject to extensive regulation by a-national sources. With the growing importance of the Net as a medium for communication, the question of its control has become an issue of deep social concern. Since its early years of popular use the net has changed from a space of absolute freedom to a more regulated environment (Lessig 2000). One of the key organizations to emerge in this regard has been the ICANN – a non-profit corporation formed in 1999 with far-reaching powers to manage the Internet.[35] Specifically, ICANN bears responsibility for managing the Internet protocol (IP) address space allocation and the domain name system. Domain names are addresses of websites and comprise two levels: the generic top-level domain name space (i.e. 'com', 'net', 'org', etc.) and the unique country-code top-level domains such as 'uk' for United Kingdom and 'il' for Israel. One of the main concerns that accompanied its creation was how to ensure that this new body would respect the egalitarian and free spirit of the Internet. To achieve this ICANN was founded on the principles of an inclusive governance structure that would utilize the unique advantages of the Internet. It was seen as a novel alternative to the traditional, pre-Internet model of a multinational governmental treaty organization.

The regulation of the ownership of domain names provides a good example to ICANN's vast powers. The registration of domain names is based on a simple registration rule of first-come, first-served. The openness of this system, however, enabled people to register a domain name with an offline counterpart that they did not hold the moral or legal rights to, such as trademarks and personal and organizational names (a practice that became known as cyber-piracy or cyber-squatting). ICANN, together with the World Intellectual Property Organisation (WIPO) developed a global, web-based, dispute settlement system for resolving trademark domain name disputes.[36] The rules became effective in October 1999 and have been employed since then in disputes involving a wide range of 'names', from Julia Roberts, to Dior, Penguin Books, and Nandos.[37] While the establishment of this system was seen as necessary to further development of the Internet, it raises difficult questions with respect to the proper balance between corporate interests (trademark holders) and the interests of the ordinary Net users.

ICANN's inclusive strategy was based on three key elements. First, it sought to provide maximum transparency by offering accurate and timely descriptions of its regulatory agenda via its website. Second, it attempted to secure public feedback, again through its website, by offering opportunities for comment on its regulatory and policy-development work.[38] Finally, ICANN sought to incorporate the public directly into its governing apparatus through its universal representative scheme, called the 'at-large membership' programme. According to ICANN's by-laws its board should consist of nine public directors from a total of eighteen.

The 'at large' programme developed and implemented an electronically mediated voting process that enabled the Internet community to elect at-large directors to ICANN's board. The global election took place in 2000.

ICANN's strategy represented a bold attempt to build a new type of global governance. However, over the last two years, its inclusive structure, and in particular the at-large programme, have been subject to increasing internal criticism. The view within ICANN was that a system of electronic voting that is based on email addresses to identify individuals – the system that was used in the 2000 election – cannot reliably represent public interest. It was argued that this mechanism is 'administratively and financially unworkable on a global scale for a sizeable electorate, and fraught with potential dangers ranging from capture to outright fraud' (ICANN-At-Large-Study-Committee 2001). The dual qualification system, which was used in the 2000 elections and required each voter to have an email and postal address as physical proof of existence, was seen as cumbersome and highly impractical (ICANN-At-Large-Study-Committee 2001). In view of these difficulties ICANN is currently considering alternative participatory mechanisms that will be less ambitious in terms of their democratic profile, but, arguably, will allow it to serve more efficiently the interests of the Internet community (Lynn 2002). Such reforms, however, were strongly criticized by external observers (Klein 2001).

Despite the scaling back of some of its participatory ambitions, these efforts by ICANN to incorporate the public in the management of the Net represents a radical departure from the notion of 'indirect supervision' contained within the state-centred model of international regime formation, as outlined earlier. As expected, the WTO and the ISO have made rather less-strident efforts to harness the technology in the service of direct democracy. It would be wrong to dismiss their efforts as merely cosmetic gestures, however. The fact that both of these pre-Net organizations have made a deliberate effort to use the Internet to open up new opportunities for participation signals a significant shift towards greater openness. Indeed, what is common to ICANN, the WTO and the ISO (albeit to varying degrees), is that they all used the new ICTs to cut the transaction barriers that have impeded the development of meaningful participatory processes in the pre-Net era. The websites of the WTO and ICANN (and to a less degree the ISO) include some of the features discussed in the second section as necessary for the emergence of viable transnational communities, such as easily available information and chat-rooms. Thus, while none of these organizations' use of new ICTs comes close to the ideals of the anti-globalization movement or of democratic purists, their activities, particularly those of ICANN, indicate a firm commitment to finding a model of e-politics that can serve as a basis for a more inclusive transnational politics in the future.

Conclusions

The chapter began with the question of whether the Internet opens the way for meaningful participation in the production of transnational norms. The answer to this question was provided in two ways. First, I explored theoretically whether the Internet could provide conditions that were supportive of participatory communities at the international level by reducing both the costs of individual participation and the transaction costs associated with the construction of a threshold community. The capacity of the Internet to reduce barriers of time and space along with its ability to sustain a high volume of multi-directional communications (connectivity), and to provide efficient archive services (memory) were seen as providing very strong potential for the efficient organization of transnational political action. I then turned to a series of 'real-world' examples of international organizations that were applying the Internet to their operating practices for some insight into how far these theoretical expectations could be realized. The evidence from our three examples of the WTO, the ISO and ICANN revealed that while not fully realizing Internet-based participatory democracy, these organizations were making notable strides towards utilizing the medium to render themselves more participatory and accountable.

One of the key lessons to have emerged from the game-theory model, however, was that despite its various advantages, the Internet does not eliminate the collective-action problem that permeates any political endeavour. The emergence of spontaneous cooperation over the Net cannot be taken for granted. This was certainly demonstrated in the three case studies analyzed, since all revealed a reliance on some form of central coordination to facilitate online participation. Such dependency on centralized direction of course introduces additional tensions in terms of the risks to free expression and the emergence of technocratic elite. The challenge here, therefore, is to devise mechanisms that could ensure the meaningfulness of the deliberation process, despite the existence of such 'residual' authority. Take, for example, the transnational process of standard setting. It is possible to imagine several mechanisms by which the integrity of the deliberative process could be guaranteed. First, the constitution of the international organization should ensure that the public is given a meaningful role in decision-making structures. The organization could be obliged, for example, to collect a certain threshold number of public comments before submitting a standard for approval, and to incorporate a specified number of these comments into the final rule. There could also be a requirement for making public the reasons for rejecting any civic proposals. Electronically available archives of public comments should allow readers to check these institutional commitments. Such obligations could counter the current tendency of public officials to discount electronic mail, which is perceived as 'cheap talk', and give more credence to traditional modes of communication (Bimber 2001: 3).

Aside from these more generic barriers to developing meaningful forms of Internet-based participation, one should not disregard the additional 'technological' challenges that international organizations face in setting up Net-based participation. One obvious challenge comes in the shape of the electronic global divide. A fair and equitable scheme of electronic participation cannot be implemented without the support of a highly accessible computer network. This is certainly not the case for many countries in the world today. There are big gaps in the percentage of Internet usage between the developed and developing regions. The 2001 UNDP annual report notes that while in high-income OECD countries (excluding the United States) 28 per cent of the population are connected to the Net (54 per cent in the United States), the percentage in developing regions ranges from 3.9 per cent in Eastern Europe to 0.4 per cent in Sub-Saharan Africa and South Asia (UNDP 2001: 13). A further threat to the project of electronic participation in the transnational realm is the potential it holds for identity fraud. The greater anonymity and remoteness of cyberspace makes authentication of individuals problematic in general, but when one moves to the global level this problem is compounded, as ICANN discovered when trying to implement its 'at-large' elections.

E-democracy, therefore, does not resolve some of the chief dilemmas of democratic political action. However, it does offer one of the most promising paths by which the public can be incorporated into the 'making' of global law. As was indicated in the third section this process has already begun. The experiences of the WTO, the ISO and ICANN provide useful lessons for utilizing the new ICTs to support new participatory schemes. The challenge society is facing today is to continue this experimentation process and extend it to other transnational domains.

Notes

1 See: *EC – Measures Concerning Meat and Meat Products (Hormones)*, Report of the Appellate Body, WT/DS26/AB/R, WT/DS48/AB/R, 16 January 1998; *United States – Import Prohibition of Certain Shrimp and Shrimp Products*, Report of the Appellate Body, WT/DS58/AB/R, 12 October 1998; *European Communities – Measures Affecting Asbestos and Asbestos-Containing Products*, Report of the Appellate Body, WT/DS135/AB/R, 12 March 2001.

2 The ISO 14000 series is a wide-ranging collection of international, voluntary environmental standards, which deals with a variety of corporate management issues. For details on the Codex Commission see <http://www.codexalimentarius.net/>.

3 This view of legitimacy stands in contrast to non-procedural accounts that are based on the compatibility of a regime with a particular understanding of the common good. Such accounts are problematic since they presuppose an agreed-upon definition of the common good, and leave unresolved the question of the criteria for determining compatibility. For more extensive discussions of these issues see Bodansky (1999), and Weiler (1997).

4 See 'The Changing Face of Protest', *The Financial Times*, 31 July/1 August 1999: 12; Guy de Jonquie 'Network Guerrillas', The Financial Times, 30 April 1998 (commenting on the successful campaign against the OECD failed Multilateral Agreement on Investment).

5 The model builds on a long tradition of threshold public-goods models, which started with Olson's 'The Logic of Collective Action'. See, for example: McLean (2000: 655), Palfrey and Rosenthal (1994), and Rapoport (1985).

6 It is assumed here that the public protest has a discrete effect: that is, the political good would be provided with some probability (e.g. α) in K, but not in $K-1$. α does not increase in K. It is possible to relax this assumption and to build a model that links between the numbers of participants and the probability of the political good being provided. I do not pursue this path here.

7 In real life, public reactions are likely, of course, to differ in their content and effect. This could reflect the lack of a clear consensus in the public, and various other factors (e.g. the fact that the identity of the commentator might influence the response of the international organization). On the assumptions of our model the debated norm will not be changed unless there are at least K people, which agree that this change is worthwhile.

8 In my model Vi is constructed as a purely instrumental variable. I thus do not assume that the act of participation holds some intrinsic value for the participator, which is independent of the instrumental value of his political action. This assumption is somewhat contrary to Downs (1957) famous calculus of voting. Downs argued that voting holds an intrinsic value for voters, which reflects a citizen's sense of duty towards the community in which he lives and his desire to preserve the institution of 'democracy'. I believe, however, that this assumption is inappropriate to the transnational game discussed here. Downs's argument takes place within a well-established community, with shared values, tradition and history. None of these exists, a priori, in the transnational context. A citizen's duty is something that evolves parallel to the emergence of a community; it is not something that could be presumed independently of such emergence. The notion of civic duty cannot provide, then, an exclusive and independent explanation to the individual decision to participate. It becomes part of the strategic calculus that characterizes the participation process, and thus cannot resolve the puzzle of its original emergence.

9 This is a reflection of my earlier assumption that raising the number of participants from N to $N+1$ does not increase the probability of the good being provided. Relaxing this assumption could change the reasoning profile of a potential contributor. In such a case, an individual might still decide to contribute, even though he believes there are K contributors (without himself), if he believes that the increase in the probability of the political good being provided (caused by his participation) would be higher than his participatory costs. This, of course, could change the game equilibria.

10 Another implicit condition is that the net value of the political action – (Vi(Pg) – Ci) – is larger than the (net) value of any alternative action – the outside option – that the individual could have pursued instead (in or outside the Net). Otherwise, even if condition (1) is satisfied, the individual will not take this path.

11 I assume that $k \neq 1$ and $k \neq N$. It is assumed also that the rules of the game, as well as the values of all the relevant factors (e.g. of K, N', α) are common knowledge.

12 Each of these combinations represents a stable Nash Equilibrium because none of the players has an incentive to deviate from it unilaterally. None of the $N-N'$ players will have an incentive to participate because for them Ci > Vi(Pg). None of the $N'-K$ players will have an incentive to participate because, although for them Ci ≤ Vi(Pg), by not participating they can save Ci but still get Vi(Pg). As to the K participants – because each of them believes (by assumption) that he is 'pivotal', he would not defect because this would mean losing Vi(Pg) – Ci.

13 Since $B/A = [(N' - c)!/(K!(N' - 1 - K)!]/[N'!/(K!(N' - K)!] = (N' - K)/N'$.

14 A numerical example could help in illustrating the dilemma facing an individual participant (i), in deciding whether to participate in a political game. Imagine that there are thirty potential participants (N') and that the size of the threshold community (K) is 10. The first solution that was noted above means that there are 30!/(10!(30 – 10)!), that is 30045015 possible equilibria (or coalitions). If the individual would rule himself out of the potential contributors there would still be 29!/(29!(29 – 10)!) or 20030010 potential equilibria. While the number of potential coalitions was reduced by one-third it remained high enough to discount any sense of individual criticality, making 'free-riding' an appealing option. Note, however, that if all the members of the community would follow this line of reasoning none would contribute. Thus, i is facing two plausible, but contradictory predictions, in which his investment is portrayed as both critical and redundant.

15 For studies that examined the extent to which the perception of 'individual efficacy' plays a role in the decision of individuals to contribute to the provision of public goods, see Colman (1995: 215–21), and Yamagishi and Cook (1993).

16 Ostrom *et al.* (1994) conducted a thorough investigation of the problem of public-good provision under various laboratory settings. Their findings indicate that adding opportunities for communication in the game yields, in a very consistent fashion, higher levels of cooperation. See, Ostrom *et al.* (1994: 145–69, 195–9).

17 The profile of any selected equilibrium (or coalition) should be treated probably as a random phenomenon, caused by accidental fluctuations and unplanned perturbations in the border between society and consciousness. A similar uncertainty exists in the case of physical systems. See Kelso (1995 10).

18 For this broad interpretation of the idea of transaction cost, see Calabresi (1991).

19 To the critical role of 'assurance' in the emergence of cooperation in prisoner-dilemma type games, see, for example, Hayashi *et al.* (1999).

20 Going beyond this image of 'transaction costs' as a constraint on the number of viable coalitions requires a very detailed description of the mechanism that will be used to counter any transaction barriers. The features of this mechanism (e.g. the intervention of a group leader seeking to construct a threshold community) will determine a new game. As it is impossible to provide a complete catalogue of these potential mechanisms, the structure of this unfolding game and the strategic dilemmas it generates, cannot be specified in advance. However, what is important in our context is that there are convincing empirical studies, which show that offering more opportunities for communication and assurance signals raises the prospects of cooperation. For an example of a concrete analysis, which explores the effect of a particular coordination mechanism (recommended contributions) on the voluntary provision of public goods, see Croson and Marks (2001).

21 Assuming some kind of institutional intervention does not mean that we should rule out the potential role of private group-leaders. Even if the public agency agrees to fund (or provide directly) some of the coordination services (e.g. website facilities) it could still leave the stage open for external leaders.

22 The introduction of the Internet should also reduce the opportunity costs of participation by reducing the time needed for participation.

23 This term is from Canan and Reichman, which gives a detailed account of the role of institutional entrepreneurs in the development of the Ozone regime (2002: 188–9).

24 As was noted earlier C_T is comprised of two elements. variable and fixed. Here I refer only to the variable element.

25 This single-shot image is also consistent with the national experience – for example, in the context of environmental impact assessment regimes which are also geared towards single-shot rounds of participation (Biswas 1992: 240–1; Dipper *et al.* 1998: 735).

26 Assuming that the political game is a repeated game (with infinite horizon) rather than a single-shot game increases substantially the number of potential equilibria. For our needs it would suffice to say that any solution of the single-shot game is also a solution of the infinite game. Thus, any viable coalition of the base game will constitute a solution to the repeated game. Furthermore, any combination of these coalitions could also serve as a solution of the repeated game (to operationalize such a solution we would need some randomizing device that would 'pick' a different coalition at each stage-game; because any such coalition is a Nash solution to the stage game such solution would be incentive compatible). See, Ostrom *et al.* (1994: 71–2).

27 An additional advantage of this time persistency is that it provides some immunity from fluctuations in the saliency of a particular transnational domain.

28 See <www.wto.org/english/forums_e/forums_e.htm>, accessed 17 July 2001.

29 A recent WTO-initiated discussion focused on 'Trade and Sustainable Development' <http://www.itd.org/forums/tsdfor.htm>. Message postings have focused on issues

such as 'Protest and WTO', 'Environment and WTO' and 'Is the WTO inherently evil?' (WTO Forum; accessed 17 July 2001).

30 See <www.wto.org/english/forums_e/ngo_e/ngo_e.htm> also, 'WTO Secretariat activities with NGOs', WT/INF/30, 12 April 2001, and the NGO information page for the fourth Ministerial Conference, available at <http://www-chil.wto-ministerial.org/english/thewto_e/minist_e/min01_e/min01_ngo_e.htm>, accessed 16 December 2001.

31 Ibid.

32 A thorough discussion of ISO 'constitutional' framework is beyond the scope of this chapter. For a more detailed discussion, see UNCTAD Report (UNCTAD 1996: 21–40). It is particularly enlightening in this context to compare the ISO to a recent global initiative – the 'Global Reporting Initiative' (GRI) – which, through a much more open and inclusive process, seeks to develop standards of sustainability reporting. For further details see the GRI website <www.globalreporting.org>

33 The details of the standard-setting process are set in *ISO/IEC Directive (Part 1): Procedures for the Technical Work* (a copy of which is available from the ISO website). A brief description can be found in the document *Stages of the Development of International Standards* <www.ISO.ch/infoe/proc.html>, accessed 1 March 2001. The ISO constitution distinguishes between three forms of membership: full members have the right to participate as P-members in Technical Committees, which gives them the right and obligation to vote on all questions submitted for voting within the technical committee, including enquiry drafts and Final Draft International Standards. Correspondent Members can only participate in the standard-setting work as Observing-Members (O-Members), which allows them to attend meetings, receive documents and submit comments. A third category – subscriber membership – usually for countries with very small economies, establishes only a very limited contact with the ISO. See, *Introduction to ISO*, available at <www.iso.ch>, and paras. 1.7 – 1.7.5 of ISO/IEC Directive (part 1). NGOs can only gain access to the ISO standard-setting process as 'Liaison' organizations, a status that enable them to observe the standard-setting process, but does not give them formal voting rights. Furthermore, to gain this limited access, NGOs have to get the approval of the ISO Chief Executive Officer. See paras. 1.15 – 1.15.5 of ISO/IEC Directive (part 1).

34 See, Weissinger (2001), and <www.iso.ch/e-balloting>. The new balloting scheme maintains the system of voting rights that was established by ISO/IEC Directive (part 1). See, *User Guide to the Electronic Balloting Application*, Version 1.1 (December 2000), available at <www.iso.ch/e-balloting>

35 ICANN was incorporated under California law as a 'public benefit corporation', for a more detailed description of ICANN and its history see <www.icann.org> and Weinberg (2000: 192–213).

36 WIPO is an intergovernmental organization (by 17 July 2001 it had 177 member-states), which is responsible for the creation of a worldwide framework for the protection of intellectual property rights; for further details see the WIPO website at <www.wipo.org>. For further details about the dispute settlement rules see *ICANN Uniform Domain Name Dispute Resolution Policy*, available at <www.icann.org/udrp/udrp-policy-24oct99.htm>. For the consultative history of this policy – known as the 'First WIPO Internet Domain Name Process' – see <ecommerce.wipo.int/domains>. It should be noted that ICANN and WIPO are not the only players in the game of 'controlling the Net'. Probably the most important co-players are governments (especially the United. States and the EU) and big private players such as Microsoft, Adobe, AOL, AT&T and IBM.

37 These disputes were dealt with by WIPO Arbitration and Mediation Center. The full text of the decisions can be accessed at <arbiter.wipo.int/domains/decisions/html>. See *Julia Fiona Roberts* v. *Russell Boyd*, Case No. D2000–0210; *Parfums Christian Dior* v. *QTR Corporation*, Case No. D2000–0023; *Penguin Books Ltd.* v. *the Katz Family*, Case No. D2000 – 0204; *Nandos International Limited* v. *M. Fareed Farukhi*, Case No. D2000–0225.

38 See <www.icann.org/participate and forum.icann.org>

Bibliography

Bimber, B. (2001) 'Information Technology and the "New" Politics,' unpublished paper <http://www.polsci.ucsb.edu/faculty/bimber/research/index.html>, first accessed 2 November 2002.

Biswas, A. K. (1992) 'Summary and Recommendations', in Biswas, A. K. and Agarwal, S. B. C. (eds), *Environmental Impact Assessment for Developing Countries*, Oxford: Butterworth-Heinemann.

Bodansky, D. (1999) 'The Legitimacy of International Governance', *American Journal of International Law*, 93, 596–624.

Calabresi, G. (1991) 'The Pointless of Pareto', *Yale Law Journal*, 100, 1211.

Caldwell, L. K. (1996) *International Environmental Policy*, Durham: Duke University Press.

Canan, P. and Reichman, N. (2002) *Ozone Connections*, Sheffield: Greenleaf Publishing.

Charnovitz, S. (1996) 'Participation of Nongovernmental Organizations in the World Trade Organization', *University of Pennsylvania Journal of International Economic Law*, 17, 331–59.

Cohen, J. and Sabel, C. (1997) 'Directly-Deliberative Polyarchy', *European Law Journal*, 3, 313–42.

Colman, A. M. (1995) *Game Theory and Its Applications in the Social and Biological Sciences*, Oxford: Butterworth/Heinemann.

Croson, R. and Marks, M. (2001) 'The Effect of Recommended Contributions in the Voluntary Provision of Public Goods', *Economic Inquiry*, 39, 238–49.

Dipper, B., Jones, C. and Wood, C. (1998) 'Monitoring and Post-auditing in Environmental Impact Assessment: A Review,' *Journal of Environmental Planning and Management* 41 (6), 731–48.

Downs, A. (1957) *An Economic Theory of Democracy*, New York: Harper and Row.

The Ecologist (2000) 'Special Report: Globalizing Poverty', *The Ecologist*, 30, 6.

Esty, D. (1999) 'Why the World Trade Organization Needs Environmental NGOs', International Centre for Trade and Sustainable Development Working Paper, <http://www.cid.harvard.edu/cidtrade/issues/environmentpaper.html>, first accessed 2 November 2000.

Hammond, A. and Lash, J. (2000) 'Cyber-Activism: The Rise of Civil Accountability and Its Consequences for Governance', *iMP Magazine*, May 2000, <http://www.cisp.org/imp/may_2000/05_00hammond.htm>, first accessed 2 November 2000.

Hayashi, N., Ostrom, E., Walker, J. and Yamagishi, T. (1999) 'Reciprocity, Trust, and the Sense of Control', *Rationality and Society*, 11 (1), 27–46.

ICANN (1999) 'The Membership Advisory Committee Commentary on the Principles of the At-large Membership' <http://www.icann.org>, first accessed 29 November 2000.

ICANN-At-Large-Study-Committee (2001) 'Final Report on ICANN At-Large Membership', <http://www.icann.org>, first accessed 27 June 2002.

ICANN-Committee-on-Evolution-and-Reform (2002) 'ICANN: A Blueprint for Reform', <http://www.icann.org>, first accessed 27 June 2002.

ISO (1999) 'ISO in Brief', <http://www.iso.ch/presse/longrang.pdf>, first accessed 1 March 2001.

ISO (2001) 'The ISO Survey of ISO 9000 and ISO 14000 Certificates – Tenth cycle' <http://www.iso.ch>, first accessed 26 July 2001.

Jackson, J. H. (1997) *The World Trading System*, Cambridge, MA: The MIT Press.

Kelso, J. A. Scott (1995) *Dynamic Patterns*, Cambridge, MA: The MIT Press.

Klein, H. (2001) 'The Future of Democracy in ICANN', *CYBER-FEDERALIST*, 11, <http://www.cyber-federalist.org>, first accessed 27 June 2001.

Lessig, L. (2000) 'Architecting for Control', Keynote address given at the Internet Political Economy Forum, *Cambridge Review of International Affairs*, Cambridge, UK, 29 May.

Lynn, M. S. (2002) 'President's Report: ICANN – The Case for Reform', <http://www.icann.org>, first accessed 27 June 2002.

McLean, I. (2000) 'Review Article: The Divided Legacy of Mancur Olson', *British Journal of Political Science*, 30, 651–68.

Murray, P. C. (1999) 'Inching Toward Environmental Regulatory Reform – ISO 14000', *American Business Law Journal*, 37, 35–71.

Ostrom, E. (2000) 'The Danger of Self-Evident Truths', *Political Science*, 33 (1), 33–44.

Ostrom, E., Gardner, R. and Walker, J. (1994) *Rules, Games, & Common-Pool Resources*, Ann Arbor: The University of Michigan Press.

Palfrey, T. R. and Rosenthal, H. (1994) 'Repeated Play, Cooperation and Coordination', *Review of Economic Studies*, 61, 545–65.

Perez, O. (1998) 'Reconstructing Science', *European Foreign Affairs Review*, 3 (4), 563–82.

Perez, O. (2001) 'Ecological Sensitivity and Global Legal Pluralism', unpublished PhD thesis, London School of Economics and Political Science.

Perez, O. (2002) 'Using Private-Public Linkages to Regulate Environmental Conflicts', *Journal of Law & Society*, 29, 77–110.

Petersmann, E. U. (1999) 'Dispute Settlement in International Economic Law', *Journal of International Economic Law*, 2, 189–248.

Rapoport, A. (1985) 'Provision of Public Goods and the MCS Experimental Paradigm', *American Political Science Review*, 79, 148–55.

Starr, P. (2000) 'The Electronic Commons', *The American Prospect*, 11.

Teubner, G. (1997) '"Global Bukowina": Legal Pluralism in the World Society', in Teubner, G. (ed.), *Global Law Without a State*, Aldershot: Dartmouth.

UNCTAD (1996) *ISO 14001: International Environmental Management Systems Standards*, Geneva: United Nations Conference on Trade and Development.

UNDP (2001) *Partnerships to Fight Poverty: UNDP Annual Report 2001*, New York: United Nations Development Programme.

Weiler, J. H. H. (1997) 'Does Europe Need a Constitution?' in Gowan, P. and Anderson, P. (eds), *The Question of Europe*, London: Verso.

Weinberg, J. (2000) 'ICANN and the Problem of Legitimacy', *Duke Law Journal* 50, 187–260.

Weissinger, R. (2001) 'Electronic Balloting', *ISO Bulletin*, 32 (April), 3–6.

WTO (2002) 'WTO Website User Survey', <http://www.wto.org>, first accessed 24 June 2002.

Yamagishi, T. and Cook, K. S. (1993) 'Generalized Exchange and Social Dilemmas', *Social Psychology Quarterly*, 56 (4), 235–48.

8 Problems@labour

Towards a net-internationalism?

Stuart Hodkinson

Introduction

This chapter takes as its context the widely recognised global crisis of *national* trade unionism in a 'globalised/networked/informatised capitalist era' (Waterman 2001), and argues that although this crisis requires a revival of union *internationalism*, the history of past labour internationalisms reveals possible 'inherent' barriers to such cross-border solidarity. This is where the Internet may come in. Some thinkers and activists in and around the international labour movement argue that while new information and communication technologies (ICTs) have been integrally responsible for national union decline, they have also provided workers for the first time with 'the means to coordinate globally in the age of the multinational corporation' (Davison 2000: 1). The aim of this chapter is to come to some preliminary conclusions about the potential of the Internet to overcome past and present obstacles to union internationalism through a critical review of what I call the 'net-internationalism' perspective. The first part of the chapter sets out the crisis of trade unionism under globalisation and examines the problematic case for a new 'union' internationalism. Part two sets out the claims of 'net-internationalism', which are then critically discussed in part three. The conclusion argues that while the Internet has provided new and important tools for labour internationalism, it is not the virtual solution to real-world solidarity building.

Globalisation, trade union decline and the dilemmas of internationalism

Perhaps one of the defining features of contemporary global capitalism is the decline of trade unionism to the extent that it 'now faces in large parts of the world almost total elimination as a significant social institution' (Thomas 1995: 4). While there is sharp disagreement in academic and trade union circles as to the long-term implications of this crisis, few contest the present malaise in a climate of mass unemployment, stagnant average real wage growth, chronic employment insecurity, dwindling union membership and the global trend towards the curtailment of trade union rights and political influence. This represents a dramatic turnaround from what is considered the height of trade union power – the post-1945 era or so-called 'Golden Age' of capitalism (Marglin and Schor 1990). Despite the deep variation that existed between different national industrial relations systems, union power was generally reflected at the level of the labour market, the labour process, public policy and civil society. Unions were particularly powerful in western Europe where they 'reached a degree of influence in the economy and a level of social protection for workers, which had never existed before' (Visser 2000: 426).

Unprecedented postwar economic expansion driven by state-led reconstruction helped create full employment conditions and thus strong bargaining power for organised labour. Collective bargaining took wages and workers 'out of competition' with each other, curtailing employers' ability to divide and rule over their workforces and enabling large real wage gains and improved working and living conditions (Visser 2000: 426). Unions' market and industrial strength translated into significant political influence with their participation in 'neo-corporatist' government macroeconomic and industrial management systems (Crouch 1992). Employers and public institutions recognised unions as their 'indispensable partners in the industrial order' and integrated them into policy-making circles (Regini 1992: 2–3, 6). Welfare states effectively removed wage-determination from competitive labour markets while the underlying Fordist mass-production manufacturing model was conducive to unionisation and collective bargaining. Crucially, the domestic capacity of states to pursue union-friendly demand-management and full employment policies was supported at the international level by the postwar international monetary system, which restricted short-term capital flows and speculation (Cox 1994; Drache 1996).[1] This political and economic power also made unions key social actors in community and class struggle.

By the 1990s, this 'Golden Age' of organised labour had evaporated and '[t]he prolonged pattern of divergence had been replaced by the convergent trajectories of union decline' (Western 1997: 21). Explanations of these trends are inevitably much disputed and while most approaches point to the impact of mass unemployment and deindustrialisation, their significance is contested. For example, business-cycle approaches emphasise the changing elasticity of demand for labour effects on union bargaining power and unionisation (Hirsch and Addison 1986); sociological approaches focus on the changing nature of work and workers, and in particular the erosion of working-class consciousness (Meiksins 1998); and Marxian political economy approaches variously highlight the crisis of Fordism, the role of class conflict and the intervention of the state (Boyer and Drache 1996; Kelly 1998; Panitch 1998). However, while all of these explanations are relevant, it would appear impossible not to conclude that a crisis of unionism that literally spans the entire global economy must have its root cause in a universal or global set of processes and dynamics. The argument adopted here is that the central material and ideological factor in trade union decline is *globalisation*.

Globalisation is a highly contested term and many even dispute its existence, but there is little doubt that something quite unprecedented has happened to the world economy in the last thirty years. In its simplest sense, globalisation refers to 'the increasing economic integration of the world' towards a *global* as opposed to an *inter*national economy characterised by growing interconnectedness and interdependence between countries, cultures and economies (Brown and Hogendorn 2000). The most important aspect of globalisation is the transformation of the production process, which is increasingly globally organised and technologically networked, incorporating 'components produced in many different locations by different firms, and assembled for specific purposes and specific markets in a new form of production and commercialisation: high-volume, flexible, customized production' (Castells 1996: 96). This deterritorialisation of production has enabled Transnational Corporations (TNCs) to quickly transfer many parts of their production line virtually anywhere in the world and thus create a 'world market for both labor and industrial sites' (Mittelman 1996a: 4). This has enabled companies to pursue a range of strategies towards decimating labour's collective power such as subcontracting work offshore (Castells 1996; Klein 2000) or by making 'plant survival and new investment dependent upon unions accepting certain new demands such as restricting wage claims or industrial activity' as well as the intensification of the work effort (Bacon and Blyton 1999). Governments too have become 'increasingly constrained in their freedom of manoeuvre by the economic policies of other states as by the investment decisions of internationally mobile capital' (Gill and Law 1988: 92). This has reduced the state's capacity to pursue policies favourable to trade union influence. Overall, the result is that capital can now 'divide and rule' over governments and workers by threatening to source from or transfer production and jobs to other countries, or to curtail future investments.

In this context, labour organising on a national scale appears increasingly at odds with a new globalising economy, and it would seem axiomatic that if they are to at least survive, unions must engage in international cooperation and solidarity with fellow workers in other countries and continents to protect global wages, employment and labour standards and confront and constrain the power of capital mobility by increasing the power and efficacy of the democratic welfare state. Indeed, the rationale of labour internationalism is contained within the very structural logic of a networked global capitalism. Global campaigns against TNCs could have a major impact because TNCs dominate many 'nominally independent employers' and set 'world-wide trends in working conditions' (Moody 1997: 62). Successful action is feasible because TNCs are vulnerable at many points of their cross-border chains and thus 'the entire production network can be brought to a standstill' through local strikes in key locations (Breitenfellner 1997: 547). And as we shall shortly discuss, the use of new ICTs by global firms in their strategies against labour can be turned to labour's advantage through cross-border union communication networks of information-sharing on corporate economic data, pay-bargaining and management strategies (Lee 1997).

However, the prospects for a new labour internationalism appear deeply uncertain. Despite the *praxis* of worker internationalism since at least 1864 with the founding of Marx's International Working Men's Association (*aka* the First International), the actual history of international worker solidarity has been dominated by failure, continually undermined by nationalism, economism, ideological divisions, organisational problems and resource weaknesses. For example, during the

Cold War, the international union movement split into two rival factions when anti-Communist unions withdrew from the World Federation of Trade Unions (WFTU) to create the International Confederation of Free Trade Unions (ICFTU) in 1949. This not only isolated Eastern unions from West, but it also 'sharpened divisions between communist and non-communist unions in Western countries' (O'Brien 2000: 537). The ICFTU and WFTU essentially became 'transmission belts for the priorities of the interests of US and USSR labor-state alliances' while domestic labour politics of developing countries were increasingly penetrated by Cold War politics through 'divisive interventions rather than assistance towards the creation of autonomous unions' (Thomson and Larson 1978; Spalding 1988; Stevis 1998: 9). Cold War divisions also scuppered the attempt to create World Company Councils (WCCs) and achieve global contract and multinational bargaining during the 1960s and 1970s (Stevis 1998: 13). Meanwhile, efforts to overcome these obstacles were continually frustrated by the poor means of communication between trade unions of different industries, countries, continents and the cost of flying officials from around the world to conferences and meetings (Lee 1997: 13).

Recent optimistic voices have argued that the end of the Cold War has removed the major 'ideological cleavage' that had previously split workers' organisations (O'Brien 2000: 536). Yet its legacy remains undoubtedly disruptive. The past 'divisive interventions' of the ICFTU and the American Federation of Labor-Congress of Industrial Organization (AFL-CIO) in particular have not been expunged from the collective memories of developing countries and the domination of international trade union structures by Cold War politics has left them weak 'with limited powers and resources' (Stevis 1998: 12). Yet even if one accepts that the geopolitical climate has become more conducive to a renewed internationalism, there exist strong theoretical arguments that the pursuit of cross-national cooperation among workers is inherently compromised. For example, when Levinson (1972) argued that the internationalisation of capital would inevitably overcome the objective and subjective barriers to full-scale international trade unionism, he was decisively countered by a sustained outpouring of writings which argued that building international solidarity would always be confronted by the natural 'disunity of labour' in contrast to the intrinsic 'organic unity of capital' (Olle and Schoeller 1977; Haworth and Ramsay 1988; Ramsay 1997: 510). In other words, while all workers share the same structural relationship to capital as wage-labour in the *abstract*, in the *concrete* they do not share the same circumstances, realities and relations 'among themselves and with actually existing employers' (Hyman 1999: 95). Hence, globalisation may erode such differentiation by compressing the global and local experience, but under acute internationally competitive conditions with the threat to jobs and livelihoods of possible capital flight, it could just as easily divide labour along national lines. Olle and Schoeller (1977) argued that internationalism could therefore only be *politically* constructed, but conceded that such a task was always threatened by states and firms appealing to nationalist and protectionist sentiments.

It is almost certainly as a result of these factors, as well as many others, that as capitalist relations have gone global, the scope of union organisation, strategy and ethos has remained nationally embedded. Indeed, virtually all union strategies aim to adapt union members to competitive business considerations and engage in 'enterprise egoism', that is, making the survival of the firm the union's top priority to ensure that *their* members maintain *their* jobs (Hyman 1999). This nationalistic approach serves only to accelerate and deepen the power of TNCs and harm the overall position of labour in the global economy – as unions compete with each other for investment and world market shares, their competitive offers on wage levels, working conditions and productivity are not one-off adjustments but form part of a constant blackmailing process that hits the poorest workers and countries hardest first and keeps going to workers *everywhere*. By accepting and engaging themselves in the globalisation process, unions are being reconstituted from both inside/outside into mere agencies of global capital.

Nevertheless, the last decade has seen signs of an upsurge in international trade union activity and cross-border solidarity and a growing number of activists and academics argue that the qualitative form of this resurgence contains one important and potentially significant difference from the past – the Internet. It is to these claims that we now turn.

Cyberspace and solidarity: the emergence of net-internationalism

Since the end of the Cold War, a pronounced escalation has occurred in the international activities of trade unions and labour movements. Most writing focuses on the 'vertical' activities of 'official' structures of international trade unionism such as the ICFTU, the International Trade Secretariats (ITSs) and the European Trade Union Confederation (ETUC) to whom national trade unions are affiliated and use to represent and coordinate their international efforts. Taylor (1999: 4) argues that through these institutions, '[t]he international trade union movement has established a common agenda for collective action at the international level in recent years'. Recent research has also documented more 'horizontal' cross-border cooperation between national unions. Lambert and Webster (2001: 337, 349) focus on the emergence of SIGTUR 'a new network/organization of southern unions...from Latin America, Southern Africa, Asia and Australasia' whose aim is 'to build a strong Southern unionism focused on global action campaigns' in alliance with other social movements. There is also significant work on the activities of internationally minded NGOs such as Women Working WorldWide involved in grassroots cross-border labour networking, bypassing official union structures and working directly with unorganised workers or independent labour movements (Hale and Shaw 2001).

This revival of labour internationalism's' is rooted in both *necessity* with the crisis of national labour organising in the era of globalisation, and *possibility* with the technological, ideational and structural processes of globalisation helping to breaking down previous obstacles and opening up new opportunities for transnational labour activism. The focus here is on the technological aspect with the role played by new ICTs and particularly the *Internet*. As Bailey (1999: 1) argues, '[c]omputer technology has created the conditions for a global communication network that is essential to the operation of capitalism today'. Yet while the Internet has been integral to the 'electronic reconstitution' of class relations, there has also been a simultaneous upsurge in computer-mediated local, national, regional and crucially *global* protest demonstrated in the now classic example of the Zapatistas in 1994, which precipitated a number of highly public uses of the Internet by different groups. It is in this context that many unions, grassroots activists and labour academics have begun purring about the possibilities and activities of the Internet for both trade union revival, and specifically, labour internationalism.

In his groundbreaking book, *The Labour Movement and the Internet: The New Internationalism*, Lee (1997) sets out the bones of what I call 'net-internationalism'. In short, he argues that the very instrument of TNC power can be turned against global capital through its adoption and adaptation by the trade union movement in its pursuit of international solidarity. His central proposition, mirroring other contributions in this area, is that while the Internet is not a panacea, computer-mediated communications (CMC) are actively (re)-internationalising the labour movement by solving some of the problems that beset previous internationalism through the annihilation of time/space/cost, in the communication of *information, organisation* and *solidarity culture*. The following analysis provides a synthesis of these arguments.

The most important aspect of the Internet for internationalism is its ability to store, process and enable additional and alternative hyper-rapid 24-hour cross-border information-sharing between trade unions all over the world. Through email, electronic messages containing anything from simple text to computer programs, databases and pictures can be sent to potentially unlimited numbers of other trade unionists in seconds and at very low cost. Websites can store text, pictures, sounds and even videos, which can be used by trade unions to publish information on virtually everything, and is accessible to anyone and anywhere when connected to the Internet. This has a number of important benefits. Members can be immediately alerted to changes in national collective agreements, negotiations, macroeconomic data, employer strategies and production techniques as well as labour disputes, strikes and employer/state assaults. By linking every national trade union website home page to the other, and to official and independent international websites, members can just as easily find out international union news as local and national news, effectively joining up all the trade union and labour movements around the world in what he calls a 'global labour information highway'. Through online strike newspapers, websites can be used to refute management or government propaganda and explain workers' actions, gain media coverage and international support by helping to 'speed up the availability of counter-information which can be used to contradict false (or the absence of) reporting in mainstream news services' (Pollack 2000: 2). Moreover, email and websites can help to by-pass the 'elite-controlled mass media in terms of both obtaining information and getting it out' (Cleaver 2000: 16). So, workers from different countries get a sense of similar struggles in other regions and countries, regardless of time, place and race through an informational flow that they would not otherwise have received and thus a struggle or series of struggles they would ordinarily not have known about.

This communication tool will also overcome many past *organisational* obstacles to coordinating international solidarity efforts. For example, by combining global interactive databases with email, online chat and videoconferencing, trade unions can hold 'virtual' international conferences and meetings for the purposes of *multinational collective bargaining* with TNC employers (Thorpe 1999: 219–20). Lee (1997: 13) argues that this 'virtual' medium for international meetings is the 'solution to the budgetary problems' faced by the WCCs in 1970s. The increasing availability of Internet translation programs, although imperfect, also enable such information to be shared to all trade unionists of whatever nationality and language. Moreover, by turning trade unions into 'e-unions' or 'cyberunions', not only can they achieve an optimum level of organisational efficiency releasing scarce resources, they can also become what Bill Gates calls in business circles 'digital nervous systems' (Darlington 2000b: 2). Lee (1997: 184) argues that as every trade union gradually comes online, it will eventually be possible to have what he calls a 'global early warning network' on trade union rights whereby through email (or phone or fax if necessary), any news story of a worker or union involved in a sudden and serious violation of their human and labour rights could be posted to every trade unionist in the world instantly asking for their support. Finally, organisation *through* cyberspace can also become militancy *in* cyberspace by using the Internet to directly target employers and states through 'hactivism' or international action sending mass emails of protest often by simply clicking on a specific link on a trade union website that has a specially designed web engine to launch 'ping' or mail bomb attacks against websites that overtax its 'reload' function or load memory banks with emails (Cleaver 1999: 17).

Reinforcing the instrumental global information and communication flows facilitating international action, the Internet is also seen as creating a new, more conducive place for reinforcing and building a shared 'global solidarity culture' of labour everywhere (Waterman 2001). Cyberspace helps forge these cross-border cultural affinities in two main ways. First, the use of hypertext and hyper-linking on the World Wide Web and its ability to instantly pick up foreign workers' news, culture and struggles '*contributes by its very nature* to internationalism and the ideals of global solidarity' (Waterman 2001: 39) and thus helps trade unionists to 'transcend their own local and national limitations' and feel 'part of a global community based not on language or skin colour, but social class – and a vision of a new society' Lee (1997: 179). Second, constructing what Hyman (1999: 107) calls an 'organic solidarity' for a new global workforce requires a continuous dialogue at every level and cyberspace provides this discursive arena. Waterman (2001: 16) argues that the very 'logic of the computer is one of feedback', thus helping unions and workers move away from a unidirectional, one-to-many, top-down instrumental flow of information towards a multidirectional, reciprocal, dialogical exchange that could take place through e-conferences, mailing and discussion lists, a dialectical process 'in which initial positions are transformed and a new synthesis reached' between workers of different countries.

Of course, the literature is still in its infancy and lacks critical theoretical and empirical investigation, and the deliberate synthesis presented here hides considerable differences in conceptual frameworks, arguments, visions, expectations and examples employed. In the space allowed, it is not possible to engage in a detailed theoretical analysis of these perspectives, but it is worth briefly mapping out a preliminary framework for future research. Generally speaking, there are three interrelated but distinct categories of net-internationalism: instrumental-organisational, organisational-solidaristic and solidaristic-communicative. Instrumental-organisational approaches fall under Waterman's (2001: 16) conceptualisation of the dominant union approach/use of the Internet as primarily a tool for 'faster, cheaper, further-reaching' communication, presenting new opportunities for organisational efficiency and mobilising trade union action and would best describe the work of Darlington (2000a,b) and Shostak (1999). Organisational-solidaristic perspectives focus on the informational and organisational benefits of the Internet for subjective solidarity-building through building a global worker-culture within the existing international trade union movement and would best describe the position of Lee's (1997) and Bailey's (1997) position. The solidaristic-communicative approach might be associated with the work of Waterman (2001: 16) and takes this theme one step further, seeing the Internet primarily as 'cyberspace' and cyberspace as a kind of Habermasian 'ideal speech situation', a place with 'unlimited possibilities for international dialogue, creativity and the invention/discovery/development of new values, new attitudes, new dialogues'. Within these three approaches, a range of expectations exist on what contribution the Internet can make to internationalism depending on both the respective analysis of the problems confronting internationalism and the relative efficacy of the Internet in solving these.

Discussion: problems@labour or problems@internet?

There is little doubt that the informational, organisational and solidaristic qualities of the Internet are being increasingly employed by national and international trade union organisations. First, of an estimated 391 million people online (www.euroktg.com/globalstats), Lee estimates that well over 60 million are probably trade unionists (Lee 2000a: 14–16) and whereas in 1999 around 1,500 labour websites existed, today there are 2,700 trade union websites alone (Lee 2001 citing Freeman), albeit dominated by North American and western European unions. In Britain, nearly all TUC-affiliated unions are online (Ward and Lusoli 2003) and there are now around 300 union websites, a substantial growth from the 211 in late 2000 (<http.dmoz.org> Lee 2000b). In the United States, fifty-six out of sixty-six AFL-CIO-affiliated unions are online with dozens more local branches networked (AFL-CIO 2001). Importantly, nearly all international union organisations are online such as the ICFTU, ILO and ITSs with multilingual website access to their press releases, campaign information, resource tools and latest international trade union news.

Second, many regional and international union organisations have been using new ICTs to develop interactive databases of information on multinational corporations, economic trends and management strategies for the purposes of national and international *collective bargaining* as well as more proactive strategies. For example, the Public Services International (PSI) has a multilingual database on privatisation and associated multinationals, with files on over 2,000 companies monitoring takeover and merger activities, financial and political developments and issues of performance, pricing, financing, employment and political relations, including corruption. The database is used to answer enquiries from trade unions affiliated to PSI, and others, on the companies and other information contained in the database. It also allows online access to information on companies, recent news and PSI-related reports and publications. The PSI is trying to develop electronic links between databases and information on privatisation between trade union and universities from Brazil, Canada, India, South Africa and Spain (www.psiru.org).

Third, the interaction between the infinite sources of corporate information located on the World Wide Web, the creation of union websites and databases and the growth of independent labour movement websites, mailing and discussion lists and web forums, has created an embryonic form of what Lee (1997) envisages as an 'online international labour press' with a built-in 'global labour early warning network'. For example, embodying and indeed forming much of this is Lee's own *LabourStart* website (www.labourstart.org) – the most comprehensive, multilingual and up-to-date global labour news service in all forms of media. The main website contains links to global labour news stories (national, regional and internationalist) usually taken from official online media and directly added to a database by 127 volunteer correspondents from around thirty different countries. The database then updates the website every 15 minutes. *LabourStart*'s home page has a summary of the latest world's major union headlines of that and previous recent days. The main site contains important features such as requests for urgent international solidarity action, discussion forums, a 'Labour News Network' to which contributors add/delete modify their own labour-related stories, directories of trade union websites and labour media, a 'Global Labour Calendar' with a day-by-week-by-month events guide for unions and software to both place a 'Labour NewsWire' on any other labour website – a live news feed of *LabourStart*'s latest five or ten headlines from either own country or globally in your own language – and a trade union web browser dedicated to unions. LabourStart is in 10 languages – Dutch, English, Esperanto, French, Italian, Norwegian, Portuguese, Spanish, Swedish and Turkish, and aims to add one more language every month through volunteers.

Fourth and perhaps most important has been the ability to rapidly mobilise international acts of solidarity through the Internet. By posting requests for solidarity on mailing lists and/or union and labour websites, campaigns such as the 1995–1998 Liverpool Dockers lockout received international prominence and saw dockers in the United States, Australia, Spain and Israel take solidarity action in their support. In 1997, the Bridgestone/Firestone dispute with the United Steelworkers of America came to an end when the International Federation of Chemical, Energy, Mine and General Workers' Unions (ICEM) helped the US union launch an international 'cyberstrike' against the tyre corporation: unionists and other web surfers were shown how to bombard the company with protests during a global 'day of outrage' by 'providing a list of addresses on its website to facilitate the unauthorised occupation of the sites and electronic mailboxes of the company's management, as well as of those of car makers and distributors, tyre retailers and other bodies with a stake in Bridgestone' (Breitenfellner 1997: 547). The Internet was vital to the success of the 1998 Australian dockers' dispute with their government in 1998. Lee (2000c: 5) argues that within days of the dispute starting, 'the threat of a boycott of Australian shipping emerged . . . largely thanks to the web and email' creating international solidarity. Finally, in early 2000, the South Korean union KCTU won the release of seventeen workers arrested and brutalised during a non-violent trade union sit-in by sending urgent appeals by email to international contacts, publishing the president's email address and urging protest messages to be sent (Lee: 2000c 7).

Yet, while these achievements appear impressive, we need to be critically aware of their actual and potential significance for 'union internationalism' itself, and this is a far more contested terrain of debate. Objectively, the Internet is providing workers and their organisations with revolutionary new organisational and communicational tools to engage in internationalism. Plenty of evidence supports the idea that the Internet is facilitating internationalism through transnational business networks, international discussion/mailing lists, cross-border political appeals for solidarity support and cross-border protest organisation. The Internet enables for the first time, in theory, a qualitative and quantitative shift in inclusivity, representativeness and internationalism. National trade union and labour groups from different countries can now meet, discuss, debate, dialogue, swap information and stories in cyberspace and in real time without having to set foot outside their offices and countries when previous means of communication were almost non-existent in relation to this. A top-down process can now become a two-way process. This is not necessarily a shift from verticalism to horizontalism, but it does enable feedback mechanisms that can transform, radically, initial positions and reach consensus.

For example, the Internet allows top-level position papers, which will eventually form the expression of the 'international labour movement's' position, to actually be downloaded from the ICFTU or ITS website anywhere in the world, disseminated to first previously marginalised national labour organisations in the South, and then, given the nature of the position being proposed, to the membership, analysed in detail and consulted upon with drafted additions and amendments. This should allow for a more representative position to be created and if it is not, then national unions and movements can produce alternative position papers or critiques, again circulating them among their membership, but also to sympathetic supporters in other countries, to build up a counter-consensus which may not only dramatically internationalise the debate, but may also lead to the 'official' body changing its position and thus gaining the support of a much larger group of the world's workers. This happened, for example, at the women's Fourth World Conference in Beijing in 1995, when the Internet was used by women's NGOs to facilitate the participation of thousands of women from around the world. As Gittler (1999: 95) argues:

> [t]he public electronic spaces for discussion and information sharing also helped demystify UN proceedings. Discussions previously reserved for a few governmental delegates and observers at the United Nations were now open to anyone able to access the medium.

However, there is much more to overcoming the obstacles to internationalism than the Internet can solve on its own, due to both the nature of these obstacles and some of the shortcomings of the Internet, which are focused on here. It is essential to reiterate that as we start to move away from the richest countries with predominantly white service and industrial workforces towards the poorest, predominantly black, Arab and oriental agricultural proletariats, computer access falls from being insufficient to almost non-existent. Only about 5 per cent of the global population are actually online and therefore the vast majority of trade unionists, actual and potential, do not and cannot use the Internet. While it is possible to use other technologies in conjunction with the Internet as the global women's movement has through 'connected' women acting as bridges to 'unconnected' groups 'by repackaging on-line information and sharing it through other communication channels such as print, fax, telephone, radio and theatre' (Farwell *et al.* 1999: 106), most of the developing world has no real telecommunications infrastructure to do even this. Moreover, both the Internet and international trade unionism remain dominated by the English language and while translation software may solve the technical side, it does not create political will. For example, contrast the resource-poor LabourStart and its volunteer system in nine different languages, growing month by month, to the relatively resource-rich ICFTU and its paltry three languages (English, French, Spanish).

Problems are also faced through the increasing employer and state offensive on Internet use and privacy. Employers in the United States, Britain and Germany have recently been given powers to legally monitor and sack workers browsing websites and using email for personal use and even union work. This highlights the weakness of email itself, which Lee (2000b) compares to 'sending a postcard… open to reading by all the computers that pass it along the internet to its destination'. Consequently, employers are actively challenging and prohibiting employee use of corporate computer networks for union activity (see Miller 2000 on the recent dispute between the *Washington Post* and its employees). Moreover, as recent research by Lee (2000a) reveals, the institutions created by the US government to manage, govern and decide the future of the Internet, primarily ICANN, are 'completely unrepresentative, undemocratic, and unaccountable… all completely dominated by transnational corporate capital'. While the implications of this control require more research, we have already seen corporations turning the tables on cyber-solidarity actions. In December 2000, the *Narco News Bulletin* – a US-based publication highlighting the role of US corporations in Narcotics production and trade – suffered a six-day shutdown after its email account and website suffered major technical problems from an alleged mail-bomb attack by the US lawyer-lobbyist firm Akin Gump who allegedly represent the Colombian government and drugs traffickers (Giordano 2000). This has been compounded more recently by the confirmed existence of ECHELON – a global satellite system for intercepting private and commercial communications including email (European Parliament 2001).

Many of these problems are openly acknowledged by cyber-enthusiasts and it is true that some are being overcome all the time through technological and software development. However, where net-internationalism is perhaps at its weakest is in its most important and radical claims concerning the solidaristic and cultural potential of cyberspace. It is not just memories of the Cold War and the divisive interventions of the ICFTU and AFL-CIO in developing countries that present fundamental barriers to internationalism. The everyday experiences of workers in a globalising economy remain nationalistic, parochial, highly localised and differentiated and are continually shaped by capitalist ideology, in particular the ideology and practice of economic nationalism. So, while a radical and effective internationalism will not be achieved without the development of what Waterman (2001) calls a 'global solidarity culture', the problem is how to get to this state and whether the Internet, or cyberspace, can help achieve this. Waterman certainly believes so, arguing that through the Internet, a 'global solidarity dialogue' can construct the kind of organic solidarity required for it to be internationally felt and adhered to.

However, Waterman and others are regrettably, if understandably, vague about the details. In practical terms, how and when is this dialogue going to take place and who will it take place between? Are we talking about the leaders and elites of the world's various trade unions, including the official international organisations, getting cosy in cyberspace? Is it a dialogue between elite and grassroots? Or is this just a grassroots thing? Given that the Internet is still only, and likely to remain so for the considerable future, largely a plaything of North America, Europe and sporadic elements in the developing world, how 'global' do we envisage this dialogue being? Waterman is right that the logic of the computer is 'feedback' – but who will be sending and who will be feeding back? If dialogue is problematic then how difficult will it be to create a solidarity culture both globally and between workers?

Tarrow (2000: 11, 13) reminds us that solidarity culture comes from social networks that provide the 'interpersonal trust, the collective identities and the social communication of opportunities that galvanise individuals into collective action'. Such identities are 'negotiated among people who know one another, meet frequently, and work together on common projects . . . identities are dependent on networks'. These vital social networks have, therefore, only been hitherto accessible to local and national people. Can they be accessible to an international community? Does the Internet recreate the necessary conditions for such global social networks to evolve into solidarity activity itself? Waterman would seem to believe so, but it his reference to the work of Escobar (1999) as his inspiration that betrays his own doubts. Escobar (1999: 32) talks of a 'cultural politics of cyberspace' best achieved and most effective if there is 'an ongoing tacking back and forth between cyberpolitics... political activism in the physical locations at which the networker sits and lives'. The power of the Internet to create a political community of feeling in this way is undeniable and can be witnessed during the unsuccessful 1996–1997 Citizens for Local Democracy (C4LD) campaign in Ontario, Canada, in the preliminary organisation of global civic movement that shut down the WTO at Seattle in 1999. Through browsing the website and becoming involved in the online cyberpolitical community, C4LD saw local people actually inspired to go to physical meetings and participate in the campaign. Just as Escobar argues, solidarity was built by what C4LD's principal web activist Liz Rykert called 'breathing in and breathing out' with members from both real and virtual worlds continually moving back and forth between the two realms, creating a community of feelings and shared values (O'Malley 1998: 22). The same is true of Seattle.

So clearly the Internet can create solidarity cultures, but can Escobar's model and those of C4LD and Seattle be applied to labour internationalism? It would appear not. Their strength lies both in the ability of activists to move in and out of real and virtual activist communities due to their proximity, and the fact that these two supposedly different worlds are actually the same because it is the *same* people doing the 'tacking in and out'. In contrast, workers engaging in internationalism cannot move as easily back and forth from cyber- to real-world activism because they do not live in the same locality nor work in the same conditions. The solidarity cultures and networks created on the Internet are unlikely to be cemented by real-world contact between say Canadian and Japanese workers, but it is this very interface between cyberspace and real place of everyday, face-to-face relations that is the key to the most important part of solidarity – building trust.

Moreover, C4LD and Seattle were essentially single-issue campaigns working towards a definite end goal in a fixed real-world location and dominated by pre-existing, and in the case of Seattle *internationally* organised, social movements and NGOs – perhaps symbolically, organised labour played a very small part in these cyber-communities. So the Internet didn't so much create a global solidarity culture as link different solidarities together globally. Groups such as the environmental movement were already coherent activist movements with an inherently global ethic and outlook and a long history of internationalism and even pioneering cyberactivism. So when Seattle activists left their cyber-communities, they re-entered their actual communities and their existing coherent activist groups and engaged in local workshops, meetings and events. Again, these ingredients do not correlate to union internationalism because the world's unions do not have a specific target, goal or project, nor do they have a pre-existing global solidarity culture. To compound this, global solidarity must form on the basis of workers and trade unions who are already suffering from a crisis of national solidarity, who are arguably inherently non-internationalist and many of whom harbour deep suspicions of the Internet as a threat to jobs and their way of life. This makes international networks, especially between trade unionists, extremely ephemeral and fragmentary, and whereas this might be a strength for horizontal social movement networks, it might be a weakness for labour internationalism.

This is supported empirically by the fact that not only is the overwhelming use of the Internet by trade unions for *non*-international solidarity purposes such as recruiting new members (customers) and providing members with legal advice (competitive service provision), but when net-internationalism does take place, it tends to take the form of a commercial 'e-greeting' card – the unidirectional sending of solidarity messages to striking or struggling workers to let them know that other people support their struggle, know about it and are behind its continuation. So, in sophisticating the medium of internationalism, the Internet is not changing the message itself.

Conclusions

This chapter has argued that although the dynamics of the global crisis of organised labour necessitate a revival of union internationalism to confront and reverse globalisation, the history of labour internationalism demonstrates that achieving effective cross-border worker solidarity is highly problematic, being continually jeopardised by subjective (nationalism, economism, ideology, history) and objective barriers (organisation, communication, resources). The Internet is actively overcoming many of these past obstacles to labour internationalism by enabling unions to mutually inform, organise and construct solidarity across national borders with unprecedented speed and reach. However, when adding together the continuing obstacles posed by Internet access, ownership and control with its shortcomings for building a global solidarity culture in a movement defined by its national outlook, it is important that the Internet does become fetishised as the virtual solution to real-world solidarity building. Navigating through this impasse may not so much mean changes to the Internet but changes within the international labour movement itself.

Note

1 Such a portrayal of the postwar 'European industrial-relations model, however, is highly abstract and many contributions have argued against this romanticised view of the Golden Age on two counts. First, comparativist approaches tend to emphasise the deep variation that existed in the levels of collective bargaining, the degree of centralisation of unions' and employers' own internal administration and the role of unions in economic and social policy, typically contrasting the virtually impotent labour movements of countries like France, Italy, Switzerland and Holland with Scandinavian countries where union federations were 'involved with the government in the *administration* of much public policy, not just consultation' (Crouch 1992: 171). Second and more fundamentally, some Marxist writers have argued that union movements' involvement in state institutions and corporatist bargaining arrangements were unsustainable ticking time-bombs that have contributed to today's crisis of organised labour. Corporatism simply enabled state and capital to co-opt powerful union

movements and reconstitute them from class organisations for the expression of workers demands to state-subservient institutions administering wage restraint through incomes policies.

References

AFL-CIO (2001) <www.aflcio.org/unionand/unions.html>

Bacon, N. and Blyton, P. (1999) *Meeting the Challenge of Globalisation*, Nottingham and Cardiff University.

Bailey, C. (1997) *Towards a Global Labournet*, paper presented to the LaborMedia'97 Conference, Seoul, South Korea, 10–12 November.

Bailey, C. (1999) *The Labour Movement and the Internet*, 2nd Seoul International LaborMedia'99 <www.amrc.org.uk.hk/Arch?3401.htm>, first accessed December 2000.

Boyer, R. and Drache, D. (eds) (1996), *States Against Markets*, London and New York: Routledge.

Breitenfellner, A. (1997) 'Global Unionism', *International Labour Review*, 136 (4), 531–55.

Brown, W. B. and Hogendorn, J. S. (2000) *International Economics in the Age of Globalization*, Ontario, New York, Hertfordshire, Rozelle: Broadview Press Ltd.

Castells, M. (1996) *The Information Age. Volume I: The Network Society*, Oxford: Blackwell.

Cleaver, H. (2000) *Computer-Linked Social Movements and the Global Threat to Capitalism*, Department of Economics, University of Texas, USA.

Cox, R. (1994) 'Global Restructuring', in Stubbs, R. and Underhill, G. R. D. (eds), *Political Economy and the Changing Global Order*, London: Macmillan, 45–59.

Crouch, C. (1992) 'The Fate of Articulated Industrial Relations Systems', in Regini, M. (ed.), *Future of Labour Movements*, London, California, New Delhi: Sage, 169–87.

Darlington, R. (2000a) *The Creation of the E-Union*, text of presentation made to an Internet Economy Conference, London School of Economics, 7 November.

Darlington, R. (2000b) *Books On Business* <http://members.tripod.co.uk/rogerdarlington/>, first accessed October 2000.

Davison, C. (2000) 'Unions Get Connected', *The Standard.com Europe*, 7 November.

Drache, D. (1996) 'From Keynes to K-Mart', in Boyer, R. and Drache, D. (eds), *States Against Markets*, London: Routledge, 31–61.

Escobar, A. (1999) 'Gender, Place and Networks', in Harcourt, W. (ed.), *Women@Internet*, London: Zed.

European Parliament (2001) *Temporary Committee on the Echelon System*, Meeting 29 May.

Farwell, E., Wood, P., James, M. and Banks, K. (1999) 'Global Networking for Change', in Harcourt, W. (ed.), *Women@Internet*, London: Zed, 102–113.

George, S. (2000) 'Seattle Turning Point', *Le Monde Diplomatique*, January.

Gill, S. and Law, D. (1988) *The Global Political Economy*, New York and London: Harvester Wheatsheaf.

Giordano, A. (2000) *About the Cyber Attack on Narco News*, December <www.narconews.com>

Gittler, A. (1999) 'Mapping Women's Global Communications and Networking', in Harcourt, W. (ed.), *Women@Internet*, London: Zed, 91–101.

Hale, A. and Shaw, L. (2001) 'Women Workers and the Promise of Ethical Trade in the Globalised Garment Industry', *Antipode*, 33 (3), 484–509.

Haworth, N. and Ramsay, H. (1988) 'Workers of the World Untied', in Southall, R. (ed.), *Trade Unions and the New Industrialization of the Third World*, London: Zed Books.

Hirsch, B. T. and Addison, J. T. (1986) *The Economic Analysis of Unions*, London: Allen & Unwin.

Hyman, R. (1999) 'Imagined Solidarities', in Leisink, P. (ed.), *Globalization and Labour Relations*, Cheltenham: Edward Elgar, 94–115.

Kelly, J. (1998) *Rethinking Industrial Relations*, London and New York: Routledge.

Klein, N. (2000) *No Logo*, London: Flamingo.

Lambert, R. and Webster, E. (2001) 'Southern Unionism and the New Labour Internationalism', *Antipode*, 33 (3), 337–62.

Lee, E. (1997) *The Labour Movement and the Internet*, London and Chicago: Pluto Press.

Lee, E. (2000a) *The Internet Belongs to Everyone*, Labour and Society International.

Lee, E. (2000b) 'How the Internet is Changing Unions', *Working USA*.

Lee, E. (2000c) 'Email Privacy is a Trade Union Issue' <www.labourstart.org/nettips1/>, first accessed January 2001.

Lee, E. (2001) 'Beyond the Website', *LabourStart*.

Levinson, C. (1972) *International Trade Unionism*, London: Allen & Unwin.

Marglin, S. and Schor, J. (eds) (1990) *The Golden Age of Capitalism*, Oxford: Clarendon.

Meiksins, P. (1998) 'Same As It Ever Was', in Meiksins-Wood, E. *et al.* (eds), *Rising From the Ashes*, New York: Monthly Review Press, 28–40.

Miller, G. (2000) 'Guild Pushes to Use Paper's E-Mail System to Reach Workers Labor', *Los Angeles Times*, December 25.

Mittelman, J. H. (1996a) 'The Dynamics of Globalization', in Mittelman, J. H. (ed.), *Globalisation*, International Political Economy Yearbook Vol. 9, Boulder: Rienner, 1–19.

Mittelman, J. H. (ed.) (1996b) *Globalisation*, International Political Economy Yearbook Vol. 9, Boulder: Rienner.

Moody, K. (1997) 'Towards an International Social-Movement Unionism', *New Left Review*, 225, 52–72.

O'Brien, R. (2000) 'Workers and World Order', *Review of International Studies*, 26, 533–55.

O'Malley, K. (1998) 'Grassroots in Cyberspace', *Canadian Forum*, January/February.

Olle, W. and Schoeller, W. (1977) 'World Market Competition and Restrictions upon International Trade Union Policies', *Capital and Class*, 2.

Panitch, L. (1998) 'The State in a Changing World', in *Monthly Review*, 50, 11–22.

Pollack, A. (2000) *Cross-Borders, Cross-Movement Alliances in the Late 1990s*, Global Solidarity Dialogue <www.antenna.nl/~waterman/pollack.html>, first accessed January 2001.

Ramsay, H. (1997) 'Solidarity at Last?' *Economic & Industrial Democracy*, 18, 503–37.

Regini, M. (ed.) (1992) *The Future of Labour Movements*, London, California, New Delhi: Sage.

Shostak, A. (1999) *CyberUnion*, Armonk, NY: M. E. Sharpe.

Spalding Jr, H. A. (1988) 'US Labour Intervention in Latin America', in Southall, R. (ed.), *Trade Unions and the New Industrialization*, London: Zed Books, 259–86.

Stevis, D. (1998) 'International Labor Organizations, 1864–1997', *Journal of World-Systems Research*, 4 (1), 52–75.

Tarrow, S. (2000) *Beyond Globalisation*, Departments of Government and Sociology, Cornell University.

Taylor, R. (1999) *Trade Unions and Transnational Industrial Relations*, Geneva: International Institute for Labour Studies.

Thomas, H. (ed.) (1995) *Globalization and Third World Trade Unions*, London: Zed.

Thomson, D. and Larson, R. (1978) *Where Were You Brother*, London: War on Want.

Thorpe, V. (1999) 'Global Unionism: The Challenge', in Waterman, P. and Munck, R. (eds), *Labour Worldwide in the Era of Globalisation*, London: Macmillan, 216–22.

Visser, J. (2000) 'From Keynesianism to the Third Way', *Economic and Industrial Democracy*, 21 (4), 421–56.

Ward, S. and Lusoli, W. (2003) 'Dinosaurs in Cyberspace?' *European Journal of Communication*, 18 (2), 147–179.

Waterman, P. (2001) 'Trade Union Internationalism in the Age of Seattle', *Antipode*, 33 (3), 312–36.

Western, B. (1997) *Between Class and Market*, Princeton, NJ: Princeton University Press.

9 Rethinking political participation

Experiments in Internet activism in Australia and Britain

Jenny Pickerill

Introduction

> We've got a desert indymedia set up in the back of a truck, trying to keep stuff away from the dust which is ... flying around everywhere ... it is participatory media so anyone can come and write a story ... giving people here an unmediated voice for their perspective.
>
> (Andrew, desert.indymedia)

Camped in the inhospitable Australian desert outside the Woomera refugee detention centre 500 km north of Adelaide, over 1,000 activists collaborated in an action against Australia's policy of mandatory detention of asylum seekers and its use of the inner desert as a dumping ground. The Woomera2002 auto-nomadic festival of freedom attracted international media attention as they physically pulled down the fences of the centre and helped several dozen refugees escape (Williams and Plane 2002). Internet and email were used extensively in both the organisation of the action(s), and in sharing the protests with the world direct through their own media.

Environmental and social justice activists[1] began using email and newsgroups in the late 1980s and by the mid-1990s several websites appeared publicising groups' campaigns (Young 1993). The use of new information and communication technologies (ICTs) by activists has since facilitated participation mobilisation, the coordination of actions and has been used as a tactical tool in itself (Lubbers 2002). While activists face constraints in their use of ICTs – such as access problems, threats from online surveillance, corporate control and the tensions of using environmentally damaging technology – many have been able to appropriate and subvert the technology to their advantage.

In addition to identifying the particular ways in which activists have benefited or struggled with the technology (Pickerill 2001b), examination of activists' ICT use can be used to explore the extent to which ICTs facilitates groups who employ different organisational forms. Crucially, are some forms of activist networks or groups better able to benefit from ICT use than others? Such questions require an examination of organisational form. Within environmental and social justice movements there is often an emphasis upon participatory democracy. Thus analyses of components of these movements serve as an important comparison to some of the more institutionalised political structures explored in this book.

The core premise of this chapter is that the use of ICTs has disproportionately benefited small grassroots groups and individual activists linked only into fluid networks using cellular structures. It is these groups who often suffer from a lack of resources but were able to be more inventive in using the technology because of their ideology and free-flowing organisational structure. Consequently, they gained a temporary advantage over some other less-inventive established organisations and helped create a degree of equality within the environmental and social justice movements.

Case studies and context: Woomera2002 and Friends of the Earth UK

In this chapter two case studies representing different forms of activism in Britain and Australia[2] are employed to investigate the questions outlined here. The Woomera2002 actions were a temporary demonstration of a diffuse and fluid network that took place in the desert in Australia in March 2002, whilst Friends of the Earth (FoE) UK is a well-established formal environmental lobbying organisation with its headquarters in London. For the purposes of this chapter the desert.indymedia network will be the main focus of analysis for the Woomera2002 case study. Composed largely of independent media activists in Melbourne and Brisbane with a grounding in autonomous (and for some anarchist) principles, the indymedia[3] group were the main employers of ICTs and were the focus for the distribution of activist media during and after the actions through the Melbourne indymedia website.[4] Furthermore, many of those involved in the desert.indymedia network had had core roles in the coordination and promotion of the Woomera2002 convergence.

Although both are located in similar environmental and social justice movements and are aware of each other's existence,[5] they operate within different organisational and national contexts. Both Britain and Australia have vibrant and diverse environmental movements. Participants range from radical green activists who engage in direct action to strong professional lobby groups who are able to work closely with sectors of government (Rawcliffe 1998; Hutton and Connors 1999; Doyle 2000). The traditions of these two countries also overlap, most obviously through the British colonialism of Australia from the eighteenth century that is reflected in Australian contemporary legislative structures, social and cultural practices and continued role of the British monarchy in Australia. Furthermore, Australian and British environmental and social justice activists have shared a direct-action repertoire, such as the use of lock-ons, tree-sits and tunnels and the use of 'manufactured vulnerability' (Wall 1999; Doherty 2000: 62).

There are of course key differences too. Australia is governed under a federal system, which gives the eight states independent governments[6] (Lovell *et al.* 1995). In comparison to Britain it is a relatively new federation that has yet to understand the needs and ways of its indigenous aboriginal population (Valadian 1990; Neill 2002). Furthermore, the Australian Green Party has been successful in gaining a foothold in parliamentary politics. This is in stark contrast to the lack of formal representation in the Westminster Parliament of the British Green Party. These differences are reflected in the ways activist groups choose to operate but as we shall see there are also strong similarities between ICT utilisation irrespective of national context.

This chapter begins by appraising the current debates surrounding the impact of ICTs on political power struggles and then goes on to delineate the divergent organisational forms of activism. The two case studies are then examined in relation to the implications of ICT use for altering the processes of political leverage, with particular emphasis upon the influence of organisational form on the use of technology.

The Internet organisations and campaigning: politics as usual?

Initially, ICTs were presented by utopians such as Rheingold (1994) as providing new spaces for social interaction free from the hierarchical and bureaucratic pressures of existing society. These democratic properties could also facilitate public participation in political processes, through the bypassing of traditional government hierarchies, and aid the development of social cohesion (Frederick 1997; Tsagarousianou 1998). Bonchek (1995) argues that the formation of collective political action is facilitated by ICTs because the use of computer networks reduces transaction costs associated with organising collective action. He also notes, however, that current dynamics lead to unequal Internet access across social strata, which result in a domination of affluent, young, male and often highly educated individuals using the technology and consequently only some groups benefit from its use. Indeed, ICTs can also contribute to an increase in marginalisation of sectors of society through the creation of intolerant 'purified communities' in online culture (Belt 1998). ICT users bring with them their existing intolerances, such as racism or homophobia. The Internet therefore remains a social space and cultural product that is as prone to antagonisms as any other media (Froehling 1997; Warf and Grimes 1997; Cleaver 1998).

Such unequal access and increasing infusion of existing social values and prejudices into cyberspace, led Margolis and Resnick (2000) to argue that over time existing political practices, leverage and power would be mirrored on the Internet as cyberspace becomes 'normalised'. Resnick (1998: 65) goes so far as to suggest that, 'for all their commitment to radical change, the presence of activists on the Net is part of the process of political normalisation . . . they represent a familiar element of democratic pluralism'. There is, however, an alternative interpretation of what this 'pluralism' of political interests on the Internet represents. Rather than simply being a reflection of existing political practice, Bimber (1998) argues that ICTs enable a plethora of issue groups to operate without institutional support or structures and to mobilise quickly at low cost. This 'accelerated pluralism' is fashioned by 'more rapid and more intense citizen responses to mobilization efforts by linkage groups' and 'the possibility of decreasing coherence and stability in interest group politics, as the group process loses some of its dependence on stable public and private institutions' (Bimber 1998: 144). According to this understanding, activism via ICTs would remain centred around groups and networks (rather than lone individuals), but these linkages would be more diffuse, fluid and short term, and the cycle of mobilisation would move more quickly. Moreover, some forms of organisation, especially traditionally resource-weak informal groups may find the use of ICTs particularly beneficial. Although the provision of more information and ability to increase communication does not lead to greater political participation in itself[7] (Bimber 2001).

In terms of participant mobilisation, most research has underlined the importance of existing inclusion in social movement networks and that this integration is dependent on face-to-face interaction (McAdam 1988; Wall 1999). Only occasionally can 'strangers' be mobilised through 'moral shocks' (Jasper and Poulson 1995). Consequently, Diani (2001) argues that ICTs will aid different types of movements in different ways. Accordingly, organisations mobilising mainly professional resources using ICTs, such as FoE, are able to create virtual communities,[8] but this does not affect their overall mobilisation potential. In contrast, organisations mobilising mainly participatory resources requiring direct participation, such as those at Woomera2002, rely more upon face-to-face interaction and hence, ICTs result in virtual extensions that maintain the importance of the existing networks. Nevertheless, most groups can at a minimum benefit from ICT use by enhancing their ability to communicate effectively with increased speed, reduced costs and ease of interaction between an internationally dispersed network (Pickerill 2001a).

Participation and the impact of organisational-structure culture and context

Organisational form is often a reflection of the ideological, cultural or economic goals of its participants. There is no particular model of organisation, or unidirectional organisational evolution, which can be applied to social movements. There tends to be heterogeneity and plurality in the forms of organisation, a constant process of 'adopting, adapting, and inventing' (McCarthy 1996). Social movement organisations tend to favour decentralisation, participatory democracy, internal solidarity and *ad hoc* short-lived leadership. Organisational models have been differentiated by Doyle and McEachern (1998) according to the degree of organisation, distribution of power and the degree of commitment required from participants. These potential differences have resulted in a panoply of organisational forms, such as: local nuclei, umbrella organisations, party models, public interest groups, movement associations and supportive organisations (Della Porta and Diani 1999).

Integral to the choice of organisational form for a group is an understanding of the strategy by which environmental protection or social justice can be achieved. There are multiple strategies for environmental change espoused by different ecological groups. These strategies can reflect contrasting approaches to the value of democratic processes (Doherty and de Geus 1996). Some appear to advocate authoritarianism in order to ensure comprehensive environmental protection and Goodin (1992: 120) suggests that 'it is more important that the right things be done than that they be done in any particular way or through any particular agency'. There are, however, many links between environmentalism and a desire for a 'particular sort of decentralised face-to-face democracy' (Dobson 2000: 120), a form of participatory democracy and commitment to local politics that seeks involvement from as many individuals as possible in societal decisions (Seel and Plows 2000). Furthermore, many environmentalists have deliberately emphasised the importance of openness, participation, decentralisation and inclusion within their campaigning (Paehlke 1988). In practice, this has taken the form of 'informal and non-hierarchical forms of organisation' (Doherty *et al.* 2000: 11). This is often evident in radical direct-action networks such as Earth First! or associated groups whose principles included being 'non-authoritarian, non-coercive and non-hierarchical' and providing a 'democratic space' for participants (Anon 1999a). One increasingly popular structure amongst environmental networks is the use of affinity groups for coordination and actions:

> The affinity group is not a form of organization that treats everyone the same, or a mode of action where people are required to make the same commitments.... The groups act as a group, it has a task, but the basis of action lies in personal relationships and the recognition of the individuality of each person.
>
> (McDonald 2001)

In this way, different roles are taken on by participants of the affinity group, such as media spokesperson or first aider, but crucially there is a sense of trust and often a buddy system to ensure that everyone works together on a task and the goals of the group are achieved[9] (Starr 2000). As such, an affinity group is a mechanism through which participatory democracy can more closely be practised through self-organisation, with spokescouncils[10] being used to coordinate between affinity groups.[11] Alternatively, the more traditional model is via a branch structure based on geographical areas. Such local groups can run autonomously but are commonly linked, guided and influenced by a central headquarters. This structure is more popular amongst large-scale membership, non-governmental organisations (NGOs) (Rawcliffe 1998).

FoE, Woomera2002 and participatory democracy

Despite sharing a theoretical commitment to the ideals of participatory democracy, FoE UK and Woomera2002 practised it in disparate forms. Woomera2002 auto-nomadic festival of freedom[12] was a temporary manifestation of activists' networks to protest about refugees, anti-nuclear issues and the dispossession of indigenous lands. It has also been described as being 'an internet-assisted campaign' (Williams 2002: 4). It was an alliance of a variety of affinity groups[13] that met in the desert and coordinated actions through spokescouncils. Consensus was not always reached because of the variety of affinity groups involved and in particular a clash with 'old left' centred forms of organising (x-trot 2002).[14]

Predominantly, however, many affinity groups reflected the Do-It-Yourself (DIY) culture and networks of radical autonomous activists common in the non-violent direct-action campaigns of forest and anti-globalisation activism in Australia[15] (Burgmann 1993; Cohen 1997; Hutton and Connors 1999; Doyle 2000). Such grassroots activism often operated in contention with more centralised forms of organisation typified by Greenpeace Australia and the Australian Conservation Foundation. Overall, there was an emphasis upon a non-hierarchical organisational structure that encouraged individual autonomy, expression and experimentation. There was no formal membership and the convergence was financed through personal commitment and donations.

In contrast to Woomera2002, FoE UK employs a hierarchical organisational structure, while still advocating staff participation in informing the strategic direction of the organisation. Launched in London in 1971, FoE has become a particularly influential NGO in British politics (McCormick 1991; Lamb 1996). Although FoE UK's perspective is rooted in an ideology that radical political and social changes are required in order to avert further environmental destruction, its choice of aims and tactics[16] prevent it from being a radical environmental group[17] (Wapner 1995; Rawcliffe 1998). It is composed of regional campaign coordinators and 250 local groups with a national office overseeing campaigns, but not determining local group activities (Doyle and McEachern 1998). However, it is still criticised by more radical groups for being too centralised, hierarchical and bureaucratic. FoE's leadership is 'authoritative rather than representational' (Lowe and Goyder 1983: 53) and Jordan and Maloney (1997) suggest that FoE members are mainly passive *supporters* of the group, rather than active *members*. In this sense, they argue, FoE's internal structure is not democratic or participatory but is more akin to a 'protest business' and local groups and individual activists have little influence upon decisions at the centre.

Organisational use of ICTs: altering the processes of political leverage?

The ways in which ICTs are adopted and utilised within activist groups and networks reflect their existing organisational forms and ideologies (Slevin 2000: 136). Moreover, the context in which ICTs are adopted is crucial in determining how it will be utilised, how quickly it is adopted and how innovatively it is employed. Available resources for use of ICTs are obviously a key stumbling block. Activists face a variety of access restraints: financial difficulties, differing skills attainment and hardware and software problems are experienced by many. Such factors result in an uneven utilisation of the technology. However, both in FoE and Woomera2002 there were efforts to overcome these access problems by fundraising, (re)using old equipment and limiting time online. Furthermore, at Woomera2002 access to ICTs was provided through a temporary indymedia centre[18] – computers rigged up in a truck at the protest camp – and there were attempts to share technical skills through informal exchanges.[19] Activists also had to overcome the paradox of using advanced technology whose production and use has extensive environmental and social consequences.

The level of leverage that activist groups have in politics can be influenced by ICTs in several ways; *internally to the organisation* – through rapid interaction, convergence of communications, innovation through freedom to experiment and challenging internal hierarchies, and *externally of the organisation* – through cohesion and swarming, and reducing containability. Each of these is now explored through the case studies.

Rapid interaction

Activists are able to use ICTs for increasing the speed and regularity of their communication, thus reducing the onus of distance. Furthermore, such rapidity can facilitate networking, improve response times and aid the gathering of information. The ability to generate support and mobilisation were also possible within a shorter timeframe by providing an easy conduit through which to notify activists about events. Activists were able to interact at an international level quickly using ICTs during campaigns at FoE, especially on actions that involved regular communication with other chapters of FoE.

The value of speed was further illustrated in the distribution of activist media reports from Woomera2002. News about the events was published quickly and such information contributed towards the construction of a rapidly evolving storyline, which was a collection of first-hand accounts, links to mainstream news, transcripts of audio links, analysis and contributions from people who were not present:

> It was unmediated . . . the article went up and it was instantaneous, you didn't have to wait for the 7 o'clock news and wait for it to go through all the corporate filters.
>
> (Barry, Brisbane indymedia[20])

In effect, the actions and its consequences unfolded on the website in only a short lag from real time and posting continued throughout the night after the main actions.

Convergence of communications

ICTs have the potential to ease some of the stresses and strains that organisations and groups face during internal communication and coordination. By using ICTs to overcome organisational communication difficulties, the technology may contribute to improving the flow of information within a group and thus, potentially, aid its effectiveness in achieving its objectives.

FoE appeared to benefit from the convergence of communications. For example, Bell, a former FoE regional coordinator, identified time savings as a result of having a website that

> cuts out a lot of wasted time and misconceptions about what we do and certainly if you see the campaigns that we are involved with it avoids the general impression that FoE can help on everything.

FoE's Intranet aided information coordination and discussion within the core of FoE (the head and regional offices). ICTs also facilitated an informality in forms of communication between departments, as email tends to be used without the associated social graces that occur with face-to-face meetings, which in turn quickened the rate of exchanges. Despite this, and an increasing number of email public enquires, most requested information was only available as hardcopy, so post had to be used in response. Furthermore, FoE's size and the large amount of information that it produced slowed its ability to update electronic information quickly and renders FoE unable to benefit fully from the speed and interactivity ICTs offers. As one former FoE official noted:

> it takes us so long to get stuff on our own web pages internally simply because there's a big queue'. Like other FoE publications, in order for new information to go on the website the information must be cleared through a procedure and a set of channels. This involves checks for content, booking time with web managers and then getting it out on-line. This can take time.
>
> (Festing, former FoE housing campaigner)

FoE's use of ICTs to converge its communications has been further limited by the sceptics within their ranks. As one local organiser commented: 'I would see the Internet as a necessary evil if you like. It's there so you've got to use it, but if there are other ways of getting the information I would use those alternative methods' (Packham, Newcastle FoE).

For the Woomera2002 convergence, ICTs were used significantly prior to the protest festival in coordinating various affinity groups' participation. ICTs were particularly useful in communicating across the large distances of Australia and across the various time zones. ICTs facilitated the linking of participants of a disparate network without the cost of individual phone calls. Not only were emails used to coordinate amongst or between specific groups (while maintaining the importance of face-to-face meetings in mobilising participation)[21] but there was a large central and regularly updated website. This outlined the issues, contacts and affinity groups and provided logistical information about campsites, health and legal support. There was also a 'rideboard', that linked together people looking for lifts and a countdown that helped build a sense of momentum towards the commencement of the protest.

Innovation through freedom to experiment

A lack of rigid organisational structure has enabled many activists to feel free to experiment with different uses of ICTs. In comparison, more formally hierarchically structured environmental organisations have a greater number of stages through which to gain approval of the use of a technology that may slow down or restrict its adoption of ICTs. Although FoE developed their website and email system as early as December 1994 and in the process were the 'first environmental campaigning organisation with a presence on the Internet' (Pipes 1996: 63), this was due to the commitment and enthusiasm of a few individuals who did not seek formal permission and constructed the website in their spare time. Had they done so, Weatherley (former FoE IT manager) suggests 'I would have been chewed out by several management team members', stalling FoE's use of ICTs as a result of senior staff 'techno-innocence' (Burt 1999). The subsequent request for official funding was hindered by the need to appeal to those in the chain of command, which caused resentment by those wanting to develop ICTs use further:

> I think FoE should have grabbed it by the reins a lot sooner... we lost a hell of a lot of ground that we'd got because FoE just would not invest in the internet, and it's almost not until almost everyone else has that they see the need.
>
> (Pipes, former FoE GIS coordinator)

FoE decided to outline boundaries on ICT use, such as suggested email etiquette and protocol, thus constraining use within policy guidelines. This is not to say that FoE have not used the technology in innovative and novel ways but that the ambitions of some if its staff were constrained by the organisational structure. FoE were also constrained in that ICT adoption required significant financial investment for an organisation of their size. Moreover, formal groups such as FoE need to retain a control over their image and the activities of their staff and might not have felt as comfortable with ICTs because they were not able to control their use as much as they would have liked and consequently felt threatened by it (cf. Mobbs 2000).

In contrast, more loosely structured groups, such as Woomera2002, with significantly less funding have to rely upon using what resources they had available and for those with access to experiment. Activists were able to utilise a small amount of technology to make a big impact, without having to worry about organisational policy. In networks such as Woomera 2002, consensus was not required before people took action. Those groups whose structure has enabled rapid and experimental adoption of ICTs have often used the technology in particularly innovative ways.

The indymedia format itself is innovative, indymedia 'software represents a confluence of interests, influences and experiences which makes it, in many ways, the state of the art in Internet activism' (Meikle 2002: 89). The site is organised using an open publishing model[22] that enables any user to upload their story or viewpoint onto the website with minimal editorial interference (Arnison 2001). The website format also enabled an easy melding of publication types – text, audio, photographs and cartoons – to be posted alongside each other. A particularly innovative aspect of ICT use at Woomera2002 was the development of the PIMP system – the Phone indymedia Patch System:

> PIMP is basically like an answering machine for indymedia. You dial the PIMP number, then go through the voice menu, selecting the appropriate options, and then leaving a message after the tone. This message is then turned into an MP3 file, automatically uploaded to indymedia
>
> (Nik, desert.indymedia)[23]

This meant that reports could be uploaded to indymedia without accessing a computer. Consequently, there were several MP3 audio reports recording as the actions took place, which were then available online within minutes. It also enabled detainees within the centre to communicate and contribute to the debates, 'there were actually a couple of phone calls from people inside Curtin [detention centre] who were doing solidarity actions' (Barry, Brisbane indymedia).[24] Systems such as PIMP are groundbreaking and all the more so for being developed with little money by volunteers.

This freedom is especially relevant to the use of ICTs because its use has spread so rapidly. In order to use the technology to their advantage, activists have had to utilise the opportunities quickly, and what was deemed as innovative and novel (and thus attention grabbing) quickly becomes standard.

Hierarchies: nuclei, formalisation and subversion

Many activist groups face a continuous pressure to formalise and to evolve into more rigid (often hierarchical) organisational forms. This is often due to the need to solve resource issues, overcome communication problems, provide a more united image and attempt to reach a larger audience. Traditionally grassroots direct-action campaigns have been viewed as temporary. Over time they either dissipate or develop into a more formal organisation fighting for their original or broader cause. In the latter case, this formalisation tends to result in oligarchy and the associated problems of added bureaucracy and hierarchical decision-making structures (Doyle 2000). How far ICTs enable activists to subvert the development of such hierarchies or merely create new ones is discussed in the following.

Woomera2002: ICTs creating hierarchies?

For Woomera2002 many strove to operate using non-hierarchical methods such as affinity groups and spokescouncils to prevent oligarchies developing and enabling decisions to be made collectively with all participants having an equal influence. However, even in groups that appear to have few organisational structures, informal or latent hierarchies develop around some tasks, often as a result of skill differentials or because some members had been involved for longer than others (Freeman 1970).

Prior to the desert camp being established at Woomera, there were only a few people directly involved in Melbourne indymedia, 'there is no real indymedia collective, there's a couple of individuals... no-one really wanted to form a group' (Sam, Melbourne media activist). The desert.indymedia collective formed with three people and grew to ten once at Woomera. It involved a collaboration of activists from a variety of Australian indymedia groups. There were no designated leaders or management chains of responsibility. Rather the collective developed around who wanted to be involved, 'there's no hierarchy, there's no news team, there's just a space for everyone to do their own thing' (Barry, Brisbane indymedia).

Due to access problems the indymedia site was uploaded via a hotel room and a local ISP, but for security reasons only a few people knew of this process, 'no one outside of a small collective knew about the location for the uploads – we wanted to keep it as secure as possible' (Nik, desert.indymedia). The decision to restrict knowledge of this space was made by the smaller collective and enforced on later participants, 'as more people came on board it was explained why we did things this way, not everyone was happy, but about six people uploaded from the space' (Nik, desert.indymedia).

Despite being a non-hierarchical group, the use of ICTs triggered the development of a cluster of those individuals who were most involved in the use of the technology.[25] An informal nucleus surrounded the use of ICTs and subsequently largely controlled its implementation. Such clusters do not represent a hierarchy, as there were no chains of command, but still serve a similar purpose to an oligarchy. In part, this reflected the limited number of participants with the necessary technical skill, 'there's a lot of pressure on those people, for one thing, and we're totally reliant on them... It all makes it quite fragile' (Adam Data, Dorks Advocating Total Anarchy).[26] There were attempts to share knowledge of how to use indymedia, but technical-skill sharing was still relatively limited.[27]

In an action such as Woomera2002, hierarchies can develop around several issues: who maintains and understands the online linkup of the indymedia centre; who gains access to the limited number of computers; whether any editorial control is operated and thus some posts get removed; and what posts get linked to through the features section of the website. In particular, hierarchies can also develop around the process of editorial control. Although the Melbourne indymedia site utilised an open publishing broadcast model, a few posts have in the past been hidden:

> The only times that we have hidden a story is when someone's published someone's personal address or when someone's published something that has impersonated someone else and it's obvious that it's an impersonation.
>
> (Sam, Melbourne media activist)

> Posts are occasionally removed... I've used my discretion and taken down two sentences of... swearing... but only very occasionally.
>
> (Adam Data, Dorks Advocating Total Anarchy)

Even this limited editorial interference caused debates about 'where's the line, how do you define who can take it down and then who are they accountable to... how do you define what is not the right content for the website?' (Alex, Melbourne indymedia). Consequently, Melbourne indymedia have developed decision-making processes and outlined how the editorial collective operate using modified consensus[28] with the aim of providing 'an unmoderated, open-publishing newswire' (Anon 2002e), which helps prevent the development of hierarchies of access to knowledge, debate and contributions.

At Woomera2002 the radicalness of the actions meant that some information (such as the locations of escaped refugees) was sensitive and thus did not get published online. Most activists were aware of this precaution, but in addition the people 'who were uploading media were aware of those issues and if something was incriminating they wouldn't publish it, and go back to that person... and just discuss with them the issues' (Barry, Brisbane indymedia).

Despite the existence of these nuclei, ICTs have helped groups maintain their non-hierarchical networks. By easing the processes of communication, the need for formal structures or centralised offices are reduced. Individuals are able to communicate cheaply and regularly through ICTs without necessarily meeting face to face, or by formalising the contact. ICTs enabled the networks to remain fluid and loose, and to adapt to the changing involvement of different participants. It also provided a cheap medium through which to attract participants and coordinate their contributions. ICTs provide a medium through which the group can remain visible even if there are few participants, little activity is taking place or they are low on funds. Their web presence can continue to evolve at whatever pace participants choose, but does not fade when not attended to. Hence, ICTs are a medium where activists can move onto other projects and yet still maintain their initial campaign, such as the indymedia site. This fluidity enables campaigns to be dynamic for longer as they do not become constrained by the resource issues that so many activists face.

A test for the exclusivity of the nuclei is the extent to which non-collective members take part in projects such as desert.indymedia. With open access through the indymedia truck 'there were a lot of people who used it who aren't actively involved in infrastructure in indymedia' (Barry, Brisbane indymedia), and there were a large number of postings to indymedia during and after the actions. The desert.indymedia collective were also making a conscious effort to break down hierarchies by eroding the distinction between activists and journalists: 'for melb.indy there is no distinction, we don't 'cover' events, we set up the conditions for people to cover them themselves. We also upload to indymedia, but we do so as activists, not journalists' (Nik, desert.indymedia). Other participants did not perceive this cluster of individuals around the technology as intentional or exclusive, and there was a feeling that people were free to become involved. This was aided by the reflexivity of collective members who tried to resolve their privileged positioning:

> power is something that we don't think and talk about enough in any sphere, just power of access and knowledge and confidence... if I have power and

> access then my responsibility is to help someone else gain that space as well or use that space to create more spaces and it's not necessarily squashing anyone else if I'm trying to create more space.
>
> (Alex, Melbourne indymedia)

One of the ways in which hierarchies can be subverted is through impermanency. The Woomera2002 group was 'only going to exist up until we go out to Woomera and then it's not going to exist anymore' (Alex, Melbourne indymedia). While the Melbourne and Brisbane indymedia collectives were longer standing there was an emphasis upon fluidity, 'there's always that feel to formalise what you're doing… I think amateurism's really important' (Nik, desert.indymedia).

In addition to ICTs being used by non-hierarchical groups to retain their forms of organisation, the technology has been accredited with flattening existing hierarchical structures (Walch 1999). FoE's hierarchy was challenged by the use of ICTs at the same time as being maintained and reinforced by it. The use of ICTs by FoE facilitated greater flows of communication between those in head office, regional offices and London. This streamlining of communications was also facilitated by the development of the Intranet and enabled a campaign to be based in (and coordinated from) Leeds,[29] which further challenged the dominance of London. ICTs eased previous communication problems between local groups:

> it has never been feasible to ring round all these groups…this is so much easier because I just write one message and it goes out to about twenty different groups round the country.
>
> (Welch, Newcastle FoE coordinator)

Although ICTs could have helped FoE improve local-group networking amongst themselves and for such groups to become 'information hubs' this did not happen (Burt 1999). There has always been a concerted effort by national FoE to encourage local networking – particularly through the funding of regional campaign coordinators. ICTs may aid this process but did not trigger it (Washbourne 2001). ICTs have been used to share information, especially through the campaign-specific email discussion lists, but barriers remain to intergroup communication and especially to sustained dialogue. The information networks still flow primarily via the head office, rather than between local groups. Thus the possibility of a non-hierarchical national network between local FoE groups seems limited. The use of ICTs actually maintains the central London head office as the hub of all information flows. Furthermore, the official stages through which information has to pass in order to be published on the national FoE website reinforces the hierarchical structure of the organisation onto any use of ICTs. The differing levels of access to ICTs available to staff also maintained the hierarchical structure by reinforcing the present division of resources. Mobbs (2000) suggests that with ICTs, decentralisation of centralised organisations becomes inevitable. At FoE, however, there remained many barriers to changing their hierarchical structures.

The traditional need to centralise (to benefit from economies of scale) was reduced by ICTs that enabled cheap, fast, decentralised communication between participants. Although ICTs increased and eased communication flows around the FoE UK network (incorporating head office, regional offices and local groups), the importance of the hierarchical network was maintained. Not only do the stages through which website content is decided preserve the traditional hierarchies, but email has predominantly been used to exchange information between central office, regional office and local groups in a linear fashion, rather than to subvert the hierarchy by using ICTs for intergroup dialogue. Thus, ICTs have not been proven to promote the circumvention of existing formal hierarchies.

Working together: strengthening the cohesion of networks and swarming

One of the main advantages of utilising ICTs are their ability to aid networking with other activist groups, aid mobilisation and generate collective and cohesive campaigns. This can also help strengthen cohesion between those involved in environmental and social justice struggles and extend links to other political activists. Furthermore, ICTs can be utilised as a component in multiple tactics that can be swarmed upon a target simultaneously.

Although many groups attempt to use ICTs to mobilise participation in their campaigns, the value of ICTs is hard to discern because of the use of multiple methods to attract participants, and the importance of non-ICTs methods is often retained. Hence, the use of ICTs did not particularly increase the ability to mobilise participation in protest events within existing environmental groups or like-minded cliques (because there are already adequate networks). Rather, ICTs served to reinforce the *strength* of existing network ties and enable quick and cheap communication within them.

A specific example of the use of ICTs by FoE to communicate with other organisations was the development of the URGENT (the Urban Regeneration and Greenfield Environment NeTwork) website. It was a separate site autonomous from FoE and has information from a variety of different organisations, including FoE, CPRE and direct-action groups. Its aim was to provide a comprehensive overview of the housing debate in the United Kingdom and links to different groups:

> it's basically about a spirit of co-operation because one of the lessons we learned from the anti-road movement was . . . Friends of the Earth . . . needs to co-operate with other groups, and it needs to be seen to be doing that in a way which is not pushing our weight around.
>
> (Festing, FoE)

For Woomera2002 the main website served as a focal point for coordinating a disparate collection of groups prior to the convergence. Furthermore, by channelling activists' news reports to the Melbourne indymedia website, part of a global independent news network with a recognisable and easy to find URL, activists were contributing to the general cohesion of online media activism. The connections made through ICTs gave the comfort of solidarity to activists (Cleaver 1998). This increases the ability of activists to network on a global scale and for wider social movements to emerge out of such coalitions. Other links outside the movement facilitate the cross-fertilisation of alternative ideas and the sharing of skills.[30] ICTs have also strengthened existing networks as they offer another media for communication. This is especially useful for radical activists who lead slightly transitory lives and do not have a permanent base for mail or phone.

Hacktivism (hacking with a political motive) and other forms of online activism such as virtual sit-ins have also been used in addition to existing forms of lobbying (Wray 1998). However, the most effective tactics combine online activism with existing forms of protest – to *swarm* targets with several techniques being used simultaneously. This was evident at Woomera2002 through physical action occurring at the same time as people posted reports and analysis to the indymedia site, and virtual interaction through the Virtual People Smuggler.[31] The indymedia centre enabled activists to have directorship over the representation of their cause and actions, to distribute their media quickly and to an international audience. This helps activists add to opponents' woes by not only conducting an action, but being able to advertise their success afterwards. Online participation was encouraged through the Virtual People Smuggler:

> a space for people who were unable to physically attend to partake in someway. So people sort of wrote pieces, messages of solidarity, that sort of thing, I think it was just an outlet for people who couldn't come.
>
> (Barry, Brisbane indymedia)

Although the virtual presence did not actually involve a targeted action, participants were able to join an online tactical bloc, express their views about the physical actions occurring and communicate with each other. The freedom of ICTs to exist beyond the barriers of national borders, 'confined neither by geopolitical limits nor the standard aesthetics of protests, the Virtual People Smuggler pays tribute to the chatrooms, spoof sites, weblogs, online gaming, independent media as virtual, vital and, therefore, actual moments in the crossing of borders' (Lovink 2002).

Containability

The ability to contain activists' concerns and publicity of their protests is reduced through the use of ICTs. Activists' views can be disseminated more freely and to a wide audience partly because of the current inability to regulate or curtail ICT use. There was a constant stream of diffuse and disparate updates of news and discussion from Woomera2002 via the indymedia website. This was especially significant given the location of the festival, near a remote town in the desert, it would have been relatively easy for news of the action to be contained. With multiple authors and opinions, the activists were able to represent the complexity of the action and its participants. This was in contrast to the mainstream media's language using terms such as 'riot', 'stormed', 'wild clashes' and depicting many of the participants as extremists[32] (Anon 2002c,d; Williams and Plane 2002). Moreover, many of the PIMP audio reports were with refugees who had escaped and were being harboured by the activists. These not only provided credence to the claims of success by the activists, but served to further humanise the reports of refugees plight, and reduce the ability of the government to manipulate the stories about refugees' motivations and conditions in the detention centres. This immediacy of the activist news might have helped influence the interpretations given by mainstream media. The use of PIMP could also bypass any attempts at preventing access to the internet or indymedia, 'we actually had the facility to do emergency uploads via mobile phone... but at the same time the PIMP system would have been just as good' (Barry, Brisbane indymedia).[33]

Despite this variety of online publication, however, most information was distributed through the one indymedia website. Although the indymedia brand is global and has received coverage from mainstream media sources, there remain issues over how wide the audience might be and whether users are able to see beyond the 'walled gardens' of choices created by ISP portals (Malina 1999). As 'a constructive space where you're actually trying to communicate to audiences that aren't necessarily familiar with the issues of activism I think open publishing needs to be questioned a little bit' (Sam, Melbourne media activist). Furthermore, not all news could be reported, because communication could have jeopardised the freedom of the escaped refugees.

Groups are also able to maintain their non-hierarchical forms of organising, sustaining a nomadic form of power and centre-less organisation, which are hard to target by the centred state authorities and hierarchical multinational organisations, thus further reducing containability. This is particularly important when opponents have tried to exercise power over some NGOs by attempting to seize assets. FoE had to withdraw from the Twyford Down actions in 1992 because such a court injunction was imposed on them (Lamb 1996). In contrast, it is virtually impossible to identify individuals or assets of loosely defined horizontal networks.

Leveling the playing field

Activists who are able to gain access to ICTs have been able to increase the speed of their interaction, integrate a variety of media in innovative ways, strengthen the cohesion of their contacts and develop novel online tactics. Although it is difficult to measure the before and after effects of ICT use, more political leverage is gained by non-hierarchical grassroot groups (such as Woomera2002) than formalised NGOs (such as FoE UK). This is because ICTs help reduce the importance of resources for smaller groups. ICTs enable cohesion of disparate networks through the ease and speed of communication – which corresponds to the loose affinity model structure of direct-action movement. By facilitating the internal and external cohesion, the operating and organisational ability to collectively organise large-scale protests is improved.

Moreover, ICTs aid groups' ability to resist formalisation, therefore maintaining the participatory democracy project and leaving power with the individuals making consensus decision-making. Furthermore, convergences such as Woomera2002 have illustrated that participatory democracy models of organisation can work.[34] There were many successful elements of the Woomera2002 actions and the use of ICTs played an important role in many crucial aspects – in aiding the coordination of the convergence and in quickly disseminating news and discussion of the actions (Pickerill 2002). The Woomera2002 network was able to remain fluid, loose and dynamic and retain a web presence even when participation or resources were low. Using the desert.indymedia case study it has been illustrated that although resources are necessary for ICT utilisation, it is inventiveness, enthusiasm and adaptability that are vital and it is these attributes that are encouraged in non-hierarchical grassroot networks.

Previously, established NGOs formed in order to benefit from economies of scale by harnessing the resources necessary to coordinate large-scale actions or lobbying campaigns. Using ICTs, however, groups are able to subvert the need for centralisation (in office space, for newsletter production, etc.) and physical manifestation (as in the physical presence of activists) (Kellner 1999). Thus they are also able to bypass the bureaucratic implications of formalisation. The larger NGOs are actually less able to benefit from the spontaneity offered by the new technology because of the tradition of centralisation and top-down control over decision-making and operations. The consequence of this trend is the increased political leverage gained by small activist-groups.

The importance of national context is hard to delineate using these case studies. However, in these cases the most influential factors were not institutional, political or social structures, but the activists' ideology of participatory democracy that shaped the ways in which they sought to utilise ICTs. As such, there appear to be similar enduring trends even in different national contexts.

There are, however, certainly threats to the political leverage gained by activist networks. ICT use is increasingly being normalised by large-scale mass utilisation and the influx of corporate ownership (Margolis and Resnick 2000: 208). This commercial commodification not only restricts the free spaces available to activists but increases the possibility of surveillance by both the state and those wishing to profit from ICTs. Activists have attempted to subvert such interference by using encryption, foreign hosts and being aware that what they post online may be under surveillance. In addition, activists are using ICTs in a similar way to their radical appropriation of some physical spaces (e.g. the Reclaim the Streets practice of occupying roads and holding parties in the middle of motorways). By claiming their own virtual spaces and developing their own brands of media (such as indymedia) activists can seek to simply maintain parallel spaces to those of corporates and continue in their experiments of participatory democracy.

Conclusions

The cases examined in this chapter have made conscious efforts to employ ICTs in a certain way, which reflects and is reflected in their organisational form. Slevin (2000: 139) suggests several strategies of using ICTs to facilitate organisations' ability to succeed in the uncertain complexity of modern society. Of these, he supports the idea of 'opening out' organisations and making them more inclusive using 'the Internet to facilitate and incorporate active bottom-up alliances'. Thus, in effect, moving closer towards models of participatory democracy advocated by the more radical activist groups. While he argues against total inclusion[35] there is an acknowledgement that moving away from hierarchical models is necessary for organisational survival, and perhaps survival for political structures too.

When examining the possibility of participatory democracy through Internet activism the context of this chapter has been very specific. The particular context of environmental campaigning (and social justice to a lesser extent) tends to be dominated by individuals who although may be resource weak in terms of capital investment, are not necessarily marginalised in society but can come from privileged social locations – often being white, middle class and tertiary educated. Therefore, while direct democracy for *all* citizens is unlikely to be achieved, certain networks are able to move towards practices of participatory democracy using ICTs. Manifestations such as Woomera2002 contributed to the refugee debate within Australia (and internationally), enabled several hundred of its citizens to make their opinions clearly heard and ICTs significantly contributed to their ability to achieve this. In contrast, FoE UK were less successful at encouraging participatory networks to develop, but have still used ICTs in innovative and advantageous ways. Whilst not all small activist-groups can benefit in similar ways from such ICT use, in certain contexts where access, skills and knowledge are present, activists organising in small-scale autonomous groups can use ICTs more effectively than more established lobbying organisations. This has implications not just for the way political participation is examined, but for the value that is placed on hierarchically structured organisations when faced with the rise of fluid, grassroot mobilisations.

Acknowledgements

This research was undertaken through funding provided by an ESRC PhD Studentship (1997–1999) and a Leverhulme Trust Post Doctoral Research Fellowship (2001–2003). This chapter advances some assertions proposed in my contribution to the Fibreculture Reader (2001, Melbourne), and I would like to thank the editors for permission to continue that theme. I would also like to thank all the research participants for their time, energy and reflections, and Stephen Ward and Michele Willson for valuable comments on this chapter.

Notes

1 The definition of an 'environmentalist' is diffuse, with an increasing number of social justice issues being taken onboard by what were traditionally explicitly environmental

organisations. Friends of the Earth UK are a case in point. One of their main campaign priorities in May 2002 was 'challenging corporate power', which clearly has environmental implications but is also concerned with issues of equality, fair trade and community.

2 The data for these case studies was collated through in-depth face-to-face interviews undertaken with participants in Britain and Australia, and from secondary sources such as group literature, publications and media reports. British fieldwork was performed between June 1997 and June 1999. Australian fieldwork was undertaken between March 2001 and March 2003.

3 The indymedia network is a global network of alternative media websites. The global website is <www.indymedia.org> with over 70 regional centres across the world, each with their own websites fashioned from the original model (Hyde 2002; Meikle 2002; Scalmer 2002). The Melbourne indymedia website was set up during the protests against the World Economic Forum in Melbourne, September 2000 (Gibson and Kelly, 2000).

4 Footage and stories from Woomera2002 were posted onto the Melbourne indymedia site – <www.melbourne.indymedia.org>. Additional footage and discussion was also posted onto the Brisbane indymedia site – <www.brisbane.indymedia.org>

5 Friends of the Earth Australia is a radically different organisation from its British counterpart, operating using a non-hierarchical grassroot participation model, its volunteers are often involved in the organisation of radical protest such as Woomera2002.

6 Federalism means that activists can attempt to assert their influence on both their state and federal governments. In certain key campaigns, such as the Franklin Dam protests in 1983 and efforts to prevent the logging of the South West forests of Western Australia in 2001, activists were able to mobilise state voting power around the specific campaigns to lead pro-environmental parties to power, the Australian Labor Party (ALP) in each case (Doyle 2000; The Wilderness Society 2001).

7 Bimber argues 'the only form of participation which is demonstrably connected to Internet use is donating money' (2001: 53).

8 'Virtual communities' refers to networks that are not based on any face-to-face interaction and have been formulated entirely through ICTs.

9 'An affinity group is a group of people who have an affinity for each other, know each others strengths and weaknesses, support each other, and do (or intend to do) political/campaign work together' (Anon 2002a).

10 A spokescouncil is a forum for delegates from affinity groups to 'discuss actions, enable cooperation and share information between lots of different groups. Decisions made at the spokescouncil are not binding – which means that any decisions of the meeting as a whole are only given effect if there is consensus' (Anon 2002b).

11 For example, during the anti-WTO Seattle protests in 1999, Starr (2000: 116) observes, 'groups with different messages, tactics and skills coexisted without attempting centralized organising… the anarchist alternative to bureaucratic top-down systems'.

12 More information is available at <www.woomera2002.com>

13 Some of the affinity groups present included: Boatpeople, desert.indymedia, No One is Illegal, Pt'Chang, Refugee Rights Action Network and xborder.

14 How to work in the presence of Socialists (such as the Socialist Worker Party and Democratic Socialist Party) is one of the main internal conflicts of recent global protest events in Britain and Australia (Anon 1999b; Anon 2001).

15 However, Woomera2002 was essentially a mix of environmental and social justice campaigning. The debate about refugees has become much more than a social justice issue in Australia – debates have raged over what population Australia can support and its environmental limitations.

16 FoE's strategy has been five pronged: (1) the use of political lobbying and legislative activity, (2) scientific research and information provision, (3) employing the media, (4) the mobilisation of the public through local groups and (5) coordination and co-operation with other groups (Pickerill 2001b).

17 Its aversion to the use of illegal direct action and its emphasis upon political lobbying and legislative activity contrasts with more radical environmental groups such as Earth First! FoE UK has also been criticised for not having a strong green philosophy (Lamb 1996).

18 Though this temporary centre itself raised logistical issues – dealing with the heavy police presence (the activists were trespassing by establishing their camp near the detention centre), generating power, finding a landline – all on a low budget.

19 Adam Data (Dorks Advocating Total Anarchy) noted 'we've had a few people contact us with technical questions and wanting to learn some programming or set up their server. So we're going to organise a Linux workshop'.

20 Barry is speaking as a participant of the Brisbane indymedia collective but not as a representative.

21 Nik (desert.indymedia) noted 'it's better not to organise a group via email, but better to... network over email, that's like a networking of the groups... you need to ground email. It's like info sharing, it's no good having the info sharing unless you print it off and give it to other people. So I think you need to ground the inspiration and ground the information... it's a networking device and I think in a lot of ways it's no substitute'.

22 'Open publishing means that the process of creating news is transparent to the readers. They can contribute a story and see it instantly appear in the pool of stories publicly available... Readers can see editorial decisions being made by others. They can see how to get involved and help make editorial decisions' (Anon 2002e).

23 Nik is speaking as a participant of the desert.indymedia collective but not as a representative.

24 The involvement of detainees in participatory media is set to be further improved through a project of Melbourne indymedia: 'one of the projects that has come into being since Woomera2002 is a mobile phone project – a project that aims at supplying phones (with media and other numbers pre-programmed in) to detainees... to let them speak in their own voices for themselves (which is what indymedia is all about)' (Nik, desert.indymedia).

25 Similar clusters of control develop around other tasks or technology due to skill differentials or access, such as the mobile phone, CB radio, camcorder, or activities such as climbing, tunnel building or media relations. However, few have the potential of ICTs to shape the campaign or protest. The consequences of such nuclei also depend upon whether other participants approve of the way in which the ICTs are being used, or whether they disagree with the way the campaign has been portrayed on, for example, a website.

26 Adam Data is a code name for an activist; he speaks as a participant of the Dorks Advocating Total Anarchy collective but not as a representative.

27 Alex (Melbourne indymedia) commented, 'I think whatever form of activism you're involved in, skill sharing is really, really difficult, but there are always, always bottlenecks of information. Like so many groups that I've been involved with get to a certain point where one or two people are carrying the whole group on their shoulders, based on their experience and knowledge and confidence and power and history with that particular organisation... because of the urgency that drives activism people don't often think that there's space for new people to do things because we don't have time for people to make mistakes or learn... I guess the other thing is that people's identity is so bound up with their activism that sometimes you don't necessarily want to skill-share... I don't think people like letting go of their identity that much'.

28 A process where if consensus does not occur initially, there is further discussion and if there is still no consensus then a 75 per cent vote can pass a proposal (Anon 2002e).

29 The Real Food campaign is coordinated from the Leeds regional office and staff use the ISDN line to connect to the Intranet and access all the files that staff in London were able to.

30 Prior to ICT use activists have still sought to learn from how other movements operated, however, ICTs have quickened and cheapened the process of communicating between often distinct identities (Rucht 1993).

31 See <http://noborder.org/peoplesmuggler> for more information.

32 However, unlike many other significant and radical actions, Woomera2002 was covered internationally by mainstream media (including the BBC in England (see Mercer 2002) and CNN in America), which facilitated the publicity of the activists' concerns. This coverage was probably influenced by the sensitivity of the refugee debate at the time, and the nature and uniqueness of the actions.

33 There were limitations even with the PIMP system however, David (posting to Fibreculture email list, 16 April 2002) noted 'problem was for the rest of us that the protesters' camp... was serviced by exactly one telephone, which was obviously quickly jammed with coins. People I knew with wireless said the mobile coverage was shocking'.

34 Starr (2000: 116) also argued that participatory democracy worked during the organisation of the anti-WTO Seattle protests, 'groups with different messages, tactics and skills coexisted without attempting centralized organising. That coexistence was the material of the blockade's success. Everyone who participated has now experienced the anarchists alternative to bureaucratic top-down systems. We saw self-organisation at work and it worked'.

35 Slevin (2000: 134) suggests that 'organisational activities would soon come to a grinding halt if the views of all those who are part of an organisation would have to be actively canvassed and balanced with respect to every decision made'.

References

Alex (2002) '3CR Talks to Alex Kelly of Indymedia at Woomera', transcript of radio interview posted to Melbourne Indymedia, 30 March.

Anon (1999a) 'The First Year of Tyneside Action for People and Planet', *Do or Die*, no. 7, Brighton.

Anon (1999b) *Vampire Alert!* Leeds Earth First! <www.leedsef.org.uk/swp.htm>, first accessed March 2000.

Anon (2001) *Monopolise Resistance?* SchNEWS: Brighton.

Anon (2002a) *What Is an Affinity Group?* Woomera2002 convergence <www.woomera2002.com/affinity.php3>, first accessed July 2002.

Anon (2002b) *What Is a Spokescouncil?* Woomera2002 convergence <www.woomera2002.com/spokes.php3>, first accessed July 2002.

Anon (2002c) 'Ruddock Critical of Lack of Police Action at Woomera', *The Age*, Melbourne, 30 March.

Anon (2002d) 'Woomera Protesters "Wasting Their Time": Ellison', *ABC News*, 30 March.

Anon (2002e) 'Melbourne Independent Media Centre Editorial and Decision Making Policies and Processes', <http://melbourne.indymedia.org/decpol.php3>, first accessed July 2002.

Arnison, M. (2001) *Open Publishing Is the Same as Free Software* <www.cat.org.au/maffew/cat/openpub.html>, first accessed March 2002.

Belt, V. (1998) 'Technological Change and Urban Change', *CURDS Working Paper*, University of Newcastle upon Tyne: Newcastle upon Tyne.

Bimber, B. (1998) 'The Internet and Political Transformation', *Polity*, 31 (1), 133–49.

Bimber, B. (2001) 'Information and Political Engagement in America', *Political Research Quarterly*, 54 (1), 53–67.

Bonchek, M. (1995) 'Grassroots in Cyberspace', presented at the 53rd Annual Meeting of the Midwest Political Science, Chicago, 6 April.

Burgmann, V. (1993) *Power and Protest*, New South Wales: Allen and Unwin.

Burt, E. (1999) 'Information and Communication Technologies' presented at research seminar ICTs: Reshaping Voluntary Organisations? at London Voluntary Section Resource Centre, 18 November.

Cleaver, H. (1998) 'The Zapatistas and the International Circulation of Struggle: Lessons Suggested and Problems Raised' <http://www.eco.utexas.edu/Homepages/Faculty/Cleaver/lessons.html>, first accessed November 2000.

Cohen, I. (1997). *Green Fire*. Sydney: HarperCollins Publishers.

Della Porta, D. and Diani, M. (1999) *Social Movements*, Oxford: Blackwell Publishers.

Diani, M. (2001) 'Social Movement Networks', in Webster, F. (ed.), *Culture and Politics in the Information Age*, London: Routledge, 117–28.

Dobson, A. (2000) *Green Political Thought*, London: Routledge, third edition.

Doherty, B. and de Geus, M. (1996) 'Introduction', in Doherty, B. and de Geus, M. (eds), *Democracy and Green Political Thought: Sustainability, Rights and Citizenship*, London: Routledge, 3–17.

Doherty, B., Paterson, M. and Seel, B. (2000) 'Direct Action in British Environmentalism', in Seel, B., Paterson, M. and Doherty, B. (eds), *Direct Action in British Environmentalism*, London: Routledge, 1–24.

Doherty, B. (2000) 'Manufactured Vulnerability', in Seel, B., Paterson, M. and Doherty, B. (eds), *Direct Action in British Environmentalism*, London: Routledge, 62–78.

Doyle, T. (2000) *Green Power: The Environment Movement in Australia*, Sydney: University of New South Wales Press.

Doyle, T. and McEachern, D. (1998) *Environment and Politics*, London: Routledge.

Frederick, H. (1997) 'Mexican NGO Computer Networking Cross-Border Coalition Building', in Bailie, M. and Winseck, D. (eds), *Democratizing Communication*, Cresskill, New Jersey: Hampton Press, 255–85.

Freeman, J. (1970) 'The Tyranny of Structurelessness', *Berkeley Journal of Sociology*, <http://flag.blackened.net/revolt/hist_texts/structurelessness.html>.

Froehling, O. (1997) 'The Cyberspace "War of Ink and Internet" in Chiapas, Mexico', *The Geographical Review*, 87 (2), 291–307.

Gibson, J. and Kelly, A. (2000) 'S11 – Become the Media', *Arena*, 49, 10–11.

Goodin, R. (1992) *Green Political Theory*, Cambridge: Polity Press.

Hutton, D. and Connors, L. (1999) *A History of the Australian Environment Movement*, Cambridge: Cambridge University Press.

Hyde, G. (2002) 'Independent Media Centers: Cyber-Subversion and the Alternative Press', *First Monday*, 7 (4) <www.firstmonday.org/issues/issue7_4/hyde/index.html>, first accessed May 2002.

Jasper, J. M. and Poulson, J. D. (1995) 'Recruiting Strangers and Friends', *Social Problems*, 42 (4), 493–512.

Jordan, G. and Maloney, W. (1997) *The Protest Business?* Manchester: Manchester University Press.

Kellner, D. (1999) 'Globalisation From Below? Toward a Radical Democratic Technopolitics', *Angelaki*, 4 (2), 101–13.

Lamb, R. (1996) *Promising the Earth*, London: Routledge.

Lovell, D., McAllister, I., Maley, W. and Kukathas, C. (1995) *The Australian Political System*, Melbourne: Longman.

Lovink, G. (2002) The Virtual People Smuggler, post to Fibreculture discussion list, 25 March.

Lowe, P. and Goyder, J. (1983) *Environmental Groups in Politics*, London: George Allen and Unwin.
Lubbers, E. (2002) 'Net.activism', in Lubbers, E. (ed.), *Battling Big Business*, Greenbooks: Devon.
Malina, A. (1999) 'Perspectives on citizen Democratization and Alienation in the Virtual Public Sphere' in Hague, B. N. and Loader, B. (eds), *Digital Democracy*, London: Routledge, 23–38.
Margolis, M. and Resnick, D. (2000) *Politics as Usual*, Thousand Oaks, CA: Sage Publications.
McAdam, D. (1988) *Freedom Summer*, Oxford: Oxford University Press.
McCarthy, J. D. (1996) 'Constraints and Opportunities in Adopting, Adapting and Inventing', in McAdam, D., McCarthy, J. and Zald, M. N. (eds), *Comparative Perspective on Social Movements*, Cambridge: Cambridge University Press, 141–51.
McCormick, J. (1991) *British Politics and the Environment*, London: Earthscan Publications.
Meikle, G. (2002) *Future Active*, Sydney: Pluto Press.
Mercer, P. (2002) 'Activists Outwit Australia's Asylum Policy', *BBC Online*, 31 March.
Mobbs, P. (2000) 'The Internet, Disintermediation and Campaign Groups', *ECOS*, 21.
Neill, R, (2002) 'Black Lives White Lies', *The Weekend Australian*, 29–30 June, 19 and 22.
Paehlke, R. (1988) 'Democracy, Bureaucracy and Environmentalism', *Environmental Ethics*, 10.
Pickerill, J. (2001a) 'Weaving a Green Web', in Webster, F. (ed.), *Culture and Politics in the Information Age*, London: Routledge, 142–66.
Pickerill, J. (2001b) *Weaving a Green Web?* Unpublished PhD thesis, Department of Geography, University of Newcastle-upon-Tyne, UK.
Pickerill, J. (2002) 'Positive outcomes of Woomera2002 actions' posted to Melbourne Indymedia, 31 March, <www.melbourne.indymedia.org/front.php3?article_id= 24633&group=webcast>.
Pipes, S. (1996) 'Environmental Information on the Internet', *ECOS*, 17 (2), 63–6.
Rawcliffe, P. (1998) *Environmental Pressure Groups in Transition*, Manchester: Manchester University Press.
Resnick, D. (1998) 'Politics on the Internet', in Toulouse, C. and Luke, T. W. (eds), *The Politics of Cyberspace*, London: Routledge, 48–68.
Rheingold, H. (1994) *The Virtual Community*, London: Secker and Warburg.
Rucht, D. (1993) 'Think Globally, Act Locally?' in Liefferink, J. D., Lowe, P. D. and Mol, A. P. J. (eds), *European Intergration and Environmental Policy*, London: Belhaven Press, 75–95.
Scalmer, S. (2002) *Dissent Events*, Sydney: University of New South Wales Press.
Seel, B. and Plows, A. (2000) 'Coming Live and Direct: Strategies of Earth First!' in Seel, B., Paterson, M. and Doherty, B. (eds), *Direct Action in British Environmentalism*, London: Routledge, 112–32.
Slevin, J. (2000) *The Internet and Society*, Cambridge: Polity Press.
Starr, A. (2000) *Naming the Enemy*, Annandale: Pluto Press.
Tsagarousianou, R. (1998) 'Electronic Democracy and the Public Sphere', in Tsagarousianou, R., Tambini, D. and Bryan, C. (eds), *Cyberdemocracy: Technology, Cities and Civic networks*, London: Routledge, 167–78.
Valadian, M. (1990) 'Australian Aborigines in the 1990s', *Sydney Papers*, 2 (1), 29–36.
Walch, J. (1999) *In the Net: An Internet Guide for Activists*, London: Zed Books.
Wall, D. (1999) *Earth First! and the Anti-Roads Movement*, London: Routledge.
Wapner, P. (1995) 'Politics Beyond the State', *World Politics*, 47, 311–40.
Warf, B. and Grimes, J. (1997) 'Counterhegemonic Discourses and the Internet', *The Geographical Review*, 87 (2), 259–74.

Washbourne, N. (2001) 'Information Technology and New Forms of Organising?' in Webster, F. (ed.), *Culture and Politics in the Information Age*, London: Routledge, 129–41.

The Wilderness Society (2001) *A Fringe of Green; Protecting Australia's Forests and Woodlands*, The Wilderness Society, Australia.

Williams, T. (2002) 'Woomera Democracy Fails Consensus Test', *The Australian*, 2 April, 4.

Williams, T. and Plane, T. (2002) 'Protesters Storm Woomera', *The Australian*, 30 March.

Wray, S. (1998) 'Electronic Civil Disobedience and the World Wide Web of Hacktivism' <http://www.nyu.edu/projects/wray/wwwhack.html>, first accessed May 2001.

x-trot (2002) 'Lessons from Woomera: A Libertarian Marxist Perspective', posted to Melbourne Indymedia, 2 April.

Young, J. E. (1993) *Global Network*, Washington, DC: World Watch.

10 Conclusion

The future of representative democracy in the digital era

Rachel K. Gibson, Andrea Römmele and Stephen J. Ward

This book began with a number of hypothesised scenarios for the future of representative democracy in the era of the new digital communication technologies. From full-scale erosion to radical reform and renewal. The question remains, therefore, what the chapters in this volume can tell us about where liberal democracies stand, in general, on this spectrum of change. In addition, what do cross-institutional comparisons reveal about the relative openness towards new technologies among these structural supports for the representative system? Are the more porous and flexible actors, such as parties and pressure groups, exhibiting a rapidity of change that stands in marked contrast to their more fixed and institutionalised counterparts? This conclusion, therefore, works first to draw some insights into the general systemic picture drawn from a variety of national contexts, and then complements that by peering beneath to compare the relative adeptness of key representative bodies in using the new technologies for participatory purposes.

Certainly, the guiding assumption for the book was that representative democracy appeared to have successfully withstood the first predicted onslaught from the new communications media, such that while some attrition might be taking place, systemic collapse was not a realistic alternative. The chapters presented clearly confirm this premise. However, in addition, they reveal that the slightly less apocalyptic but still gloomy prognosis of limited usurpation appears also to be inaccurate. Indeed of the four scenarios presented in our introduction, it is the third alternative – limited but effective reform and modernisation – that appears to be the most valid descriptor for the changes observed.

In a theoretical piece, Charles Raab and Christine Bellamy (Chapter 2) take Dahl's 'problem of the unit' as their point of departure. What relationships do we find in a polity made up of different units, the mixed polity? What role do ICTs play in a polity composed of a mixture of different, and not obviously compatible, political forms? Are new ICTs reinvigorating or marginalising formal political institutions, especially parliament? Two scenarios are pointed out by the authors: First, would ICTs serve to encourage the emergence of a wider range of more open, less easily manipulated interactions between parliamentary elites and members of the public, thus reinvigorating representative democracy? Or will it be 'politics as usual' and simply reinforce existing problems and trends?

The central finding of their work is that although we might see signs of more direct democracy through ICTs, we will most likely be faced with a mixed polity in which postmodern novelty will coexist with institutions from modernity. And it will most likely be government regulating the diffuse, overlapping networks of governance and by doing so may be faced with intensified problems of managing political complexity. Thus, far from withering away, central political institutions will continue to play a central role.

Catherine Needham (Chapter 3) outlines trends at work in the executive and legislative branches of government in the United States and the United Kingdom towards e-government and the more elusive citizen-oriented e-democracy. At minimum, it is clear from her work that MPs and public servants clearly understand the increasing importance of using the technologies to improve their image with voters. The chapter is overwhelming in terms of its cataloguing of the numerous policy documents commissioned by politicians to investigate the possibilities offered by new ICTs for improving government performance. Such a flurry of activity, however, more importantly, has not just simply taken the form of words. Commitments to extensive entry portals to government services and experimentation with e-consultation show a willingness to deploy new ICTs in a meaningful and innovative public way. Such initiatives are indeed particularly notable within the UK parliament. Overall, however, between the two stories of effective e-democracy reform and modernisation, her chapter does plump for the latter as being the main headline. Governments have clearly devoted more resources to improving service delivery and meeting 'consumer' demands than enriching citizens' participatory lives.

Thomas Zittel (Chapter 4) looks more specifically at the challenges of e-democracy for parliaments from a comparative perspective, both in terms of external relations with voters and for internal organisation and communication. His examination of the Swedish Riksdag, the US House of Representatives and the German Bundestag reveals that the process of putting all three parliaments on the Net has opened up some new channels for voter participation, although they are very moderate in ambition and scope. Certainly the notion that the floodgates of direct democracy have been opened is soundly rejected, particularly by the German and Swedish cases. The comparative approach adopted by Zittel, however, allows him to temper criticism of such the slow pace of change by reference to the political context. His analysis reveals that there are crucial differences between the structure of representation underlying the Swedish Riksdag and the German Bundestag on the one hand, and the US House of Representatives on the other that need to be taken into account when assessing their openness to using new ICTs in these participatory ways. Parliamentary systems like Sweden and Germany, provide little incentive to their representatives to focus on particular constituents and to structure the representative process in a more participatory way. The point of reference of an individual representative in parliamentary democracies is on the party more than on the voter. Parliaments in presidential democracies, however, show less party discipline and individual representatives have closer links to their constituencies and to voters.

Joachim Åström's essay on the Swedish local government (Chapter 5) further confirms the idea of institutionalised logic driving, or perhaps more accurately, slowly prodding the process of new ICT adaptation. Given Sweden's very high rates of Internet access, the prospects for digital democracy might be considered better than in many other countries. However, while the attitudes of elites, in this instance, the chairmen of municipal executive boards, may be optimistic towards using the Internet to develop more participatory forms of democracy, very few local governments are found to have actually attempted to implement such ideas. Of those local governments that have sought to use the Internet more extensively, the analysis reveals an emphasis on modernisation and efficiency rather than e-democracy reforms. Such conservatism, as Åström points out, while it is founded on a variety of factors, also reveals a basic institutional inertia among Swedish local governments. Government leaders clearly do place a high priority on online participation but the concrete political and technological changes necessary to realising these ambitions escape them.

Turning to look at the response of the more porous and flexible aspects of the representative system to the challenge of the new ICTs, the findings are, in certain respects, rather surprising. Adaptation among the more institutionally linked actors, namely the individual representatives and those seeking office, as described by Greer and LaPointe (Chapter 6), is arguably less adventurous than the efforts made by legislative institutions more generally (as described by Needham). While on the one hand, the developments in website content across the 1998 and 2000 US elections revealed an increasing boldness among candidates for using the media to campaign, these initiatives are not necessarily geared towards developing the participatory potential of technology. Very few candidates undertook to develop dialogue with voters, or to make themselves accountable through their sites, and in fact the figures showed a decline among incumbent candidate sites in providing constituent help in 2000. Information became more plentiful but sites also became glitzier and perhaps, most significantly, more negative. Thus, despite the new media presenting a plethora of novel communication tools and offering a basis for a new style of political campaigning, the movement towards 'politics as usual' seems to be one of the more discernable and pronounced trends among candidates for office, at least in the United States.

Chapter 7 by Perez turns our attention to organisations at the international level and how they are adapting to new ICTs as a way of creating greater openness and accountability. The chapter covers a range of organisations that exhibit differing levels of institutionalisation Thus, in addition to the highly state-centric and formalised regime of the World Trade Organisation (WTO) we also learn about the efforts being made by the less government-oriented International Organisation for Standardisation (ISO), as well as the more recently created virtual entity, the Internet Corporation for Assigned Names and Numbers (ICANN). Overall, a similar story of modernisation and limited reform emerges with the WTO and ISO revealed as having taken some small and halting steps towards using the new technology to open themselves up to greater scrutiny from the public. More constructive uses, however, have been made in regard to making their internal processes more transparent. Somewhat surprisingly, ICANN, despite being an internet-formed and focused entity, is not revealed as a trail blazer in terms of incorporating more participation from its global constituents via the new media. Indeed, if anything it seems to be retreating from its earlier commitments to canvass Internet users for decision-making purposes. Of course, as Perez's analysis also points out, the more restrained efforts by international regimes in terms of mobilising popular opinion and input, should be placed in context of their more pronounced collective-action dilemma. With a global constituency, an individual's return on their participation to achieve a public or even private good is more diluted than at the national level, inevitably lowering their incentive to contribute. However, in what is perhaps one of the most instructive parts of the book, Perez also demonstrates how the Internet actually forms one of the most effective tools for reducing the transaction and coordination costs for international political actors. Thus, ultimately, the chapter places the responsibility with these regimes, rather than the technology or the public, to ensure more participatory uses are made of the new ICTs.

One of the increasing challenges for representative institutions and organisations and indeed representative democracy more generally is the growing internationalisation and globalisation of politics and economic markets. Many policy issues now have an international dimension and supranational structures, such as the EU and the WTO, have become increasingly important. Yet, for the most part, representative organisations, such as parties and trade unions, remain rooted in the nation state. However, one of greatest areas of participatory potential of the Internet is its ability to provide a tool for creating transnational links and internationalising protest. As Hodkinson notes (Chapter 8), there are an increasing number of examples of international action facilitated by new ICTs. Yet, Hodkinson also reminds us strongly that protest in cyberspace should not be seen in a vacuum. Organisational/institutional culture, history and context are crucial to understanding the dynamics of net-based protest. In the case of the labour movement, it would appear that inherent long-term barriers to international cooperation cannot be overcome altogether by use of the technology. Indeed, in the case of the labour movement, ICTs may create new barriers to international solidarity and mobilisation – not least because of the global digital divide but also because some workers view the technology as a threat to their livelihoods.

Overall, the official labour movement and national trade unions have been relatively conservative in their use of the technology largely concentrating on providing basic information or trying to modernise their appeal via e-service provision. The innovation that has emerged from Labour movement has tended to come from activist networks or even individual campaigners. Whilst much has been made of the ability of technology to create new ties and links, Hodkinson suggests that in the case of trade unions, technology has so far rarely created brand new international ties and even when it has, it has been difficult to sustain them. Face to face activism remains crucially important in building long-term trust and solidarity.

Pickerill (Chapter 9) similarly underlines the importance of issue-context and organisational structure as catalysts for net mobilisation but paints a more positive picture of the value of ICTs in this case for environmental activists. Whilst noting overall that environmental movements have been some of most active users of the Internet-based technology, Pickerill outlines marked differences between different types of environmental organisation. In part, it should come as no surprise that the environmental movement has used the technology creatively, since it has a long-established record of expanding the repertoire of protest activities. Nevertheless, Pickerill suggests that the Internet is likely to be of particular benefit to more loosely organised, direct-action focused, protest networks. As with the labour movement, this is not to suggest that the technology creates protest. For the most part, core activist networks are already in place, but where there is a focused issue and shared goals, Internet technology makes it easier for such networks to punch above their weight and generate greater awareness of their campaigns than would otherwise be the case. The fluid structures of protest networks mean that they are free to experiment with new ICTs, and unlike representative institutions and organisations they have less to lose. In part, this is because they are not formally answerable to anyone except themselves. They are not spending public money, if they make mistakes they are under less scrutiny from the traditional media than formal organisations and they lack hierarchies of control.

Clearly the growth of direct-action protest and so-called dis(organisations) pre-dates the emergence of Internet technology. However, what this study suggests is that such technology may accelerate some of the broad pre-existing trends within representative politics – in this case the facilitation of issue-based protest politics. This does not necessarily mean the usurpation of representative organisations or the promotion of particular models of protest activity. As Pickerill illustrates, ICTs can assist most organisations, (from formal pressure groups to protest networks), to achieve their aims more efficiently but she argues that the latter have the most gain from deploying the technology effectively.

Thus, based on the evidence presented in this volume, it would appear that modernisation and reform are the watchwords that best characterise the impact of the new ICTs on representative democracy as a whole. From the more formal structures of executive and legislative power to the looser intermediaries of environmental movements, there is evidence of genuine enthusiasm for deploying the technologies towards more democratic and reformist ends. What we do not see as yet, however, is much evidence that this adaptation is producing any fundamental change in how these units operate or the ends that they pursue. From the descriptions offered here, it seems that our democratic intermediaries are mostly interested in the technology as a means to continue performing their existing functions, only to a better level. This seems to be the case whether they are the older and more embedded institutional structures or more fluid and flexible organisational actors. Thus, our initial propositions about the different aptitude displayed by macro- and meso-level representative bodies towards making innovative use of the interactive properties of the new ICTs do not appear to be supported.

Whether these patterns will continue into the future is an open question. Hopefully, however, this book has provided something of a benchmark for studying the pace and direction of those future developments across a broad range of political actors, as representative democracies move further into the digital age.

Index